CALIFORNIA

1963-1967

SPACESHIP EARTH

A Memoir

Joseph Mark Glazner

CALIFORNIA 1963-1967 SPACESHIP EARTH

Copyright © 2022 Joseph Mark Glazner
Published by Joseph Mark Glazner
Toronto, Ontario, Canada
Publisher's email: glaznerbooks1234@gmail.com

Cover design by Joseph Mark Glazner. All artwork and images © Joseph Mark Glazner. Cover painting by Joseph Mark Glazner, *Big Sur,* 2001
Formatting and Interior design by Woven Red Author Services

California 1963-1967 Spaceship Earth / Joseph Mark Glazner—First Edition
ISBN ebook: 978-17750058-8-9
ISBN paperback: 978-17750058-7-2

California 1963-1967 Spaceship Earth is based on my memories, journals, published and unpublished writings, more than five hundred personal letters to and from me, interviews with many of the people mentioned in the book, and researched facts about relevant historical events. In many, but not all, instances, I have changed the names and the identifying characteristics of private individuals to preserve their anonymity. No composite characters or events were created. Finally, I have used literary license to reconstruct the conversations from the 1960s to reflect the intrinsic nature, style, and emotions of the times.

California 1963-1967 Spaceship Earth
is dedicated to my love, Joanie Shirriff.

"We travel together, passengers on a little spaceship, dependent on its vulnerable reserves of air and soil; all committed for our safety to its security and peace; preserved from annihilation only by the care, the work, and, I will say, the love we give our fragile craft. We cannot maintain it half fortunate, half miserable, half confident, half despairing, half slave—to the ancient enemies of man—half free in a liberation of resources undreamed of until this day. No craft, no crew can travel safely with such vast contradictions. On their resolution depends the survival of us all."—ADLAI STEVENSON, US Ambassador to the United Nations, addressing the Economic and Social Council of the United Nations, Geneva, Switzerland, July 9, 1965, five days before he died.

PROLOGUE

Everything was changing, and nothing could stop it.

Optimism and rage lived side-by-side with sexual revolution, mind-expanding drugs, and music that changed the world.

Friendships promising to last forever competed for our attention with soaring racial unrest and a war tearing America apart.

Living in California between the last months of President Kennedy's White House (1963) and the Summer of Love (1967) was like looking out the window of a spaceship and catching a glimpse of the future. That spaceship was planet earth. We were traveling together, destination unknown.

The rules were changing. We felt it. We tried to define it and redefine ourselves to make more sense of the best and worst parts of the journey. We were desperate and curious enough to try anything. No matter what happened, nothing would ever be the same again.

This is what I remember.

CHAPTER 1

August 1963, Los Angeles

I made it to California but not where I thought I would land.

The previous summer, I spent a half day driving around Los Angeles with my older brother Ray. It was a small part of our ten-day car trip up the coast from San Diego to San Francisco, camping on the beaches and staying at discount motels.

Back East during a bitterly cold winter in rural New Jersey, when I first thought of applying to the University of Southern California in Los Angeles, I recalled a beautiful campus my brother and I drove past the summer before. It was filled with acres of perfectly manicured lawns, gardens, palm trees, and Spanish-colonial buildings with red tile roofs and white stucco walls in a fashionable section of town. I imagined it must have been the USC campus.

It wasn't, and it wasn't even close.

Hollywood, Sunset Strip, Beverly Hills, Westwood, Santa Monica, and the beaches and ocean—all the places I had heard about or briefly glimpsed the year before—were miles away and well beyond the borders of the suburb I had landed in for school.

I arrived this time by Greyhound bus with my guitar, a typewriter with sticky keys, and a duffle bag filled with everything I hoped I would need for the next year. I couldn't afford a return trip during the school year, so, this was my new home.

USC was five miles from downtown. It sat like a tiny anomaly in the sixteen-square-mile sprawl called South Central Los Angeles. The district was made up of mostly poor and middle-class Black neighborhoods of small, single-family bungalows; cheap, low-rise apartments; light and heavy industry; and rundown commercial streets like I had seen in Black ghettos back East.

The city busses along the streets through South Central took forever to go a few miles. With no car and no prospect of owning one, I was hours away from the ocean, movie theaters, and the city life I dreamed of.

The only thing I recognized from the year before was the thick, gray-brown smog that made my eyes water, hurt my lungs, and gave me a hacking cough whenever I took a deep breath.

Like it or not, I had to adapt. This was my chance to make something of myself.

I had nothing to return to in New Jersey. Money was tight. My dad's health continued to deteriorate. Early-onset Parkinson's disease was destroying him. His small, leather glove factory was on its last legs. My mother warned me before I left home that the modest amount of money she would be sending me for room and board might run out. I had to be careful about what I spent. If I wanted any extras, I had to look for a job.

If I hadn't won an academic scholarship, USC would have been my last choice. At $1,200 a year for tuition alone, it was among the most expensive schools in the nation and far out of my league.

I arrived before the fall semester started, hoping to get oriented before classes began.

I came with a stellar academic record from high school, but I owed that to nothing short of hard work and help from the second smartest kid in the class who had coached me through chemistry and the advanced math classes. Deep down, I was worried that university would be over my head.

I saw almost no cars or people on the streets around USC. I found a fraternity brother who was living in one of the near-empty houses. He let me stay in one of the rooms for free until my dorm opened.

I walked around the deserted campus and surrounding neighborhoods on my own, trying to make sense of my new physical surroundings.

Fraternity row was two blocks long and lined with well-tended, grand old three-story mansions with large, perfectly maintained front lawns and flower gardens. The neighborhood had been wealthy in the teens and Roaring Twenties, home to silent movie stars, oil barons, and business tycoons. Except for a few of the old homes, which had been torn down and replaced with boxy modern structures, I could easily imagine myself on a street where characters in *The Great Gatsby* might have lived.

The opulence of fraternity row ended at its edges. The residential neighborhood between fraternity row and the university had once been prosperous, too, but the money had moved on long before I arrived. Many of the old houses were in rotten shape with peeling paint, sagging porches, burned-out lawns, and palm trees badly in need of trimming. Many had been broken up into rooms or apartments for rent to students once school opened again. The neighborhood was like a metaphor for my future—affluent, bright, and shiny if I succeeded and shabby and down-trodden if I failed.

The campus itself was nothing like the acres of sprawling lawns and Spanish-colonial buildings I had seen the year before and imagined was the school I had applied to.

The USC campus was tiny, running for two blocks along a section of University Avenue closed to cars—the only closed-off street in the area. Both sides of the street were lined with old sycamore and magnolia trees, gardens, and imposing stone and brick buildings. [1]

The grandest, most impressive building on campus—the Edward L. Doheny, Jr. Memorial Library with its long walkway, gardens, and fountain in front leading to huge bronze doors—took my breath away. The massive stone building was a work of art. The fraternity brother I was staying with told me he had been a freshman and had seen then-Senator John Kennedy speak to the student body from the steps of the library a week before Kennedy had beaten Nixon for the presidency in 1960. [2] [3]

I felt comforted and thrilled knowing President Kennedy had walked where I was walking.

Kennedy had been president through most of my high school years. He was like a movie star who had walked off the screen and into our lives. He was part of something bigger, a feeling I couldn't quite describe. It felt like he was leading the country through a doorway into another world, a better world.

The last couple of years felt uplifting. The civil rights movement was growing. Freedom riders—young Northern whites and Blacks and Blacks in the Deep South—were riding busses through the old Confederate States to bust segregation. The ban-the-bomb movement was gaining in popularity especially after President Kennedy had stopped a nuclear war with the Soviet Union the year before during the Cuban Missile Crisis. A sweeping folk music revival with singers like The Kingston Trio; Peter, Paul, and Mary; Odetta; Pete Seeger, the Freedom Singers; and newcomers my brother's age, like Joan Baez and Bob Dylan, were openly talking about social problems, the dangers of nuclear proliferation, equality, the power of love and hope, and world peace. We—kids like me—thought we were winning. The big issues could be resolved. Good people like President Kennedy dreamed the same dreams we dreamed of. Kennedy acted and spoke like he knew my generation mattered.

I wanted to matter.

I had this unshakable belief that our president could and would fix all the world's problems, and it made me feel full of hope despite my own worries about how well I would do at university.

I made it this far, I reminded myself once again. I'm in California.

I shook away the restlessness and thoughts of the past, of rural New Jersey, New York City, Greenwich Village, and everything else that I felt pulling me backward whenever the future seemed terrifying.

For better or worse, I reminded myself, I'm here to study pre-med, and secretly write a novel in my spare time—secretly, because I had told no one in my family or in California that I dreamed of becoming a doctor and a writer.

CHAPTER 2

The abandoned neighborhood around the university burst to life as the school began to reopen. New students, returning students, and faculty members flooded the streets. The parking lots and streets in every direction filled up with cars, many brand new and expensive.

Every time I turned my head, I saw a sea of new faces as young as me—young women so striking they took my breath away; young men so fit and tanned I couldn't imagine any of the beautiful women ever giving me a second glance. The entire student body looked like actors playing college students in a Hollywood movie.

The size of the student population was intimidating. Nineteen thousand in all, and five thousand undergraduates alone. My freshman class had fifteen hundred students—twice the size of my regional high school—and every single student a potential friend or a competitor for grades.

I spotted the freshman with ease—bright-eyed, determined to succeed, scared, looking around, and making furtive eye contact with whomever would look back. The older students looked right past us as if we didn't exist.

I wanted to fit in. I was tempted to stay on my own, but I didn't know the rules. I didn't yet know myself as well as I thought I did.

CHAPTER 3

I moved into the dorm and joined a fraternity, hoping the fraternity would make me feel less anonymous.

A few of the brothers and fellow pledges seemed interested in civil rights and folk music. Dan, a tall, dark-haired junior with a big, friendly laugh, had just returned from the March on Washington for Jobs and Freedom. He had heard Martin Luther King, Jr. give his "I Have a Dream" speech and had sung "We Shall Overcome" with folksingers Joan Baez; Peter, Paul, and Mary; Bob Dylan; Pete Seeger; and two hundred and fifty thousand other protesters who attended the march.

Dan played the guitar badly but enthusiastically like me. We knew a dozen folk songs in common like "We Shall Overcome," "This Land Is Your Land," "If I Had a Hammer," "Ain't Gonna Study War No More," and "Where Have All the Flowers Gone." I felt lucky when he became my big brother at the house.

My assigned roommate in the dorm was from Los Angeles and had his own friends and family in the city. We had no classes together. So, we rarely saw each other.

I slept in the dorm but ate most lunches and dinners at the frat house. I studied at the dorm, the frat house, and the library.

I took a job at the fraternity as a dishwasher to pay for the extra costs.

The first semester of basic biology—the first of my courses in my major—was held in Founders Hall in an auditorium-sized classroom with close to four hundred students. The class was twice the size of my entire high school graduating class. The only time I had done well in science in the past was in my freshman high school biology class because I was good at managing fruit flies for the genetics experiments.

The grading for biology at USC was strictly on a curve and based on three tests and a lab mark. It was factory learning. Word around the dorm and the fraternity was that biology was one of the hardest majors at USC. The first two semesters were the boot-camp semesters, designed to discover the geniuses and get rid of the rest.

Older students who had taken the course told me, most got 2.0s or C's while only about 10-15 percent got B's and 5 percent got A's. I needed one of those A's, or at the minimum, a B, with a lot of A's in other science courses to be even considered for medical school or more importantly, a medical scholarship, in four years. I saw success in my first semester of biology as the keystone to my future.

The course met three times a week plus an additional three-hour lab in the science building.

Philosophy, German IV, political science, and swimming rounded out the rest of my week.

I threw myself into every assignment, knowing I had to outwork at least four out of five others who were as smart or smarter than me, not only in biology but in all my classes. I needed a B average at the end of the year to keep my scholarship. Without it, I was gone.

CHAPTER 4

The Santa Ana winds caught me completely by surprise.

I had been living in a cloud of gray-brown smog since arriving in Los Angeles. Visibility had been only a few blocks in any direction. I thought this was normal.

Then, without warning, the hot Santa Ana winds from the deserts to the east swept through the city, blowing the smog out of the basin and revealing the Santa Monica Mountains to the north, and the even more spectacular San Gabriel Mountains to the east—some with peaks nearly two miles high. I had no clue mountains could be seen from the campus. For the first time since arriving, I was able to breathe clean air.

The joy was short-lived.

The Santa Ana winds also brought a heat wave that was more paralyzing than the smog. On September 26, the official temperature in the city reached 109 degrees, the second hottest temperature in Los Angeles since 1877 when records began to be kept (and three years before USC had been founded). Few people on campus could escape the heat. My classrooms, the frat house, and dorm were all without air-conditioning. The low ceilings and brick and cinderblock construction turned Trojan Hall, my dorm, into an oven. My roommate went home. A couple of us left behind found a door to the roof and spent the nights on top of the building.

Some kids skipped classes the next day. Some with cars went to the beach. I toughed it out. I kept up with my reading assignments. I began writing my essays in philosophy, political science, and German.

I went to USC's first home football game with my fraternity brothers in 105 degree heat and held giant flashcards over my head along with hundreds of others to spell out words that were shown on national television while our team lost to Oklahoma 12-17.

The worst of the heat wave ended after a week.

The winds blew again from the west, trapping the smog in the basin. I found myself coughing less from the smog as the days went by, not because there was less smog but because I was getting used to it.

On November 2, 1963, my mother's fifty-first birthday, South Vietnam's President Ngo Dinh Diem and his brother, Ngo Dinh Nhu, his most trusted adviser and head of the secret police, were assassinated in a coup d'état and replaced by the South Vietnam general who led the assault on the presidential palace.

The incident was discussed in my freshman political science class. The professor said the police action in Vietnam was a subject we might be hearing more about. "The outcome may determine the future of much of Asia."

My professor was a former US Army paratrooper, who had been on standby toward the end of World War II, waiting to invade Japan right before the Americans dropped atomic bombs on Hiroshima and Nagasaki.

"Those bombs that destroyed two cities and killed more than a hundred thousand civilians also saved hundreds of thousands of lives of Allied and Japanese soldiers and civilians, prisoners of war, and all the rest who would have died if the Allies had to continue to fight the Japanese inside Japan," he told us one night. "The bombs ended the war. It should have ended all wars, but it didn't."

He gave us some recent history of the situation in Vietnam. Vietnamese rebel forces, the Vietminh, led by a much-loved intellectual and charismatic Communist leader Ho Chi Minh, had fought hard against the Japanese invaders during World War II and then had driven the Colonial French government out of the country in 1954.

To protect the minority Catholics and pro-Western interests in the country against the Communists, the Americans took over from the French. Through the Geneva Accords of 1954, the Americans helped the wealthy Catholic minority establish a pro-Western government in the south half of the country. The US sanctioned the split of the country, leaving the north half under the rule of Ho Chi Minh and the Communists, and the South in the hands of a small clique of Catholics (with strong ties to France and America) and a coalition of local warlords—some steeped in new-age religions and others who were members of organized criminal enterprises.

"At the time of the split, the division of the country was to be temporary. A free election was supposed to be held in 1956, two years after the ouster of the French. Both halves of the country had been promised they would be able to vote on whether or not to unite as a single nation," our professor informed us. "Does anyone know what happened?"

No one raised a hand.

The professor continued. "In 1956, President Eisenhower's advisers informed him a free vote would overwhelmingly elect the very popular Ho Chi Minh. Eisenhower reneged on the free elections and began to send more military advisers and money to South Vietnam to prop up the unpopular Catholic government. He was afraid of the domino effect or Domino Theory, which said if Vietnam went completely Communist, other Asian countries in the region would be sure to follow."

He explained that the idea of two Vietnams, like the two Koreas before it, had become American dogma, and a much-hated solution by the majority of the Vietnamese who were Buddhist or Communist but nevertheless agreed with each other on two things—they both wanted one country under majority rule, and they wanted foreign forces to leave.

"So, where does that leave America as the defender of democracy?" he asked. "Do we support the will of the people on the other side of the world and learn to live with their choice, or do we prop up a minority government that is anything but democratic?"

My professor was worried America would once again be dragged into a war like the one in Korea. "The only thing we need to worry about right now is whether the military men running the country in South Vietnam after the coup will be able to hold onto power without dragging America into combat."

What I did know by then was that tensions were high in South Vietnam between the Catholics and Buddhists. Six Buddhist monks had poured gasoline over themselves and burned themselves to death in public in South Vietnam since June. They were protesting the loss of civil rights, draconian restrictions, and prejudices against Buddhists in South Vietnam by the ruling Catholic minority. The latest self-immolation had taken place a week before on October 27.

The images were shocking and had haunted me since I had seen photos in the media of the first monk burning to death. I had been trying to turn a blind eye to what was happening, but I kept coming back to the question: What would be so horrible in my life that I would do something like that? Burn myself to death. What was the Catholic minority doing to the Buddhist majority?

I felt sympathy for the Buddhists. They were fighting for equality much like the Blacks in the US South. In the past five months, white racists in the Southern States had gunned down Black civil rights leader Medgar Evers in Mississippi, used dynamite to kill six Black children in a church in Alabama, and continued to terrorize the Black population in the South in every way they could. The Blacks and the Buddhists were feeling dangers I could only imagine tucked away in the little island of tranquility I had landed in.

We focused on another subject in our next class and never mentioned Vietnam again, which was fine with me. I had a much bigger problem— my upcoming biology mid-term exam.

I needed to worry.

The test was rapidly approaching, and I was already in trouble in my major.

My biology mid-term, my future ticket to medical school, was scheduled for the week before Thanksgiving. I was determined to do better than I had on my first exam. Despite all my studying, I got a C on the first of the three biology tests that would make up ninety percent of my grade for the semester. The other ten percent came from my lab mark, and I was doing even worse in the lab than in the classroom.

I was a wreck. Everyone taking biology was studying like mad. The system was weeding out the weak students faster than I expected.

As my biology exam approached, I was also excited about my date with Sarah.

Sarah was tall and dark-eyed with short, curly, dark hair. She was in my swimming class, a freshman like me, and a good swimmer, also, like me.

One day when we were both leaving the gym at the same time, we started talking and ended up at the student union drinking coffee for an hour.

She was still trying to figure out what she wanted to major in. "I feel like I'm waiting for someone to give me permission to start being me," she said.

"What would you do if you could do anything?"

"I'd like to paint or play an instrument if I had any talent. I wish I wrote better. I wish I had the courage to quit university and go to the South where they need people to go door to door to register voters. We're at war down there, but I haven't the nerve to do anything. So, I go to school here and take English, history, French, and art appreciation while waiting to discover what I'm supposed to do."

She loved Kennedy. She thought if anyone could, the president would break the cycle of hate between the races. "Kennedy's like the big brother I always wanted. Someone who would stop all the insanity, stupidity, and unfairness. The next time there's a big march on Washington, I bet he'll go to it and speak. Wouldn't that be amazing?"

She told me she thought I was lucky because I was studying to be a doctor and would help people.

I thought about telling her that I was secretly planning on writing a book, but I had already told her I was pre-med. So, I decided to wait until we met again.

Before we parted company, we arranged to meet on Saturday night, the day after my mid-term biology exam.

She said she could borrow a friend's car. "Call me on Friday afternoon."

I felt a connection with her. I sensed she was feeling the same way.

The upcoming date with Sarah made me study even harder. I wanted to be able to celebrate with a good conscience after my Friday test.

I went to sleep feeling confident that I was as ready as I could be for the exam the next day.

My first class on Friday was my philosophy class at ten o'clock in Mudd Hall on the south side of the campus. It was immediately followed by my biology class in Founders Hall two long blocks away. I had five minutes to get from one class to the next. The biology test started at exactly eleven. I was determined to be on time.

I raced along University Avenue, weaving in and out and around the slow-moving crowds of students streaming in both directions.

I only slowed down when I neared the front of Founders Hall and noticed a large crowd of students milling about on the sidewalk.

Something wasn't right. I recognized several students from my biology class. They should have been inside getting ready for the exam.

I spotted Trish, a tall, redheaded freshman history major who was involved in student government. She was always up on everything.

"Hey, Trish, what's going on?"

She looked like she had been crying.

"The president's been shot. Classes have been cancelled."

"President Topping?" I asked in disbelief. I couldn't understand why anyone would shoot Dr. Norman Topping, the president of the university. It didn't make sense.

"President Kennedy," she said, bursting into tears.

CHAPTER 5

Friday, November 22, 1963

Eleven o'clock Pacific Standard Time. One o'clock in Dallas.

My biology exam had been postponed until further notice.

I saw Kim Charney, a friend and fellow pre-med student who was supposed to take the same exam. He had just come from another class. He told me a bunch of frat boys in his class clapped when the professor told them the president had been shot. [4] [5] [6]

Shot.

That's all we heard.

No one knew whether the president was alive or dead.

School was closed until further notice.

Shock and fear were on every face I saw. No one knew more.

I headed for the frat house. I tried to think logically. I had to wash dishes to pay for my lunch.

The few kids at the frat house looked stricken. Several were openly crying. Around eleven thirty California time, we learned the president was dead.

I reversed the charges and called home from the pay phone in the frat house.

No one answered.

I tried my father's shop.

"Why are you calling now?" Dad asked. "It's the most expensive time of day."

"The president's been shot dead," I said.

"A terrible thing, but there's nothing anyone can do about it."

"Is Mom there?"

"No. She's gone to New York."

"I thought I should call you," I said, trying to justify the expense, knowing how worried he was about money.

"There's nothing anyone can do," he repeated. "I have to get back to work. You can reach Mom at home later when the rates are lower."

I hung up knowing I wouldn't call later.

My father was right. What the hell was the point? He could do nothing to reassure me. No one could.

I had to think clearly, keep my eyes open, and try to understand what was happening.

One of the older brothers in the frat house with a car drove three of us downtown to Pershing Square, a park taking up a square block in downtown Los Angeles facing the Biltmore Hotel. The hotel was where President Kennedy stayed during the heated Democratic Convention of 1960 when he had won the nomination in a bitter contest against Texas Senator Lyndon B. Johnson. Once Kennedy secured the nomination, he turned around and named Johnson as his running mate. Vice President Johnson had just been sworn in as president.

I bought the extra edition of the afternoon newspaper.

Kennedy Slain. Suspect in custody.

We were witnessing history.

People hurried past on the streets surrounding the park with their heads down, going, I supposed, to somewhere where they would talk about what happened with family or friends.

On the way back to the campus, we heard on the radio the border with Mexico had been sealed off.

Back on 28th Street, we learned that someone had smashed the car windows of a brother in another frat house down the street because the car had Texas license plates.

I felt empty and alone. I didn't know what to think.

In seconds, the world had gone from a place where anything seemed possible to a world where nothing mattered.

Those gunshots, I realized later, were the real start of the Vietnam War and the troubles ahead.

CHAPTER 6

I called Sarah's dorm from the frat house. No one answered. After a dozen rings, I gave up.

Most of the brothers and pledges who lived in Los Angeles went home and took the out-of-towners with them. A couple of brothers offered to take me home, but I chose to return to the dorm so I could hunker down and keep studying for my biology exam, which would inevitably be rescheduled as soon as school reopened.

By Friday evening, fraternity row, the campus, and the neighborhood around the university were deserted.

I called Sarah's dorm again. One of her dorm mates answered and told me, she wasn't in her room. No one knew where she was.

I left a message for her to call me when she got in.

Only a handful of students remained in the dorm on Saturday, the day after the president's assassination. I took a break from studying and went for a walk with Richard, one of the older kids in the dorm, who had stayed behind.

Richard was a junior, two years ahead of me. Tall, sandy haired, and handsome, he was the star punter for the Trojan football team and one of the best college punters in the country.

He was one of my friends at the dorm who had discovered the door to the roof with me during the heatwave. Three weeks before the assassination, we had nearly been arrested for jaywalking across Exposition Boulevard. [7]

The day after the assassination, Exposition Boulevard was empty when we crossed it and headed toward the Coliseum. Richard was supposed to play in the crosstown football rivalry between USC and UCLA that afternoon at the Coliseum. The game had been postponed like most public events across the country.

Kennedy had accepted the nomination of his party in 1960 at the Coliseum. This was where he had delivered his famous "New Frontier" speech. [8]

Richard and I circled the giant stadium, trying to find a way in, but the place was locked tight. We wandered back to the dorm without speaking. We were all out of words.

On Sunday, while sitting in the lounge at the dorm watching TV along with Richard and a couple of other dorm mates, we saw the police escorting suspect Lee Harvey Oswald through the basement of the Dallas Police Headquarters. We witnessed the live broadcast of Oswald being shot by Dallas nightclub owner Jack Ruby.

We looked at each other in disbelief. We had just viewed a man being shot on TV in front of us. Not just any man. The man accused of shooting the president.

I had trouble catching my breath. The acid boiled up in my stomach. I could feel one of my bad headaches coming on. I went for a walk to try to calm down.

I walked to the women's dorm and found someone who knew Sarah. She wasn't in. The dorm was nearly empty. No one knew where she was.

CHAPTER 7

I ran into one of Sarah's friends after classes resumed. She told me Sarah got sick. She went home. Her friend said she lived in Cincinnati and wasn't sure if Sarah would be coming back to school.

Her friend told me a few days later that Sarah had all her clothes shipped home and wasn't coming back. I hoped she would be all right and find what she was looking for. I missed the feelings of intimacy she had stirred up in me.

I scored higher on my second biology test. I got a B, but my lab grade kept sinking. My lab partner Jeff and I made a mess of every frog and sea urchin we tried to dissect.

It was hard to admit, but I didn't like lab work or biology. I wasn't naturally good at either one.

Thanksgiving was only six days after the president's assassination. Dan, my big brother at the fraternity, took me to his family's dinner at the home of one of his cousins. We tried to put the gloom behind us by playing our guitars and singing folk songs for his relatives. My stomach was still so tied in knots I was only able to eat a few bites of the Thanksgiving meal. I tried to stop thinking about the assassination but it continued to gnaw at me.

CHAPTER 8

The Beatles' songs "I Want to Hold Your Hand" and "I Saw You Standing There" were released in the US the day after Christmas 1963, thirty-four days after President Kennedy had been shot and killed. [9] [10]

The Beatles did not wipe out the malaise I still felt from the assassination, but they were a much welcome distraction. I felt as if they were giving me permission to let go and be happy again or at least, try to be. Their music built on all the American rock 'n' roll I had listened to since the mid-1950s when rock had been born and Elvis, Little Richard, Fats Domino, and Jerry Lee Lewis had exploded into our lives. And yet the Beatles were fresh and somehow new and different, not least because of their pleasant British accents.

Within days of the release of their first two songs, Beatles music blasted out of the fraternity and sorority houses up and down the row. Turn the dial on the radio, and it seemed like someone was playing the Beatles somewhere in Los Angeles.

Not since Elvis had any musical group or individual made such an impact on so many young people at once. It was like another channel had been added to the TV, and we were all glued to it.

Bob Dylan's album *The Times They Are A-Changin'* was released in January just as the Beatles were becoming the most popular band in the US.

The Beatles appearance on *The Ed Sullivan Show* on Sunday, February 9, 1964, cemented their hold on America. They were clean shaven with bangs down to their eyebrows, dressed in white shirts, ties, and matching suits. They were full of energy, laughter, and sexual innuendo—everything I wanted to feel right then. [11]

CHAPTER 9

As far as I could tell, most people I knew had returned to who they had been before the president's assassination. If President Kennedy's death still bothered them or if it had changed them, they didn't show it or talk about it.

I envied them.

I pretended to return to the person I had been, but something inside me had changed. I was adrift, brooding, waiting, and not sure what I was waiting for.

I ended my first semester on shaky grounds. I got a solid B on my final exam in biology, but it wasn't enough to rescue me from my poor lab mark. My final mark for biology in my first semester was a C, my worst grade.

The A in German and Bs in my other two courses gave me a 3.0 for the semester, the bare minimum I needed for the year to keep my scholarship.

I moved out of the dorm into the fraternity house at the beginning of my second semester.

My big brother Dan became inactive so he could concentrate on getting into grad school in psychology. I rarely saw him, but he got me thinking about psychology, a subject students couldn't take at USC until their sophomore year.

I remained in pre-med with a major in biology for my second semester.

About a third of the kids in my first semester biology class didn't return for Biology II. Those who took the second semester of biology were at the higher end of the bell curve. The competition and chance to get a B or better would be more challenging, but I was committed to giving medicine one final try.

I also took an English class run by a young woman working on her doctorate who seemed to hate teaching and looked down on her students. After our first assignment she told the class everyone had gotten a D or an F on their first paper except for one person—me. She gave me a B. And yet, we never warmed to each other. She was just marking time.

I studied great plays with William Wintersole, a young theater and Hollywood actor moonlighting as a professor. He introduced me to Pirandello, Beckett, and Chekhov. I wondered what it would be like to write a play.

The Beatles continued to grow in popularity. By April, the top five best-selling singles in the US were Beatles' songs: "Can't Buy Me Love," "Twist and Shout," "She Loves You," "I Want to Hold Your Hand," and "Please Please Me."

CHAPTER 10

Leslie's sorority Alpha Chi Omega and my fraternity Sigma Alpha Mu were paired together for Songfest, an annual event at USC where fraternities and sororities created original musical productions and competed against each other. I barely managed to land a part as one of a dozen backup singers in our production.

Leslie, a blue-eyed, redheaded sophomore, was the female star of our show. She was not only beautiful, poised, and fearless, but she had the strongest and best singing voice of anyone in the program. She was our campus sweetheart, the one everyone fell in love with.

Half of my fraternity brothers pursued her relentlessly. I didn't care. I just liked looking at her. Her eyes sparkled when she sang. They lit up her face and sent a thrill through me whenever our paths crossed. She smiled at everyone, so I felt good but not special.

Our show parodied current Broadway and pop tunes. We rehearsed relentlessly. I saw her almost every evening at rehearsals, but we never exchanged more than a few words.

On the night of the show, we played to a near-capacity crowd of eighteen thousand university students, faculty, parents, friends, music lovers, and talent agents at the Hollywood Bowl, one of the largest natural amphitheaters in the world. The Beatles would play their first Los Angeles concert there at the end of the summer. Songfest was covered by local radio stations and some of the Hollywood brass. [12]

We came in first in our division and second for the festival after an argument and a second ballot by the judges. We had been robbed, everyone said, but the only thing that mattered to me was that Leslie and I hit it off at the party later that night at the home of one of her sorority sisters.

The house was high up in the Hollywood Hills with a spectacular view of the city spread out below.

I got to the party early with a couple of my fraternity brothers to help unload the cases of champagne, which was really a cheap Californian sparkling wine that tasted like vinegar mixed with beer.

I was one of the few who turned their backs on the champagne when the paper cups were handed out and the toasting began. I noticed Leslie halfway across the living room holding a cup, toasting others, but not drinking.

By chance, we ended up together shortly afterward, and I got to tell her how great her performance had been, something she had been hearing from everyone.

"We all deserve the credit," she said graciously. "I would clink glasses with you, but you're not drinking."

"That stuff is poison. If you drink it, drink only a few sips or you'll be sick tomorrow."

"I was thinking the same thing, but I wasn't sure," she said. She put her cup down on a side table, and we walked to the back of the house looking over the city and talked. She was a theater major but was thinking about switching to psychology, like me.

I told her I was going to be a writer. She thought that was interesting, not odd.

"I'm planning to write a novel over the summer," I told her.

"What's it about?"

"I'm not sure yet. I have to start it and see where it goes."

She nodded like she understood perfectly.

She said she planned to be in New York over the summer and suggested maybe we could meet. We exchanged addresses before she was called away by the sorority sister who was taking her home. I wanted to believe the kiss and hug she gave me before leaving the party meant something to her.

I visited the student affairs office and asked what would happen to my scholarship if I switched majors from biology to psychology. The adviser said as long as I maintained a 3.0 average and went to school full time, I could keep my scholarship. My major didn't matter. Scholarship students switched majors all the time.

I studied hard for finals, like I had been doing all semester. I got lots of rest in the last couple of days, so my mind was sharp. After each exam, I felt I had done my best. If I survived, it was because I deserved to be at USC. If I didn't, someone else should take my place. That was only fair.

Like everyone else, I left self-addressed postcards with my professors so they could send my final grades to me. I addressed the postcards to New Jersey.

I left nothing behind in Los Angeles. I sold my ratty typewriter and shipped a footlocker of books, term papers, notes, and clothes to my father's factory by rail. I left with my guitar and the same duffle bag I had arrived with. I gave myself a fifty-fifty chance of getting my scholarship renewed and returning in the fall.

As my bus pulled away from the downtown terminal in Los Angeles in early June, I made a mental list of what I'd learned in nine months in California:

- I could get used to the smog.
- Los Angeles got much colder in the winter and hotter in the fall and spring than I imagined.
- Brief trips to Palm Springs, Lake Arrowhead, San Diego, and up the coast to San Simeon, Big Sur, and San Francisco reminded me that Los Angeles was a small part of California.
- I learned I had no chance of having sex or finding true love in Los Angeles without a car.
- I realized the fraternity wasn't for me. I was better on my own like I had been in high school with friends in different circles without belonging anywhere.
- I discovered that I could try to be a doctor or a writer but not both. I was never going to be smart enough to be both.

Vietnam had again receded far into the back of my mind.

I knew nothing of the secret, US-backed, bombing raids by mercenaries against the Ho Chi Minh trail inside Laos.

Why should I?

CHAPTER 11

My brother Ray met me at the bus station in Gallup, New Mexico and drove us back to the Navajo reservation where he had just finished his first year of teaching. I had stayed with him for a few days the previous summer before taking the bus the rest of the way to California. This time, we camped at a remote hunting lodge in the woods with the Boy Scout troop he had cobbled together during the year. He was in his element, teaching the kids all the outdoor lore he had learned in Scouts. The kids loved him. One of the Navajo kids I had briefly befriended the year before had bought a guitar and was learning to play it. Another one was getting ready to go into the Army. The third boy had moved away with his family.

My brother and I left New Mexico a couple of days later and headed to New Jersey via New Orleans and the Gulf Coast where neither of us had been.

Large parts of the interstate across the country were still under construction, so we took old state and county roads as we headed east. We drove long hours and slept on the side of the road in Texas in sleeping bags.

We found a cheap motel on the outskirts of New Orleans on the second day and splurged on dinner at Antoine's in the French Quarter. Afterward, we roamed Bourbon Street like a couple of hicks, fending off strip-joint barkers and panhandlers, and finally sitting down at a bar to drink beer and listen to a local New Orleans jazz band.

In Mississippi at a truck stop where we were chowing down on greasy burgers, I started talking loudly about how it was unfair to have separate washrooms for colored and white. My brother got angry with me when I wouldn't stop. Once we paid our bill and were outside, he told me if I ever shot my mouth off again in a place like that, he'd drive off and leave me.

Ray was sure the two men in the pickup truck that caught up to us a few miles from the restaurant and tailgated us for five miles were out to get us until they finally turned onto another road.

"You could have gotten us killed," he scolded me.

"The world's changing," I said. "People like that can't win."

"The world's never going to change," my brother insisted.

My brother, four years older than me, had been different but close growing up. I had been small, weak, and overweight. I was thin-skinned and often got injured or sick. I learned to avoid fighting and bullies. Even after I shed the fat and grew to a trim, fit five nine and a hundred and thirty-five pounds in high school, I thought like an undersized person, wary of dangers far and near. I planned everything. My brother planned very little. He had been one of the taller kids in his class, overweight and slow but tough. He was nearly six feet tall and weighed a hundred and ninety-two pounds when he played football for Western New Mexico University. When we were young and he got into fights with neighborhood kids, he wore out his opponents because he could take more punches than most kids. If he connected with one of his punches, it was like getting hit with a bag of rocks. He disliked school and authority of most kinds, leaving me the chance to be the scholar in the family.

I played army and cowboys and Indians because he did. I eagerly marched off to YMCA camps, Scouts and Scout camps because he did. My interests in the Civil War, guns, fireworks, wilderness camping and canoeing were because of his interests. If he did it, I wanted to do it, and do it better. I was always trying to outdo him. I collected more guns and Civil War artifacts than he did. I took more chances when driving. I even went farther out West to university than he had gone in part because I was determined to outdo him. I tried following him into hunting, the sport he was most passionate about. I tried hardening myself to killing. I could kill, but it didn't feel good. I didn't crave it like he did.

Now, he was supporting Barry Goldwater in the upcoming election. I was for Lyndon Johnson.

Lyndon Johnson was no Kennedy. Johnson was only nine years older than Kennedy, but he seemed to be a generation older. Kennedy had been my president. Johnson belonged to my parents' generation. Johnson, as far as I could tell, was pushing ahead with all the civil rights legislation that President Kennedy had been planning. Johnson was for peace and deescalating tensions between the US and the Soviet Union. I thought he was a good man, but I felt no visceral attachment toward him like I had toward Kennedy.

Goldwater was running in the Republican primary against New York's Liberal Republican Governor Nelson Rockefeller. Goldwater was an arch conservative. A right-winger in bed with the John Birchers, Goldwater thought desegregation should happen on its own. He was an isolationist and most likely to start a nuclear war. Some said the hate groups he pandered to had created the climate that had gotten President Kennedy assassinated.

I couldn't understand how my brother could like someone like Goldwater. I was irked that Ray could vote in the 1964 election and have a say in my future, and I couldn't.

My brother thought the Beatles were okay but preferred American music over music by foreigners.

Neither of us knew it, but we were on our last long road trip together.

Neither of us knew that three civil rights workers our age would be murdered in Mississippi weeks after we passed through.

CHAPTER 12

The home I had left almost ten months before and where I had lived from the time I was two years old was in Warrenville, New Jersey off a lightly traveled county road and down a short dead-end street. Ray and I, weary from our two thousand mile road trip, drove down the hill past a half dozen post-war, cinderblock and stucco, two-bedroom Cape Cod houses. Our house was the last one on the block. We bought it new in 1947 from an anxious developer who had built six houses out of seventeen in a cow pasture four miles out of town and couldn't sell any of them that spring because all the basements flooded with a foot or two of water after every rain.

My parents bought it anyway because they were desperate and needed a place to stay after Dad's first Plainfield factory fell on hard times.

My father was handy. He had worked in construction in his youth and could fix anything. He hired men from the factory he was managing at the time to work with him to dig drainage ditches around the house to keep the basement dry. In 1953, he hired another crew to help him add a master bedroom and bathroom over the attached garage, finish half the basement with wood paneling and a wet bar, and extend the back of the house to create a huge kitchen, dining room, and sunporch overlooking the giant plant and tree nursery behind our house. My mother designed the kitchen. It had a panoramic view for a half mile across the farms, fields, and woods of the mile-wide valley all the way to the Mt. Bethel Gap.

My parents got lucky. The two older Italian half-brothers, who owned the eighteen-acre wholesale nursery directly behind our house, became instant friends with our family the day we moved in. Uncle Tony, who died just months before I left for California, had practically raised me from the time I was two until I went to school. Over the years, he had remained a close family friend and helped my mother turn the barren dust bowl around our house into a showcase of gardens and trees. I had been able to pass most of a merit badge in Scouts just by identifying the different fruit and decorative trees we had around our house. My mother's large vegetable garden produced carrots, lettuce, celery, cucumbers, zucchini, tomatoes, radishes, corn, rhubarb, raspberries, squash, and strawberries.

The house looked the same. Outside, nothing had changed.

Inside, I was shocked to see my father for the first time in almost a year. He seemed to be trembling much worse than when I left. His gait was so unsteady that at times he started to walk backward instead of forward before catching himself.

Dad was only fifty-three. He looked a hundred.

His illness frightened me. The doctors said no one could catch Parkinson's from another person, but they also said they didn't know what caused it. So, why were they so sure I couldn't catch it or inherit it?

Before Parkinson's, my father had been the picture of health. In his prime, he was only five feet eight inches tall, but he was powerfully built with arms and hands as strong as Popeye from hard work changing tires and working as an auto mechanic, farm laborer, roofer, contractor, and shipping clerk in a clothing factory before he learned to be a manufacturer from my mother's father. He was fast on his feet from playing stickball in the streets of Brooklyn as a kid. He had dark, wavy hair combed straight back, dark brown eyes, and a handsome square face. He had been an amazing athlete in just about any sport he tried in his youth and young adult years. Before dropping out of high school at sixteen, he made the varsity football team of his tough, inner-city Brooklyn school as the team's star running back in his sophomore year.

His once kind smile was now frozen behind his Parkinson's mask. He was in pain all the time.

My mother was fifty-one. She was five feet two with a slim build, fair complexion, narrow blue eyes, and wavy, dark brown hair that hung down to her shoulders. She easily looked ten years younger than her age, but the last year had noticeably tired her. I could see the weariness in her face and eyes and the hopelessness in my father's.

My mother gave me the four postcards that had arrived from my professors with my grades on them. There was also one from Evelyn, the woman I thought I had been in love with the year before. We had spent a night together in her East Village basement apartment before she had taken off to backpack around Europe, the Middle East, Asia, and parts unknown, just as she had the previous year.

I held my breath and looked at my marks first.

B in English. I thought it should have been an A.

An A in my great plays class. I was proud of that and prouder that my drama teacher thought I wrote well.

B in comparative religions.

B in biology. Respectable enough to continue in pre-med if I wanted to.

I didn't want to.

My grade average was 3.25 for the semester, and over 3.12 for the year, just enough to keep my scholarship.

I'm going back to California, I told myself gleefully. This time, I'm going to be a writer, have a car, and find true love.

The front of the postcard from Evelyn was a glossy picture of a beach and ocean with the name *Ibiza* scrawled over the sea in big red letters. I had no idea where Ibiza was. On the reverse side was my name and New Jersey address on the right panel, and in tiny, neat printing on the left panel was a note:

Dear Joe,

I hope you found all you were looking for in California. I wanted you to know that I did find happiness. I have been traveling with a beautiful man. We have settled here for a while. Our child is due in a couple of months.

If you haven't yet found what you're looking for, keep looking.

I hope you are still writing.

She signed it Evelyn with a little heart after her name. No return-address.

I smiled. She was one of the very few people I had told I wanted to become a writer. Now, I was ready to shout it to most of the world except for my father, who I knew would need a great deal of time to absorb my change of plans.

My Uncle Sam, my mother's tall, fit, movie-star-handsome, youngest brother, represented George Elliott, one of the top commercial photographers on Madison Avenue. Sam knew everyone in the advertising business. He belonged to a small circle of men and women who had started their careers after the war. He was friends with Andy Warhol, Richard Avedon, and other creative people of note. I hitchhiked the two miles from our house in Warrenville to North Plainfield and took the hour-long bus ride into Manhattan so Sam could take me to meet art directors and copywriters at some of the biggest advertising agencies in the country. Unfortunately, no one had any work for a nineteen-year-old writer with no experience.

Instead, I got two part-time jobs close to home in a frenetic effort to make enough money to fund my escape from New Jersey as quickly as possible. I worked three, sometimes four days a week at the nearby Lyon's Veterans Hospital as a short-order cook in the canteen, making hamburgers, grilled cheese sandwiches, Westerns, and fried egg sandwiches for the psychiatric patients and staff. I got good enough to crack an egg on the edge of the grill with one hand while flipping burgers with the other.

In my spare time, I worked at my dad's factory, the Plainfield Glove Company, filling in for the men, swinging between two different jobs depending on where I was needed. I cut leather and fur on one of the heavy-duty clicker machines and pressed the finished gloves on the hot irons. Both jobs required precision but were monotonous and tedious though dangerous. The clicker machines could crush a finger or hand beyond repair, and the hot irons could deliver a nasty burn to a presser's arms or hands if he got careless.

Dad's shop was down to three dozen elderly workers. It had lost a quarter of its workers in the past two years when Dad moved the shop from the loft on Park Avenue in Plainfield to try to save money. He had moved to even smaller quarters in a two-story workshop behind a rooming house in North Plainfield.

Despite the move to cheaper quarters, the business continued to die. American glove-making had been moving overseas for several years. My father's failing health meant that he hadn't the energy or the financial resources to adapt. I wondered if any of the tired, old workers—some who had been with my dad for years—would ever find jobs if the shop closed.

The toughest part of my job was watching my father trying to repair an old sewing machine or cutting linings for gloves with his hands shaking so badly I only glanced at him out of the corner of my eye so I wouldn't humiliate him.

"Don't end up like me," he told me. "Be a doctor. You'll never have to worry about making a living."

I hadn't the heart to tell him I intended to switch my major to psychology. I thought psychology would help me write better characters. Psychology also had no three-hour labs. I had already determined that I would need the extra time to work after classes to support a car and live in an apartment off campus. I had no intention of returning to the fraternity house or the dorm.

President Johnson signed the Civil Rights Act of 1964 on July 2, making it illegal to discriminate on the basis of race, religion, color, or national origin, and providing the government with the powers to enforce desegregation. I was heartened that Johnson was continuing to push President Kennedy's civil rights policies.

I continued to grow more restless than I had ever been. I was looking for something, and I couldn't quite put my finger on what it was. I continued to feel a great change in the air, and I wanted to understand it and be part of it if I could. I had felt it during the Kennedy years. It had intensified after JFK's assassination.

After work and on my days off, I sometimes took the hour-long bus ride into New York and hung out in Greenwich Village as I often had during my last two years of high school.

I wrote down folk songs I heard in the coffeehouses. I listened to conversations around me and heard whispers of pot, grass, weed, marijuana, dope, and drugs that expanded your mind.

I overheard talk in the coffeehouses and on the street that Bob Dylan smoked marijuana. Aldous Huxley wrote about mescaline.

I was offered a "stick" of marijuana for ten dollars by a thin, creepy kid outside Café Wha? on MacDougal Street. When I asked to see it, he said he had to have my money first, and then, he'd go get it. It was stashed somewhere else. I told him I'd think about it.

I wished I knew how to get in touch with Evelyn. She had mentioned experimenting with drugs on her travels. I was only half listening. All I wanted that night was sex. At least I knew now what she meant by tripping.

I heard of two psychology professors—Dr. Timothy Leary and Dr. Richard Alpert—who had been kicked out of Harvard the year before for experimenting with mind-expanding drugs like LSD. They were carrying on their experiments on an estate in upstate New York. I wondered what would happen if I showed up at their door.

The idea that our minds could be expanded intrigued me.

A riot broke out in Harlem on July 18 after a white policeman fatally shot a Black teenager. The violence was contained to small sections of Black neighborhoods in the city.

I was in Greenwich Village that day and didn't even know about the riot until I returned home and heard about it on the radio.

Six days later, a race riot broke out in Rochester in upstate New York in the Black ghetto. It lasted three days. Governor Nelson Rockefeller sent the National Guard to the city. By the time the rioting ceased, four people had died, 350 had been injured, and 1,000 had been arrested—85 percent of those arrested were Black. Over 200 stores were looted or damaged.

Small riots took place during the summer in a number of cities in other states between the East Coast and the Mississippi, including Chicago, Illinois; Philadelphia, Pennsylvania; and Jersey City, Paterson, and Elizabeth, New Jersey. The riots were mainly in Black neighborhoods and quickly vanished from the news.

CHAPTER 13

I barely saw my brother even though we were sharing our old bedroom. He was working at our district Boy Scout camp where different troops hired him to be their Scoutmaster for the week. He spent his free time with his girlfriend, Linda, who lived at home with her parents in a town near the George Washington Bridge. Ray met Linda in his freshman year at Rutgers. She had started her science degree at Douglass and had a bachelor's degree in nursing from Columbia University in New York. They were talking about getting married. My brother decided to quit his job in New Mexico and lined up a new job teaching middle school in a nearby town near our house for the fall. He planned to live at home, get a master's degree, and save money, something he had never been very good at before.

I was happy for him. He had found someone who cared about him.

I saw my father at the shop when he was fixing a machine or working on the shop floor, but we rarely talked. He never gossiped, and he liked listening more than talking. I had nothing I could tell him that would make sense in his world.

My sister Daisy, four and a half years younger than me, worked as a counselor at a day camp in the township. She spent her evenings reading or with her friends from the neighborhood or friends she knew from one of her singing or musical groups from high school. Since I rarely ate supper with the family, I hardly saw her.

My mother was as busy as ever. Besides looking after the office work and sales at the factory, she served on the high school board of education—an elected position that she'd won the year before. She also remained active in local and county politics, and a dozen local charities, half of which she and my father co-founded. She looked after the house-work and shopping. Since Dad could no longer drive long distances, she drove Dad and herself to Newark, Brooklyn, or Long Island several times a month for regular family gatherings and celebrations. They both came from large families, and Mom, though living an hour to two hours away from the old neighborhoods in New York City and Newark and our rela-tives, was still in touch with everyone.

At least a few times a month, Mom would attend one of her stamp or coin clubs and visit several local antique shops where she hunted for vin-tage clothes and costume jewelry, art glass, pictures and prints, old books, and anything broken that she thought was worth a fortune if it only could be fixed. "If I didn't keep busy, I would go crazy," she told me.

I knew beyond a shadow of doubt that I would go crazy if I stayed much longer.

I blew my savings on a six-year-old, bubble-back, cherry-red 1958 Volvo. The previous owner had souped it up with spinner hub caps, a chrome shift on the floor, a fancy wood-and-steel steering wheel, and a few other extras that gave it a sporty look. I thought a Volvo made me look im-portant and intelligent.

When I took my new car for its first high-speed test drive, I blew a hole in the muffler at ninety miles an hour on the dead-end segment of the new interstate that ran through the township.

I bought a new Smith-Corona portable typewriter at a discount through a great uncle who lived on Long Island and sold business machines.

I sat down at the keyboard and tried to think of something to write but came up empty.

I need to return to California, I told myself. Then, I'll be able to write.

On July 27, President Johnson sent another 5,000 military observers and other personnel to Vietnam, increasing the American presence there by more than 30 percent from 16,000 to 21,000.

CHAPTER 14

I wrote to Leslie, the star of Songfest, right after I found out my marks were good enough to let me return to USC.

She took nearly two months to write back. She told me she and her sorority sister Kate were coming to New York. They were staying at the Plaza Hotel for a short stop before boarding one of the big ocean liners for Europe. She wanted to know if I could meet them and give them a tour of Manhattan.

I thought she had forgotten me. Now, she was coming to New York and wanted to see me.

I wrote back, yes, of course, I would see them.

I could hardly think straight.

On August 2, the day before Leslie arrived in New York, the top news story of the day was an "unprovoked" attack on a US destroyer, the *USS Maddox*, by three North Vietnamese torpedo boats in the Gulf of Tonkin. US Navy fighters from the aircraft carrier *Ticonderoga* sank one of the North Vietnamese patrol boats and damaged the other two, killing four North Vietnam sailors and wounding six. Unknown at the time to me and most Americans, the *US Maddox*, which took a single hit from a machine-gun round and sustained no casualties, was secretly providing logistics to an illegal CIA-supported, presidentially approved plan that had been sending South Vietnamese-manned speed boats into North Vietnam waters to knock out radar installations along the coast.

I barely noticed the news. All I could think about was meeting Leslie. The morning after she arrived, I hitchhiked to North Plainfield and took the hour-long bus ride into the city to meet the two sorority sisters at the Plaza Hotel. It was a bright, clear, sunny day.

They were excited to see me. I was equally thrilled to see them, especially Leslie. Her beautiful eyes and smile, her shiny red hair, and her laugh took my breath away. They had no idea what they wanted to do or see. They only knew where not to go. Kate's mother had been very worried about the recent race riots. So, the girls had arrived with explicit instructions to stay clear of Harlem.

I assured them they would be safe with me. I gave them my Holden Caulfield tour of Manhattan, showing them landmarks mentioned in *Catcher in the Rye*, including the carousel, zoo, and sailboat pond, and the sprawling fields and paths across the park that took us nearly halfway across the city. I showed them Rockefeller Center, the Empire State Building, and the Village. I pointed out to them where I had spotted Mary Travers, the glamorous blond singer of the trio Peter, Paul, and Mary. She had been strolling through Washington Square one Sunday afternoon when folk singers brought their guitars to the park and sang for free.

Leslie and I walked everywhere with our arms and hands all over each other. During dinner and wine at an Italian restaurant in the Village, Leslie and I had a good laugh about how sick many of my fraternity brothers and her sorority sisters had been from drinking the crappy fake champagne at the party after Songfest. Leslie kept thanking me for warning her off the rotgut. That night, Leslie and I curled up on her twin bed and made out as best we could. I was sure more would have happened between us if Kate hadn't been in the bed beside us.

The next morning, Leslie and I said our goodbyes with lots of kisses, hugs, and secret feels of each other that left me dizzy with happiness and seemed to leave her equally giddy. She promised to write to me while touring Europe.

"I can't wait to see you when I get back," she told me as their cab pulled away from the hotel.

I took the bus to New Jersey, my mind dancing with thoughts of what it would be like to return to USC in the fall and maybe get a place with Leslie.

CHAPTER 15

While I was entertaining Leslie and Kate, the second incident in the Bay of Tonkin took place.

I didn't hear about it until after I said my goodbyes to the two women. The public was told that the *USS Maddox* had been attacked a second time and had returned fire. Years later, investigations and secret documents would reveal that the destroyer had not been attacked. This government lie had major political consequences. The Republicans had just nominated right-wing Senator Barry Goldwater as their presidential candidate. President Johnson, who worried he would be labeled soft on Communism in the upcoming election, sent US war planes to attack North Vietnam gunboats and land targets on August 5 in retaliation for the faked second Gulf of Tonkin incident.

I barely noticed.

I was struck by the follow-up stories in the newspaper from the previous day—the discovery of the bodies of the three murdered civil rights workers—James Chaney, 21; Michael Schwerner, 24; and Andrew Goodman, 20.

Their bodies were found in an earthen dam near Philadelphia, Mississippi after the FBI paid a reward for the information.

My brother and I had been driving through Mississippi just weeks before the murders. I felt sick hearing the news. My brother had been right. I could have gotten us in trouble talking about segregated bathrooms in rural Mississippi. I was seriously chastened.

The Southeast Asia Resolution was passed by an act of Congress on August 7, 1964. Popularly known as the Tonkin Resolution, it was a document written in response to the falsified news of the two Bay of Tonkin gunboat incidents—one of them provoked by secret, illegal war acts by the US and the other simply fabricated. The nearly unanimous resolution gave President Johnson war powers—authorization to use military force in Southeast Asia without a formal declaration of war.

Debate on the resolution was minimal. It passed the US House of Representatives unanimously. Two Senators I'd never heard of voted against it—Senator Wayne Morse, a Democrat from Oregon, and Ernest Gruening, a Democrat from Alaska.

The only thing I thought about was Leslie and getting back to California where I could start writing for real. I hadn't written more than a few dozen pages all summer—all of it pieces of stories that went nowhere. Like me, incomplete.

CHAPTER 16

By the middle of August, I had enough money saved from my two jobs to return to California.

As I set out from New Jersey, my greatest concern was making it to Los Angeles without my car falling apart.

In the few weeks I had owned my Volvo, I had lost a lot of confidence in it. In addition to the blown muffler, which I had replaced, the engine was burning far more oil than it should, and at times, the entire car seemed to shake unnecessarily when I drove over potholes or bumpy roads.

My fears grew worse a few hours after I started on my trip when the tow truck driver, who stopped to help me repair a flat on the Pennsylvania Turnpike, asked, "What the hell are you driving, kid?" He'd never seen a car like it before.

Somewhere east of Pittsburgh, I passed the last Volvo I would see for days.

I was determined to make it. I let the road, the speedometer, and gas tank indicator hypnotize me. I drove straight through to Columbus, Ohio and slept in the car in a gas station parking lot on an air mattress on top of my steamer trunk in the back seat—the same steamer trunk I had bought in June in California to ship my things home.

I started out from Ohio before dawn. I drove through Indiana and Illinois the next morning, crossing the Mississippi in the early afternoon.

I battled storms and tornados for the next six hours while crossing Missouri, white knuckling through sheets of rain so thick I took it on faith I was still on the road. The storm finally let up as I crossed the border into Kansas. I took secondary roads most of the time so I could see the countryside and the small towns. I parked beside the two-lane road in farm country and slept another six or seven hours in the back of the car.

After driving across Kansas and eastern Colorado the following day, I discovered my heater didn't work as I headed at dusk into the Rockies west of Pueblo, Colorado. I had originally planned to sleep over with friends of my brother who lived there, but at the last minute I decided to keep going.

The first miles up the side of the mountain were easy enough. Then, my heart began to race as I heard my engine sputter and cough as I drove higher.

I had to shift into second, and then, first gear to make it up some of the steepest parts of the winding road. A handful of cars came from behind and zoomed around me like I was standing still. I caught whiffs of something that smelled like burning rubber and oil. I wanted to believe they came from the other cars or the road, but I suspected the odors were coming from my car.

Few homes and fewer services were located along the road. I kept going, afraid if I stopped, I would have to abandon my car.

When night arrived, I saw even fewer vehicles. Most of the time, I was alone. I had only my headlights and a bright moon to light the way up the narrow mountain highway.

Somewhere in the night I crossed the Continental Divide. I breathed a sigh of relief that my engine survived the steep climb. I hoped my brakes would hold on the way down. I was also freezing to death. My heater gave off nothing but a weak stream of tepid, smoky air. I drove with my front windows open as I followed a snake-like silvery river down the mountain.

Down, down, down.

Mile after mile.

Hour after hour.

The only changes were the sharp turns in the road and the reflections off the river from the moon.

The only vehicle on the road was mine.

Without warning, something big—a deer, an elk, Big Foot—ran out in front of me.

I almost drove off the side of the road into the water.

It scared the hell out of me.

Shaking, I pulled to a flat spot beside the river to take a rest. It was too cold to sleep, but I was happy. I was alive. I was more than halfway back to California.

The only thing that would have made me happier would have been having someone—Leslie, preferably—sitting beside me resting her head on my shoulder, seeing what I was seeing. I had received a couple of postcards from her before I'd left—one from Denmark and one from Germany—apologizing for not writing more often, and signed "Love, Leslie" with instructions on which American Express office to send my reply.

She was returning to California from Europe in a couple of weeks. I couldn't wait.

CHAPTER 17

I got my first glimpse of marijuana shortly after I returned to Los Angeles.

Jeff Weiss, my biology lab partner from my first semester, said I could stay at his parents' three-bedroom apartment in the Fairfax District until I found my own place.

My trip across the US took just over four and a half days—even more remarkable because I had driven most of the way at a speed of about forty-five to fifty miles an hour. In addition to the four sandwiches, two bananas, two apples, one box of cookies, and six sodas my mother had packed, I had eaten four fried egg sandwiches, two cheeseburgers, five additional sodas, and three chocolate milks at roadside diners and truck stops along the way. According to Jeff's bathroom scale I lost seven pounds, down from 135 to 128.

The mechanic at the Volvo dealer in Beverly Hills informed me I had driven across the US with carburetors that were on their last legs. Worse, my motor mounts were completely gone. The motor was sitting in the frame with nothing holding it in place but gravity. The mechanic said the mounts had likely been broken for a long time, and I had driven across the country that way. He warned me against driving the car until everything was fixed. I gave him the go-ahead and spent the rest of the day driving around with Jeff in his tow truck.

Jeff looked like a tall, athletic, wavy-haired, blond Viking with a goatee and narrow lion eyes sitting behind the steering wheel of the truck as we barreled along the freeway. As lab partners we had been a disaster, but we had remained good friends. Jeff was a year younger than me but had skipped ahead in high school, graduated at seventeen, and entered USC six months ahead of me. He had spent his vacation in summer school, picking up a few extra classes, putting him even closer to getting his bachelor's degree than me. He wanted to be a psychiatrist and was leaving for Vienna in a week to study psychology for a year.

During the final weeks of summer, he drove a tow truck for his father's scrapyard in Torrance. Jeff's job was to drive around Los Angeles County to garages and impound lots, pick up unclaimed cars, and tow them to the yard. His truck could haul three cars at a time—one over the cab, one over the bed, and one with its front wheels on the truck and its rear wheels on the street. Our last stop of the day was an impound lot on the edge of Hollywood, north of downtown. The manager in charge of the lot told us the car we were picking up had been impounded when three Mexican nationals had been stopped by Los Angeles police, then arrested when the police found a large stash of marijuana hidden behind the dashboard.

The car was a sunbaked, fifteen-year-old, four-door Dodge sedan. When Jeff opened the driver's door to release the emergency brake, I looked inside the car and couldn't help noticing shreds of green-brown dried plants, stems, and seeds scattered across the front seat and floor. It was just lying there.

Jeff didn't seem to notice.

I was tempted to grab some of it, but I didn't have the nerve. I kept my thoughts to myself as we hitched the car to the rear of the tow truck and headed to the yard.

Halfway back, Jeff said, "My cousin Laurie's on pot all the time. He says it's fun."

"You ever tried it?" I asked.

"No. Of course not." He looked at me like I was crazy.

I didn't say anything. I wasn't sure how he would react if I told him I was interested in trying some.

In New York, five days after the Beatles' Hollywood Bowl concert, and a few days after I had seen my first grass, Bob Dylan introduced the Beatles to pot at the Delmonico Hotel. And the four pill-popping guys from England took their first psychedelic trip.

The music and the musicians changed in other ways that summer as well when a new group from England, the Animals, led by singer Eric Burdon, released the world's first folk-rock song—their version of an old standard folk song, "The House of the Rising Sun." Burdon's soulful voice was backed with an electric guitar, an electric organ, and a rock beat. "The House of the Rising Sun" had been sung by folk heroes of mine like Woody Guthrie, Lead Belly, and Bob Dylan as a folk song. It was one of the first songs I learned on my guitar. The Animals' version was the first crossover. By September, it was the first non-Beatles number one hit by a British rock band in the US. This song inspired Bob Dylan to begin experimenting with electronic instruments and rock 'n' roll.

CHAPTER 18

By the time Jeff left for Vienna a week later, I'd found a roommate, an apartment, and a job.

My new roommate, a tall, pleasant sophomore I'd met in the dorm during my freshman year, was working his way through USC on a Naval Reserve Officer Training Corps scholarship. The only thing we had in common was we were both just scraping by and we were willing to battle cockroaches together.

The apartment building was at 2625 Ellendale Place about a half mile from the north entrance to the campus. The old two-story, stucco, L-shaped, Mission-style building had been constructed in the 1920s on the site of an old mansion. Each apartment had its own entrance opening onto a sidewalk with a long, narrow fishpond filled with bright orange carp and water plants running along it. Our place in the middle of the building had its own flight of stairs to our second floor apartment. The apartment door opened into a small living room. Off to the right was a four- piece bathroom. In the other direction, around an open arch was a small dining room and a kitchen.

I slept in the dining room on a cot and typed and studied on the small dining room table. Tim slept in the living room on the Murphy bed that pulled down from the wall at night and was raised in the morning. He had to go through my space to the kitchen, and I had to go through his space to go to the washroom and front door. The setup gave each of us a bit of privacy.

I found a job with a crew of about twenty other students loading cartons of books on a university pickup truck at Doheny Library, the main library on campus, and unloading them at a storage area in the basement of the old, recently decommissioned armory located in Exposition Park a couple of blocks south of the library.

I worked with Buddy and Rick, two locals who had gone to Hollywood High School together and were trying out for the USC freshman football team. They were using the heavy lifting and hauling to increase their strength and agility. I was always looking for a way to keep in shape, so, I fit right in. The three of us moved far more boxes than the others for the sheer fun of it. A couple of times, a few men in suits came to watch us. One of these men, a short, slim, older, sandy-haired man with glasses, came by a few times alone and silently watched the workers.

The sandy-haired man turned out to be Dr. Lewis F. Stieg, the head of the Library School and USC's library system. When the original moving job wrapped up just before classes started, Stieg called Buddy, Rick, and me into his office in Doheny Library and offered all three of us a chance to stay and work on other jobs. Buddy and Rick declined because they were heading to football tryouts. I gladly accepted.

My new job was to drive the new Cushman electric golf cart assigned to the library around campus, hauling individual volumes and cartons of books between the main library, the half dozen other libraries on campus as well as the two outside storage areas. The closest storage area was the annex, a boxy, brick building in the middle of a parking lot a block from the rear of the library. The other storage facility was in the old armory in Exhibition Park where the library had rented several large rooms in the locked basement for storing some of the overflow and new acquisitions from the Special Collections library and other libraries.

The first day was almost my last. I ran the golf cart into the side of a building and put a dent in the vehicle. When I told Dr. Stieg, he just laughed and said he'd done something similar with one of his first cars.

My salary dropped to $1.30 an hour, the new California minimum wage that had just come into effect, but Dr. Stieg immediately put in for a raise, and I was soon earning $1.50. The best part was that I could set my own hours and work as little or as much as I wanted. I reported directly to Dr. Stieg.

I quickly got to know the library staff in Doheny and all the specialized libraries on campus. Because I made my rounds at all hours, I was given a master key—the only one that I knew of besides Dr. Stieg's—to all the library buildings on campus plus the annex and dungeon at the armory.

Another great benefit was access to the stacks, the vast labyrinth of rooms in Doheny where the main collections of books and periodicals were kept. Normally, only graduate students, professors, and library staff could venture into the stacks at will. In an instant, I had gained another leg up. I didn't have to waste time filling out requests for books and waiting for them to be delivered to the reading room desk. I could simply roam the inner sanctuary on my own and flip through as many books and periodicals as I wanted to right on the spot. I could instantly see if they were the right ones for whatever research I was doing.

Occasionally I worked with one of the Special Collections librarians or other librarians setting up exhibits in the main library Treasure Room.

I picked classes that only met on Tuesdays and Thursdays. I started my first class at eight in the morning and finished my last night class at nine at night. By taking classes that met only two times a week, I had five days off to study, work, and figure out how to write a novel.

I also took my first psychology course, a basic overview of the discipline's history and its many branches. My other classes were modern literature, modern history, and short story writing.

A free speech movement began at the University of California at Berkeley nearly four hundred miles to the north. The movement started after several students were banned from distributing civil rights literature on the school's property and the Berkeley administration demanded a loyalty oath from faculty members. The skirmishes between students and those running the university dragged on for most of the fall semester. During an arrest for trespassing at Berkeley's Sproul Hall, a leader of the Free Speech Movement, Jack Weinberg, provided one of the most enduring slogans of the times. He told a *San Francisco Chronicle* reporter in November, "We don't trust anyone over thirty."

The free speech movement was largely ignored at other universities around the country, including USC.

I worked with one of the young librarians putting together an exhibit at Doheny Library on the late Aldous Huxley. We got to sift through some of his personal papers.

The Bel Air fire had swept through Huxley's house in 1961, destroying many of his personal effects, manuscripts, old letters, photos, and books. The display was limited to odds and ends, including some of Huxley's personal notes on an LSD trip he took in the hills behind his home with several Hollywood luminaries. On display were also first editions of his most famous book, *Brave New World* and a yellowed copy with margin notes of his great 1936 pacifist essay, "Words and Behavior," where he wrote: "What is absurd and monstrous about war is that men who have no personal quarrel should be trained to murder one another in cold blood."

We also displayed a copy of his most controversial book, *Doors of Perception*, published in 1954, about his experiments with mescaline.

Huxley had died across town in Los Angeles on the same day President Kennedy was assassinated. Huxley insisted on taking LSD on his death bed. He thought the experience was that good.

Huxley had taken psychedelics with a wide range of people. He had not turned into a lunatic or an addict. [13]

I was fascinated by the idea that a drug could expand one's mind. I wondered what it would do for me. I wanted to be a pioneer. The prospect of exploring a new frontier was fascinating and frightening.

I was majoring in psychology because I still was only half convinced I could earn a living as a writer. Unless I got really good—to me that meant writing a novel and getting a lot of money for it—I would have to earn a living at something else.

Psychology had been around for fifty years or more, but it had only begun to be mass marketed in the past few years.

Ordinary people—not elites, not intellectuals, not the leaders in industry and government—but the masses, especially young people, were openly beginning to talk about what they were thinking and feeling for the first time in history.

Psychology, sociology, anthropology and a dozen new fields were playing new roles in everything, especially in rich countries, as the need for more knowledge and knowledge workers exploded.

The first thing I did on my own was look up the psychology of writing and creativity. I found Graham Wallas, a British psychologist and Fabian, who created a four-stage model for creativity in 1926 that included preparation, incubation, illumination, and verification or implementation. Others had added or refined his list.

As far as writing a novel, I was still stuck somewhere between preparation and incubation.

The teacher for my short-story writing class, Glenn Meeter, was a tall, thin, pale, clean shaven, young Midwesterner with glasses and a timid smile. He was fresh out of the Iowa Writers' Workshop, a celebrated two-year master's program in writing. Meeter was a poet and short-story writer working on his doctorate. He taught just like my favorite high school English teacher, Robert Lee Miles. Miles was a Princeton grad fresh out of the equally renowned Wesleyan College masters writing program when he came to our high school to teach. Miles had taught us high schoolers everything he had learned. Everything Glenn Meeter was teaching us was exactly what I had learned from two years of English with Bob Miles. Meeter thought so, too.

After only a few assignments, Meeter told me one day after class he was impressed with my writing. He said I knew as much as him. The best way for me to get better was to keep writing. He let me write whatever I wanted. I wrote short stories that were more like chapters of books. It was good to be writing again. It was like being with an old friend.

One day while driving along Wilshire Boulevard, I suddenly looked up at a certain angle and saw the beautiful campus with acres of lawns and beautiful Spanish-colonial-style buildings that I thought I had applied to. It was the West Los Angeles Veterans Hospital. I laughed out loud.

I hadn't heard from Leslie in almost a month, and when I did, the news was good for her, bad for me.

She and her sorority sister Kate decided to stay in Europe. They had rented a flat and were shuttling back and forth between Edinburgh and London.

Leslie was in love with a rock musician in London and then a cooper (barrel-maker) in Scotland. Leslie and Kate had made so little contact with their folks back home after leaving New York that Kate's mother flew to London from California and got Scotland Yard involved in finding the two young women.

Leslie had missed the start of school and wasn't sure if she'd ever come back.

Vietnam popped up again a few times. The Army was drafting more people. Everyone said it would get worse if Goldwater was elected president.

Thankfully, President Johnson beat Senator Goldwater in a landslide. Many voters feared Goldwater might start a nuclear war. Johnson, I hoped, would reassure the world that the US wanted peace.

I mused in one of my letters to my mother that I might go to Mexico if the draft came after me.

While the Free Speech movement continued at Berkeley, students at USC ran riot and lit bonfires on fraternity row in protest when the Athletic Association of Western Universities chose Oregon State over USC to go to the Rose Bowl. The AAWU's decision flew in the face of USC's record for beating not only tougher teams but defeating number-one- ranked Notre Dame in a spectacular upset. The USC riots did nothing to change the AAWU's decision.

During the same week as the bonfires, a plaque was dedicated to the get-out the-vote speech Senator John F. Kennedy made on the steps of Doheny Library to the USC student body weeks before the election of 1960.

Only a smattering of students attended the ceremony. The speakers shouted to passing students to come join the gathering, but their pleas were ignored.

It became increasingly difficult to ignore the escalating war in Vietnam where the South Vietnam Army with US advisers was fighting against not only the army of North Vietnam but against the Viet Cong, the very tenacious Communist guerrilla army inside South Vietnam.

On December 4, 1964, the Viet Cong launched a series of attacks across the country against the South Vietnamese Army.

On December 27, a battalion-sized force of Viet Cong overran the village of Binh Gia, forty miles east of Saigon. A South Vietnamese Ranger battalion and a South Vietnamese Marine battalion, along with several US military advisers and observers, retook the town without a fight and then engaged a heavily armed Viet Cong fighting force outside the village. The battle and mop up continued into January 1965. The South Vietnamese armed forces suffered losses in the hundreds. Five American advisers were killed, and most of the other US servicemen were wounded.

Singer Sam Cooke was shot to death under mysterious circumstances six-and-a-half miles south of me in the heart of Watts on December 11, 1964, at the Hacienda Motel on South Figueroa. His single "A Change Is Gonna Come" was released two weeks later and became an important anthem of the Civil Rights movement.

CHAPTER 19

Leslie spent most of December worried she was pregnant with the child of her working- class Scottish boyfriend as she and Kate bounced around between the UK, France, Spain, and Italy. She agonized over how all her dreams for her future might be lost.

When Leslie discovered she wasn't pregnant at the end of December, she left Europe, greatly chastened, and returned to her parents' townhouse in Burbank.

We saw each other almost every day after she arrived home. She didn't have a car, so I drove to her place. We went out to drive-in theaters, the only place we could be alone. We were both film nuts and the drive-ins were always playing double features with old movies we hadn't seen.

We spent a lot of time in each other's arms and talked about being in love. The attraction was still strong, but there was a wall. She had already been through two great love affairs since our New York adventure.

After a while, I realized whatever spark had existed between us had gone out. We went back to being friends.

I went back to dreaming.

Life was good. The newly opened Santa Monica Freeway was so empty I could leave my apartment on Ellendale, drive down Vermont Avenue to the ramp, take the new freeway all the way to the exit in Santa Monica, and be on the sand at Venice Beach or the State Beach in Santa Monica with my books in twenty minutes flat.

I could live here forever, I told myself. I was already almost supporting myself on my part-time work.

I was taking courses that were relatively easy for me, so I had no fear of failing. I had stuck to my old habits to overcome my painfully slow reading ability. I bought and started reading every required book the first day of class. I started every written assignment the day it was given, even if it was only to write a paragraph or two. I attended every class and took copious notes. I turned in every paper on time and finished reading well ahead of any tests. Before each test, I reviewed, reviewed, reviewed, and then, relaxed going into the test by being well prepared in advance. I got a good night's sleep before every test. I worked hard and let nothing get in the way of school.

I headed into finals at the end of January with a fair amount of confidence.

Tim decided to move to another apartment with some of his Naval ROTC friends, so I had a few weeks of wondering if I could find someone to share expenses, which ran to about a hundred a month for rent and utilities in total for two people. I could afford fifty dollars a month but not a hundred. Luckily, Jeff came back from Vienna after only one semester. He hated freezing his butt off in his tiny room. More importantly, he couldn't get all the classes he needed for the spring semester.

Jeff's parents agreed to let him room with me since they had just moved out of Los Angeles to a new place in the San Fernando Valley, an hour away, sometimes two hours, depending on traffic.

The first time Jeff drove me there, we laughed ourselves silly, making gorilla noises in the car like King Kong because Jeff's parents had moved to a new luxury subdivision in a town in the Valley called Tarzana, which to us sounded like Tarzan, a movie, book, and comic book character who lived in Africa among wild animals.

Jeff's parents' new home was a large ranch house with a large swimming pool and a spectacular view of the Valley. Jeff's parents told us at dinner the development was on land that once formed the giant ranch owned by the late William Rice Burroughs, the author of many books including the *Tarzan* series. His ranch was called Tarzana.

I was pleased when my postcards arrived with my grades. I had earned a 4.0 for my first semester as a sophomore. I got my name in the school newspaper, *The Daily Trojan*. I was far enough ahead in overall grade points that I was no longer worried about my scholarship. For the first time since I had started university, I felt I was heading in the right direction. Nothing could derail me. I would work toward getting a degree in psychology. It was more like medicine than literature, and besides, by then I knew the secret of writing was writing. My dream was to write a novel good enough to make a living off it by the time I graduated. If I didn't, I could go to grad school and become a psychologist, something I thought I might be good at.

I began to relax. As I ended my teenaged years, I felt I was making progress toward a good start in life. My optimism lasted only a few days.

CHAPTER 20

In his inaugural speech on January 20, 1965, President Johnson spoke ominous words to the boys and men my age. It started off benign enough: "The American covenant called on us to help show the way for the liberation of man."

Johnson went on to say, "Change has brought new meaning to that old mission. We can never again stand aside, prideful in isolation. Terrific dangers and troubles that we once called 'foreign' now constantly live among us. If American lives must end, and American treasure be spilled, in countries we barely know, that is the price that change has demanded of conviction and of our enduring covenant."

War was on the horizon. I was just the right age to be sent halfway around the world to kill or be killed. Jeff and I were both in the crosshairs. No one I talked to in or out of school was for war. Nobody I knew could convince me how more American troops in Vietnam were saving America from the Communists.

By February, we were hurtling toward a point of no return. War was inevitable.

CHAPTER 21

For President Johnson, the last red line was crossed on February 7, 1965. It came at the start of my second semester of my sophomore year. The National Liberation Front commandos attacked a US military airbase at Pleiku in the central highlands, killing eight US military personnel and wounding more than a hundred.

Johnson immediately ordered the US Navy to bomb military installations inside North Vietnam. Three days later, twenty-three US servicemen were killed by a bomb set by Viet Cong sappers in a US enlisted men's hotel in Qui Nhon.

Following this attack, America evacuated US dependents of servicemen and civilians from South Vietnam.

The majority of Americans thought the US should retaliate harder than it had in the past against the Viet Cong and North Vietnamese.

I was in that minority of Americans who thought the US should get out.

On February 21, 1965, Black leader Malcolm X was gunned down in New York by gunmen believed linked to the Nation of Islam. The killing was the culmination of a war between Malcolm X and his former colleagues in the American Black Muslim movement over whether to join with other civil rights leaders to fight for equality as Malcolm X wanted or remain a Black nationalist movement as the Nation of Islam's leaders favored.

The Impressions' new single "People Get Ready," written by Curtis Mayfield, quickly became a new unofficial anthem for the Black community fighting its own war for equality and civil rights inside America.

CHAPTER 22

I took my second writing class with Glenn Meeter in my second semester in my sophomore year.

It was a night class for serious writers. It started at seven and got out at nine.

Another student, Garry, caught my attention in our early classes when he read one of his stories out loud. His story was about a car accident he had in New York when his taxi flipped over near the George Washington Bridge and how he had traveled through the Middle East for six weeks looking for hashish and enlightenment while somehow putting the back pain from his accident out of his mind. He talked about Aldous Huxley and *The Doors of Perception* and the beatnik writers.

Garry was a couple of inches taller than me with long, straight, dark hair, dark eyes, and caterpillar-like eyebrows and a moustache. The car crash had left him with a wobbly gait.

The next class fell on my twentieth birthday. I was feeling adventurous.

I arrived before class started. A handful of other students were already there. Garry was sitting by himself. I sat down beside him and asked him flat out if he had ever smoked pot. He said he had.

I said, "I'd like to try some."

"Anytime. I have some at my place."

"What about now?" I asked. Glenn Meeter had just arrived along with a couple of other students. Always cheerful, Glenn smiled as he looked over at Garry and me.

While Glenn took his seat at the desk at the front of the room and began preparing his notes, I turned to Garry on impulse and said, "We could go now. I had one of Meeter's courses last semester. He doesn't care about attendance as long as you spend your time writing."

I couldn't imagine a better time to try pot than my twentieth birthday while the country was on the brink of war.

Garry shrugged. "Okay." He stood and headed for the door. I followed, giving a nod to Glenn who smiled cheerfully as Garry and I walked out. I had already turned in more pages than anyone else in the class. I was writing all the time. Garry had already turned in a half dozen stories. This was a class where performance mattered more than attendance.

Garry lived in a tiny, stand-alone, furnished, one-bedroom house. It was located behind a larger house on Ellendale Place, a short walk down the block on the other side of the street from my apartment. He lived there alone, he told me, but he had a girlfriend who slept over sometimes and might drop in that night.

Garry was unlike most of the friends that I had made at USC who were studying to become doctors, lawyers, dentists, pharmacists, and businesspeople. He was immersed in turning himself into a writer. He was miles ahead of me. His bookcases were overflowing with books I had heard of but never read—the *I Ching*; *The Alexandria Quartet*—*Justine, Balthazar, Mountolive*, and *Clea* by Lawrence Durrell; the *Epic of Gilgamesh*; *The Cat's Cradle* by Kurt Vonnegut; *One Flew Over the Cuckoo's Nest* by Ken Kesey; the sacred Hindu scripture, *Bhagavad Gita*, and *The Psychedelic Experience, A Manual Based on the Tibetan Book of the Dead*, co-authored by onetime Harvard psychologists Timothy Leary, Richard Alpert, and Ralph Metzner.

Garry's record collection was like nothing I had ever seen. He had all the albums of Bob Dylan and the Beatles, lots of albums of Ray Charles, Joan Baez, Ramblin' Jack Elliott, Sonny Terry and Brownie McGee, Dave Van Ronk, and many more albums of artists that I had never heard of.

He talked about his back. He was always in a lot of pain. He had spent weeks in traction after his trip to Europe and the Middle East, and two years later, his back still gave him problems. Smoking pot helped ease the pain.

We talked about the impending war and agreed that everything about it was senseless.

He asked if I'd like to hear a new album he'd just bought. It was by a woman named Buffy Sainte-Marie, a Cree Indian from Canada. He thought I'd like to hear a song called the "Universal Soldier."

He played it on his record player. The woman sang in a voice that was pure, powerful, and haunting. The words were simple and true: Soldiers, if you hear me, don't be used by the powers that promote war. Don't go. You have the power to stop war.

Was it that simple?

Garry played along with her music, strumming a big, gutsy Epiphone acoustic guitar. He was as good as half the guitarists I'd heard in the coffeehouses in New York.

He let me play his guitar while he retrieved from his desk some rolling papers and a small plastic bag about a quarter full of grass.

"I just got this today. I haven't tried it yet," he said, sitting in a chair opposite me while he poured a portion of the grass into the lid of a shoebox balanced on his lap, I watched as he cleaned the grass, separating the seeds and stems from the dried, crumbly leaves.

When he had a nice little pile of cleaned grass, he licked one sheet of rolling paper and stuck it to a second sheet to make a doublewide sheet. He then sprinkled a line of grass on the rolling papers and rolled a joint about half as thick as a regular cigarette, twisting the ends so the grass wouldn't fall out.

He lit it, took a drag, held his breath for a half minute, and finally let the smoke out. It filled the air of the tiny living room.

The smell was unusual. Swampy, dark, sweet, not unpleasant.

He handed the joint to me.

He told me to take a slow drag and not get too much smoke in my lungs until I got used to it. Otherwise, I'd just cough it up.

I had lots of practice learning to breathe without coughing from the smog, so I had no trouble inhaling the smoke and holding it in my lungs for a half minute before letting it out.

We passed the joint back and forth a few times.

"I don't feel any different," I said.

"Sometimes you won't the first time."

"What should I expect?"

"Whatever's inside your head. Some people spend all their energy trying to control it. They try to shape what they feel into something they want to see. Some people just let their mind go where it wants to. It's all in your head. The drugs just take away the filters. We miss a lot of what's happening around us because we're always in a hurry or trying to control what we're seeing and thinking."

I wasn't sure what he was saying, but I knew what he meant about controlling your thoughts.

He played disk jockey, while I sat back on one of his old stuffed chairs and wondered if I would feel anything.

My father once spoke to me about marijuana. I was sixteen or seventeen. We were driving home from the factory after dark. He said for no particular reason, "I was at a party one time where I was offered some marijuana. I turned it down."

That's all he said. I hadn't responded because I knew nothing about marijuana at the time and didn't know what to say.

Jeff's cousin smoked pot. The beatniks, the avant-garde, the bohemians, Bob Dylan, and Aldous Huxley smoked pot. I suspected the Beatles did, too.

I felt relaxed.

I let whatever was happening take over. I felt sensations of floating, tumbling, falling, and flying without moving an inch off my seat.

The poster of a Paul Klee painting tacked to Garry's wall became three dimensional, the colors more vibrant.

I picked up Garry's guitar and sang along with the Lead Belly record Garry had put on. I felt bayou heat, swamp, sweat, poor men on a chain gang swinging sledgehammers, breaking stones for a road, and remembering love affairs that ended badly.

My hearing seemed to become more acute. I could pick out notes and instruments on a Dylan album I had previously missed.

I opened my notebook and began to draw—faces, figures, frogs, turtles, flowers, sunsets—whatever came to mind. I was amazed at how fluid my drawing was.

Time slowed down.

My mind sped up. I thought of new ideas for my novel—brilliant ideas worth writing down. The whole novel formed in my head.

I told myself not to worry. I would remember everything.

Seconds later, my brilliant ideas vanished into the smoke-filled air.

I broke out laughing.

My birthday cake was a couple of cookies left over from one of Garry's parties and a cup of mint tea.

I stayed until Garry started to look like he might fall asleep in the chair opposite me.

"I should be going," I told Garry, getting to my feet. "Thanks for the experience. I wrote a whole novel in my head. I just can't remember it." I laughed.

"Done that a few times myself," he laughed, walking me to the door. "Happy birthday, man."

Just as I was leaving, his girlfriend arrived. She was a tall, pale woman with narrow eyes and long, wavy, reddish-brown hair. We knew each other from a class we had taken together. I said a quick goodnight and began walking away.

Garry called after me as I headed down the driveway, "Drop by any time."

CHAPTER 23

On March 7, 1965, hundreds of peaceful Black demonstrators marched into Selma, Alabama to protest against voting rights discrimination. They were met with a wall of police and deputies who mercilessly beat them. The televised beatings of the protesters on that day, known now as Bloody Sunday, were broadcast nationally and stayed at the top of the news for days.

On March 8, 1965, the day after Selma and less than two weeks after my twentieth birthday, two Marine battalions of about 3,500 soldiers arrived on the beach in Da Nang, marking the beginning of the American ground war in Vietnam.

I felt a sense of foreboding and panic when I received the notice from my New Jersey draft board that I had been reclassified from 2-S (student deferment) to 1-A (immediately eligible for the draft). I fantasized in my letters home about the possibility of leaving town with no forwarding address.

The reclassification turned out to be a clerical error. USC had failed to send the necessary paperwork to my draft board. It took a few weeks of letter writing to reestablish my 2-S. I breathed easier, but I was now growing increasingly wary of the draft.

I no longer felt free or carefree. I had simply been given a stay of execution. The undeclared war had started in earnest. [14] [15] [16] [17] [18]

CHAPTER 24

I dropped into Garry's place a few times a week.

Marijuana had kicked me out of my complacency. Somewhere along the way to being twenty, I had stopped seeing, tasting, hearing, smelling, and feeling. My life and thought processes had become one dimensional and dull.

Grass stimulated my senses.

One of the benefits of getting high after the first time was that I didn't have to wait twenty minutes to feel the effects of the drug. I knew what to look for, and so I could feel the effects in a minute or two. Like Garry said, it was a mind drug. The grass just lifted the filters. The inhibitions weren't the same ones that alcohol lifted. Alcohol was an anesthetic. It lowered my inhibitions but dulled my senses. Grass lifted me up and energized me. The blinders that came off gave me a rush of new thoughts and new ideas that I hastened to put down on paper as drawings and notes.

I was also wary of smoking too much. If I did, it could also wipe me out, leaving me sitting around feeling lazy, rubbery, and guilty about doing nothing.

Knowing grass was illegal bothered me but not enough to make me consider stopping. I wasn't rebelling. I wasn't tearing myself away from society. I was doing something illegal, but it was something no more terrible than drinking while underage in high school or in California where I still wasn't legal and had been drinking freely since arriving.

Prison time for grass was many times worse than for drinking under-age, so, I was careful and told no one I was smoking grass, not even Jeff or Leslie. I had no idea what I'd do if I ever got busted. [19]

On March 16, 1965, an 82-year-old American widow, Alice Herz, who had left Germany after Hitler came to power, set herself on fire in Detroit in protest of the escalating war and "a great country trying to wipe out a smaller country for no reason." She died ten days later.

The trick to getting high for me was to not get too high—and not all the time. Visiting this alternate universe was like traveling to a different, equally interesting reality. Each of my two realities gave me a different way to look at what I was writing, drawing, composing, and thinking. I had twice as many chances, I felt, of being equally brilliant or delusional with two states of mind available to me.

Garry called my writing cinematic. I tagged along when he and his friends went to a movie house playing Armenian movies. A few nights later, the same gang went to another theater playing Indian movies. Both movies had no subtitles. We sat through the films and afterward tried to piece together the storylines from the images. On one excursion, Garry and another girlfriend of his took me to the midnight underground mov-ies at the Cinema Theater on North Western Avenue in Hollywood. I was seeing different ways to tell universal stories.

I studied hard in all my classes, and nowhere more so than my writing class, which I rarely attended but turned in copious amounts of stories. I pushed myself against the mind-bending task of trying to create a long story, not just a short story or a piece of a book or movie, but a story that pulled the readers in, held their attention, and let them out the other end enlightened, changed, and craving more.

Bob Dylan's album *Bringing It All Back Home* was released on March 22. It rewired our minds.

It sounded like nothing else that I had heard before. It featured songs played on an acoustic guitar on one side. On the other side, an electric rock 'n' roll band accompanied Dylan. Songs like "Mr. Tambourine Man,"

"Subterranean Homesick Blues," (released later as a single and becoming Dylan's first top 40 hit single), and "Maggie's Farm" injected a new, high-octane energy into the old folk music. It was folk music on drugs.

The launch of the album turned into a rolling event. Garry got a copy the day it was released. Day after day I showed up at Garry's and found a small gathering of his old and new friends listening to the record. Most of Garry's friends like Mike Vosse, David Anderle, Sherril Forbes, Jack Rowe, Tom Costello, and others were from USC's theater school. Sometimes stoned, sometimes straight, I listened with the others to each cut repeatedly, trying to make out every word, every note, every hidden message.

I wanted to write like Bob Dylan.

Everyone did.

I wanted in, not to the music world itself but to the feelings and emotions of this new scene.

Something was changing. I was determined to be a witness.

CHAPTER 25

The first teach-in was organized by the Students for a Democratic Society (SDS) at the University of Michigan on March 24-25.

More teach-ins were held at dozens of the largest and most liberal universities around the country. Attendance grew at each new rally.

Professors and peace activists at these events gave lectures. People brought instruments and played music. No one had anything good to say about the war.

The teach-ins and protests were largely ignored at USC and most other colleges and universities in the country.

I started writing the beginnings of more novels. I turned out ten to twenty pages of whatever came into my head. When I could no longer sustain the momentum, I started another ten to twenty pages, and another ten to twenty pages.

Each time, the story collapsed into nothing.

Is it because I haven't yet lived long enough to have experienced stories with sufficient twists and turns to become a novel? Did we write short stories, poems, and songs in our youth because our own life experiences were so short? I bombarded myself with questions about the psychology of writing.

I tried to get my mind around what I would have to do to write a novel. I had no idea how to do it, but I already knew that learning how to do it was going to be the most interesting part. Writing was work. Every sentence was an effort, but it was good work and rewarding. Discovering my way of doing it would be the only way I could develop my own style. I wondered if it was even possible to be able to write a novel while I was still in school.

I thought of the war all the time. Was there a story for me in that mess?

Originally, I had been interested in the psychedelic experience because I wanted to be part of the vanguard of a new way of thinking. I wanted to write about it. But I knew nothing compared to Garry. He had been smoking pot for three years. He and his friends were the avant-garde, the trailblazers.

Garry had done research on the mystical connections between religion and psychedelics. He had taken his first LSD trip in his first year at university.

Garry arrived at USC a year ahead of me as a pre-med student. He had struggled with biology in part because his father had been stricken with brain cancer and suffered through surgeries that did little to stop the disease. Like me, Garry realized he hadn't the will or skills to be a doctor. After his father's death, he made up his mind to see if he could make it as a writer.

He took off on the trail of William Burroughs and the beatniks who had lived in or passed through Morocco and other Middle Eastern countries. When he returned to California, he got busted for marijuana and hauled off to jail. Garry's rich uncle had bailed him out and made sure Garry got off with no additional jail time. Garry laughed about it. It was one more adventure to write about. I craved more experiences. I was still under the illusion that the only way I could write something meaningful was to turn myself into a character in a book.

That character in a book would have to find something else to write about. But what?

On April 7, President Johnson increased the ground troops in Vietnam to 60,000.

CHAPTER 26

Garry asked me to his family's Seder. He had an ulterior motive for inviting me, which I didn't understand at first.

In the week before Passover, Garry began telling me more about his family.

His father, the late Lou Rusoff, had been a film and TV writer and producer. The family was originally from Winnipeg, Canada. Garry's father moved their family to Hollywood in the late 1940s and began writing for radio and television. [20]

Shortly before his death, Garry's father wrote and co-produced the highly successful teen movie *Beach Party*, starring Robert Cummings, Annette Funicello, and Frankie Avalon. Most of Lou Rusoff's movies were written or produced for the most famous, low-budget movie studio of the day, American International Pictures (AIP). AIP was founded by Lou's brother-in-law, a lawyer turned movie producer, Samuel Z. Arkoff, and Sam's partner, James H. Nicholson. Sam Arkoff's wife, Hilda, was Lou Rusoff's baby sister and Garry's aunt.

Garry told me how sad and broken he had felt when he had taken his father with his head in bandages in a wheelchair to the set in Malibu where they were filming *Beach Party*. His father had not lived to see its release and success.

Lou Rusoff, I was told, was a man full of natural warmth and charisma. He had been the de facto spiritual head of the Winnipeg Rusoff clan in Los Angeles until his death in 1963. Since then, Garry's uncle, Sam Arkoff, had become the one whom everyone deferred to—except Garry.

Garry was a rebel, a Hollywood *enfant terrible*, the non-conformist, the pothead, and acid head. An angry and very disappointed Uncle Sam,

Garry told me, had been the one who bailed Garry out of jail. Sam Arkoff was a very big man in Hollywood.

All of this was news to me and quite fascinating.

Part of my role in going to his family's Seder was to reassure his relatives that Garry was traveling the straight and narrow path at school. I was supposed to be his normal friend, the scholarship student, someone who had been on the Dean's List, a poor Jewish kid who had no place to go for Passover.

I dressed like Garry suggested—white shirt, tie, sports jacket, and slacks—instead of my usual T-shirt, jeans, and army surplus coat.

We drove to the Seder in Garry's 1958 Triumph TR3 since my Volvo was acting up again.

As we entered his house through the side door into the kitchen, I was hit with all the familiar aromas of roasted chicken, matzo ball soup, and other treats I recalled from Passovers past in New Jersey. Garry's mother, Suzanne, was a warm, attractive woman with friendly eyes, red hair, and a reassuring voice. She was surrounded by sisters-in-law and other relatives who were putting the last-minute touches on the Passover dinner.

The women greeted me with hugs, warm handshakes, and hellos like I was a member of the family. Garry had already informed Suzanne that I was, like Garry, planning on writing great novels. My ambitions didn't seem odd to her. She had been a writer's wife. She made me feel comfortable.

The house, too, was comfortable and inviting. Garry's father had custom-designed their home in the 1950s. It was a large ranch on a slope in a hilly section of Studio City on a street that branched off the Valley side of Laurel Canyon Boulevard. The house had a large pool in back. At the time, the slope above it was empty of other houses, giving it total privacy from its neighbors. The inside was a writer's paradise. Beyond the kitchen was a dining room that opened onto a large living room with a beamed ceiling. So many people were attending the Seder that they had turned the living room into a giant banquet hall. I wondered where I would be sitting.

On one side of the living room was a long hallway with bedrooms on both sides. Garry showed me his old room and his collection of guns, including a military-style carbine that he used to shoot at a rifle range at the other end of the Valley. He had shot it once in the hills behind his house, and someone had called the cops. Like me, he thought every kid growing up in America should own a gun and know how to use it. Also like me, he had been reevaluating this idea for the last several years. He joked about trading his guns for a big block of hash or a key of grass. He would do just that several years later.

On the other side of the living room was Lou Rusoff's old study where he had written many of his screenplays. Garry let me look around the room where his father had worked. I was mesmerized.

So, this is how a writer lives, I thought. It was the first time I had seen the inside of a real writer's workshop.

Lou Rusoff's study was nearly as large as my apartment on Ellendale. The walls were lined with bookshelves filled with books and old film scripts. Garry showed me a copy of the script for *Beach Party*. It was the first time I had seen a movie script. The study was only a few steps away from the kitchen, dining room, and living room—a perfect place to get away and at the same time remain close to the family.

I was getting a glimpse behind the scenes of Hollywood.

I wanted to be Lou Rusoff.

Garry introduced me to his Aunt Hilda and Uncle Sam Arkoff. Hilda was dark haired and pretty. Sam was ruddy and pudgy. Both greeted me warmly. Garry made sure I met his tall, handsome, older cousin, the Chicago-born, Canadian-raised, veteran Hollywood TV and movie character actor, Sheldon Allman and his latest new wife, a beautiful former Las Vegas showgirl. Garry saved his warmest introduction for actress Helene Winston, another Winnipeg transplant and long-time friend of the Rusoffs—and one of the only other people besides me who wasn't a relative or a spouse. Most of the relatives were involved in some way in show business.

Through the whirl of new faces and names I also noticed a very pretty, young woman, about my age, helping the older women with the food. We made eye contact a few times, and I got the feeling she was interested in me. I didn't get to meet her until the start of the Seder when the only free seat turned out to be between the pretty girl and one of Garry's aunts. The aunt patted the seat between herself and the pretty woman and ordered me to sit down.

Lucky me, I thought, sitting down, and introducing myself to the young woman named Donna. We had no time to chat as the Seder got underway. The ceremony was presided over by Uncle Sam, with all the attention focused on reading the *Haggadah*, and eating and singing, with outstandingly beautiful solos sung by Garry's cousin Sheldon, who was also the singing voice for the talking horse on the TV show *Mister Ed*. [21]

During lulls in the ceremony, I turned my full attention to the young woman beside me. She was well-read and laughed when I tried being funny. She was curious about everything. We talked about psychology, folk music, Henry David Thoreau's *Walden*, and the new Bob Dylan album, and how everyone's mind had been blown by Dylan's new sound that mixed folk music with rock. I told her about a haunting story by Mark Twain called the *Mysterious Stranger*. I liked it because it was one of Twain's most personal pieces. The reader got to look inside the head of Mark Twain and see him wrestling with his own inner struggles and mortality.

When the meal ended, we all left the table.

Donna disappeared into the kitchen to help the women. I rejoined Garry. He was smoking a cigarette on the patio beside the pool.

"I see you hit it off with my cousin Donna."

"Oh, so she's one of your cousins." Garry had mentioned several of his cousins would be at the Seder.

"She really likes you," he said with a mischievous smile.

I had seen her speaking with Garry briefly after the Seder.

"I really like her."

"She's Uncle Sam's daughter."

Awkward, I thought. Garry had a love-hate relationship with his Uncle Sam. I wondered what Uncle Sam might think about his daughter seeing a friend of Garry's.

"I'm thinking of asking her out."

"I'm sure she'd like that." Garry's grin widened. "But you know, Joe, Donna's only fourteen."

I was speechless.

Garry laughed.

"She's in eighth grade."

I couldn't believe it. "No."

He continued to chuckle. "Don't take it so hard. She's very mature for her age, and she's one of the smartest in the family. You aren't the first one to be fooled."

I had been right about a few things. She was beautiful. She was very smart. She did genuinely like me. I liked her.

But Donna Arkoff was *fourteen*.

Garry couldn't help teasing me relentlessly on the long drive back to USC. I think he was half hoping I would be crazy enough to ask Donna out so I could rile his uncle.

The world is already crazy enough without me adding to it, I told myself.

CHAPTER 27

The next day, the Students for a Democratic Society and the Student Non-violent Coordinating Committee led 25,000 relatively peaceful protesters in an anti-war march on Washington, DC. It was Saturday, April 17, the first full day of Passover and the day between Good Friday and Easter Sunday.

A small opposition to the war in Vietnam was beginning to find its legs. I was heartened to know that it wasn't just draft-eligible kids like me who were against the war. The protesters came from all ages as they had during the civil rights marches.

Three weeks after the release of Dylan's new album, the Los Angeles-based Byrds launched their recording career and pushed what became known as folk-rock to new heights with their souped-up version of Dylan's "Mr. Tambourine Man."

At the end of April, the US launched a blockade of Santo Domingo and sent in thousands of Marines and paratroopers to fight beside the right-leaning rebels against the left-leaning government forces in the country's short, bloody civil war. The US troops were there under the pretense of protecting Americans—though none had been killed or injured. In reality, the US appeared to be there to stop another Communist country taking hold in the Caribbean.

One night, I tagged along with Garry and his friends Michael Vosse, David Anderle, and Sherril Forbes to see *The Freaks* at the midnight showing at the Cinema Theater. The movie was made in 1932 by MGM at the height of the Depression. It was about a group of deformed circus freaks who get revenge on a trapeze artist who tries to swindle them.

Around this time, we started calling ourselves freaks.

CHAPTER 28

My childhood friend Fred showed up in California in the middle of my second semester. Fred had dropped out of college and come to California by bus to try to make it as a flamenco guitarist.

He didn't seem to have a clue how to go about it. His entire game plan had been to simply get to California with his guitar and his knowledge of flamenco music and see if he could get work. He was already good enough to play at some of the clubs in Greenwich Village.

I heard he had arrived in California through my mother who had heard it from his mother.

Fred was living at the YMCA in Long Beach. I called there and left a message. He called me back that evening after he got off work.

He was trying and struggling to make ends meet by working at a car wash.

I showed up at the Y the next day just after he finished his shift. He had no bankroll and couldn't find anyone in Long Beach who had even heard of flamenco music, much less knew where it was played. He was appalled by the Y.

"Joe, you have no idea how crazy it is here. The other morning, I went into the shower, and there was a turd floating in the drain on the floor. What kind of people shit in the shower?"

I had no idea.

Fred had arrived in California with the same naïve idea I had two years before—that Western cities were like Eastern cities with good public transportation systems.

He had been in California for a few weeks and had yet to visit the clubs in Los Angeles where he thought he might get work or at least try to build some connections like he had in the Village. Fred was one of the smartest people I had ever known, but as gifted as he was—he had impressed the top flamenco players in the Village with his skills by the time we left high school—Fred remained clueless when it came to street smarts. I did my best to help. Over the next week, whenever I had free time, I drove him around Los Angeles, taking him to the one club on Sunset Boulevard near downtown where flamenco was played and to several other clubs along the Strip where we soaked up the rock scene. On the weekend, we drove to Tijuana, two and a half hours to the south. We had a few beers in several bars and strip joints so we could listen to the local music. We chased leads all over Tijuana, looking for the elusive flamenco bar that everyone knew about, but no one seemed to know how to get to.

Back in Los Angeles, I got Fred an interview at the USC library for a full-time job, but it wouldn't start for another month. By this time, Fred was missing Cecelia, his high school sweetheart who was in her freshman year in college in New Jersey. Fred was also terribly demoralized by how low he'd sunk since arriving in California. In the end, I lent him enough money for bus fare home, with a parting warning, "Get yourself back in school, Fred, or you might get drafted."

All Fred wanted to do was to play his guitar, be with his girlfriend, and live out his life in peace. All I wanted to do was write books, draw, learn how to play the guitar better, find the right woman, and live out my life in peace.

It was still early 1965. Student deferments were relatively easy to get for anyone attending college or university full time. The ground war in Vietnam was still in its infancy, but no one was kidding anyone anymore. We were at war. The military-industrial complex that Eisenhower had warned us about in his farewell speech was growing an insatiable appetite for boys and young men like Fred and me.

I was happy and a little envious to find out that Fred did get called for his physical a short time later, but a history of seizures when he was young earned him a permanent deferment. I was glad he was out of harm's way. He had been incapable of surviving Long Beach. I knew he would never make it in Vietnam. I was worried that I might not either.

My first deliberate anti-war act was to buy a used record player for nine dollars at a pawn shop on Vermont Avenue and a copy of Buffy Sainte-

Marie's first album, *It's My Way*, for a dollar. I played "Universal Soldier" over and over until I knew it by heart.

CHAPTER 29

With great diligence, I continued to absorb the nuances of the underground psychedelic world that I had stumbled into.

Lysergic acid diethylamide or LSD; mescaline in its raw state as peyote buttons and in its manufactured state; and psilocybin in its natural state as magic mushrooms and in its manufactured form—were all legal. LSD continued to be manufactured by the Swiss pharmaceutical company Sandoz. [22]

LSD was relatively easy to make. Student and amateur chemists were turning out batches in many of the top schools in the country like Harvard, University of Chicago, Columbia, and UC Berkeley. The most famous manufacturer of street acid at the time was unquestionably Augustus Owsley Stanley III, scion of a politically prominent family from Kentucky. Owsley, as most people called him, was the first underground cook to manufacture large batches of very high-grade LSD, much of it sold for three or four dollars a hit or given away free. It came in liquid form in vials, in capsules, and eventually as dried liquid residue on blotter paper. After his first lab was busted in Berkeley in early 1965, Owsley sued the police for illegal search and seizure and won because LSD was not illegal to make or ingest. He used the proceeds to set up manufacturing operations in Los Angeles during the spring of 1965, producing thousands of doses, which made their way across town through friends of friends in the movie and music business to tiny cells of freaks like Garry and his friends. Garry had connections to Owsley through friends in Hollywood. I had yet to try it but I was inching closer by the week.

Fear of being busted for smoking pot was a constant worry in the spring of 1965. The incumbent Los Angeles Mayor Sam Yorty was in the political fight of his life. He was running for reelection against US Congressman James Roosevelt, the eldest son of the late President Franklin Roosevelt. Yorty, who was being considerably outspent by Roosevelt, made his appeal to the voters through increased raids on prostitutes, numbers rackets, and illicit drugs.

The strategy was successful.

Yorty was reelected.

The pot busts continued.

The paranoia increased, and so did the number of people who dropped over to Garry's place to get high—some for the first time—and join a growing underground of freaks and pot and acid heads.

I began to write and draw more. I carried an unlined notebook everywhere and drew constantly in it with a felt-tip pen. I drew faces and people, animals, and bugs. Sometimes I wrote a few sentences of what I was thinking or seeing.

I loved the new nomenclature—pot, grass, weed, dope, shit, ganja, hemp, boo, Mary Jane, cannabis, m, and dozens of other epithets. A marijuana cigarette was called a joint. When the joint burned down to the very end, it was called a roach—because it resembled a cockroach in size, shape, and color. Paper clips and alligator clips were used as roach clips to smoke the last precious end of a joint.

I loved the rituals, the sharing, the common bond, the generosity, the peacefulness, the feeling that I belonged to a group of ill-defined outsiders.

The peace sign and hugs began to replace handshakes as greetings among stoners and friends. Ever so slowly, the ankh and peace symbols replaced crosses, stars of David, and mezuzahs.

Speed and downers occasionally showed up, and some experimented once or twice with joints dipped in a paregoric solution to get a mild opiate high.

I rewrote an old story I had written and rewritten in high school. I had written it the first time in Mr. Mile's honors English and again for honors English in my senior year. It was called "Mud Christmas." It was my reaction to Erich Maria Remarque's *All Quiet on the Western Front*, an anti-war novel set during the horrors of World War I. Remarque's story was told from the point of view of a German soldier who not only suffers through the horrors of the war but finds himself alienated from the very homeland he is fighting for. In the end, he is shot and killed in the most insignificant way.

My story, "Mud Christmas," was written from inside the mind of a French soldier on leave from the front during World War I as he walked the last miles home from the train station. He thinks about the meaninglessness of what he is doing and the insanity he has witnessed as he walks along the dirt road turned to mud connecting his village to his family's farm. He thinks about what would happen if he didn't go back but deserted instead.

I thought about how so much of the history I knew—especially American history—was defined by war, not peace. Patriots were heroes. As a kid, I had collected war junk—arrowheads from old encampments near our house, and swords, bayonets, buttons, old uniforms, canteens, carbines, and cartes de visite of soldiers of the Civil War from antique and junk shops we visited on family outings. In one shop, I had purchased two small leather Civil War medical kits filled with scalpels to cut open bodies, catheters to treat rampant venereal disease, and needles and silk thread for sewing up wounds. I wanted to be American. I thought collecting war junk put me closer to the heart and soul of America.

Now, I saw no glory, only wounds that were deepening. America was shooting itself in the heart, choking itself on misplaced hubris in Vietnam.

Some humans were better off with religion, some not.

Some were happy and more relaxed with alcohol, some not.

Some got their highs running, fasting, eating, meditating, traveling, creating, or destroying.

Grass was like that. It was a force, like so many of the forces humans had discovered.

Like alcohol, guns, love, sex, food, money, writing, art, music, and sports, and all things that can bring ecstasy and pain, grass needed to be treated with respect.

I was satisfied I could respect grass. I would have been one of the people drinking alcohol in moderation during Prohibition.

As I headed toward finals at the end of the second semester of my sophomore year, I began looking for a new place to live. Jeff was moving to his parents' new house in Tarzana at the end of May. He was planning on transferring to the University of California at Riverside over the summer. We had to be out of our apartment on May 31, a few days after my last final, or I had to pay the entire rent and utilities.

CHAPTER 30

In addition to Garry and Jeff, I had maintained my friendship with Buddy, one of the two football players I had worked with in the fall at the library.

Buddy was hanging around with a circle of sorority sisters from one of the most exclusive sororities on the row. He was crazy about a freshman named Teri, a dark-haired, dark-eyed sister who was beautiful and smart. Teri liked Buddy, but she had her sights set on one of the older jocks at the school. By the end of the year as everyone was buckling down for finals, Teri turned her parents' home in the wealthy enclave of Hancock Park into a study hall for her friends. Buddy and I spent long afternoons and evenings there with Teri and a few of her sorority sisters, in part because her parents had a well-stocked refrigerator and an ample liquor supply, and in part because Teri and Teri's friends were fun to be with.

None of them smoked pot or showed any interest in it, but with the exception of Buddy and Teri, the others thought nothing of popping diet pills and sleeping pills, which they freely passed around to anyone who felt sleepy, bored, or too wired to sleep. [23]

We were experiencing a golden age of medicine, an era of almost unbridled optimism about pharmaceuticals. Deadly scourges, which had killed and crippled generations of humans as far back as the origins of the species—from polio and tuberculosis to gonorrhea and syphilis—could now be prevented or cured. There were pills for the heart, for cancer, for Parkinson's. Nervous or sad? No problem. Take a pill. Can't sleep, eating too much, can't stay awake, feeling a little crazy? No problem. More pills.

The most amazing pill was the birth control pill. For the first time in history, the birth control pill and intrauterine devices put the decision for preventing unwanted pregnancies in the hands of women. Overnight, one little pill had metaphorically liberated half the world's population. Overnight, women, who had access to the pill, had become equal partners and leaders in the sexual revolution. I wondered how fast the new knowledge society would progress with the smartest people regardless of sex leading the way. In politics, it couldn't come soon enough for me. I didn't know a single woman who was for war.

In the middle of finals, I also located a new apartment I could afford on my own. It was a self-contained furnished place between fraternity row and 32nd Street at 3028½ University Avenue, a quiet residential street between the campus and fraternity row with light traffic in both directions. It would be turned into a pedestrian-only walkway a few years later. My new home was an efficiency apartment built on the top of an old 1920s two-car garage. It sat at the end of the driveway behind a 1920s, Mission-style, pink four-plex that had been renting apartments since John Wayne had played for the USC Trojan football team.

My little apartment had its own outside staircase on the north side of the garage leading to an uncovered balcony running across the front of the second story of the building. The inside of my new apartment contained a small kitchen, a main room, a huge walk-in closet, and a bathroom. Each room, including the bathroom and walk-in closet, had a window of its own. I had an abundance of light. The main room had a built-in dresser; an ancient, scarred, oak table and chair; and a pre-war, three-quarters-sized bed—48 inches wide. The wood trim, doors, windowsills, and built-in dresser were painted brown with thin, wavy, black pinstripes to make the surface look like natural wood grain. An old bronze, three-bulb light fixture hung from the middle of the ceiling in the main room. The bathroom had a sink, toilet, and a giant, cast iron, clawfoot tub but no shower. The kitchen was just big enough to fit a tiny table with one chair in front, one on the side, a stove, sink, and refrigerator, all nearly as old as my parents. Both the stove and refrigerator were powered by natural gas and had pilot lights that added to the heat in the hot weather.

At forty dollars a month with another fifteen dollars for gas, electricity, and phone, it was a steal. I could also save on parking, gas, and wear and tear on my car since I could walk to all my classes and my job at the library in five minutes.

My new home also had a few negatives. The apartment had previously been occupied by one of the university groundskeepers. The sharp metallic smell of fertilizer had been ground deep into the rug. The place was crawling with cockroaches, ants, and spiders. I was far from discouraged. At twenty, I had achieved a life goal. I had a place like *Walden's* author Henry David Thoreau—a little, self-contained house where I could think and write. I was the Urban Thoreau. The concrete pad in front of my house and the ribbons of sidewalks and streets were my Walden Pond and the streams that fed it. The rundown houses, the smog-choked palm trees, and the telephone poles were my forest. I was ecstatic.

I was lucky. I hadn't accumulated much in the past year, so, I was able to move everything from my old apartment to my new apartment with a couple of short trips on the last day of the month.

I had worked hard all semester, so I was pretty sure I would do well in all my classes except my statistics exam in psychology. It was the hardest class I had. When I finished my stats exam, I was pretty sure I had done okay. Even with a shaky mark in statistics, my cumulative average was high; my scholarship was safe.

I felt good at the end of my second year. I was on my own. I had a great place. I didn't have to go back to New Jersey to earn money. Dr. Stieg had offered me a fulltime job that paid $350 a month. I could keep my own hours. I would be doing warehouse work again, but I was happy to do it. It was a job with no homework, no day-to-day boss, and no employees to supervise. I could start when I wanted.

I decided to postpone unpacking and getting the telephone installed and the electricity and gas turned on. Instead, I decided to head home to New Jersey for a few weeks.

CHAPTER 31

During my sophomore year at USC, I discovered why Volvos were reputed to last an average of twenty-one years—because only stupid, stubborn people like me bought them and believed the Volvo propaganda, which in turn caused owners to spend untold amounts of money for repairs to prove that their Volvo would live up to its billing.

I still loved my seven-year-old car, but I was fully aware that it wouldn't make the trip to New Jersey and back.

Flying was out of the question. Only people with money flew. A bus was my obvious choice, but since I had yet to unravel the mysteries of writing a novel, I wondered if hitchhiking to New Jersey might provide something original to write about.

I had seen very few hitchhikers on surface streets in Los Angeles in the two years I had lived there. I had seen none on the freeways since it was illegal to hitchhike or walk on them in Los Angeles. The only hitchhiker I had seen while driving across the US the previous summer had been a local teenaged farm kid I picked up on a patch of rural highway in Kansas. He was going only a few miles down the road.

All of my hitchhiking in New Jersey had been over short distances. I had never once hitchhiked more than five or six miles away from our house. Although I often hitchhiked the two miles to North Plainfield to catch the bus to New York, I had never thought about hitchhiking *into* New York.

Hitchhiking across the US seemed like an adventure I shouldn't pass up.

Buddy and Teri volunteered to drive me to Barstow, a small desert town on Route 66, about a hundred miles away and halfway across the state. There, after an early lunch of burgers, fries, and milkshakes at a roadside diner, I waved goodbye to my pals, stuck out my thumb, and hoped for the best.

I was traveling light, dressed in rough leather, half-calf boots, jeans, T-shirt, and a brand-new moustache—the third one I'd had tried in the past year. This one had filled in enough to look like a real one instead of a dirty upper lip. Moustaches and face hair of any kind were still rare, even among freaks. Most of the rockers and folk-rockers were still clean shaven. I was hoping the moustache would add a few years to my looks. I carried my army surplus jacket and a small canvas gym bag with my toilet kit and a change of clothes.

After an hour, I began wondering if I had made a terrible mistake. The hot June sun beat down mercilessly. I thought about backtracking into town, locating the Greyhound stop, and catching the next bus heading east.

I was in limbo, uncertain whether I was heading home or leaving home. I wanted to think of Los Angeles as home. I had spent most of the past two years there. Still, the East had a special hold on me. I had spent most of my life there. Most of my immediate family and extended family for four generations back—including six of my eight great grandparents and all four of my grandparents—all Russian-born Jewish immigrants—had lived, died, and were buried within a fifty-mile radius of where I grew up.

A trickle of cars and trucks passed by. None of them slowed down. The drivers pretended not to see me.

It took another hour in the desert sun before I got my first ride.

The driver was a sailor in uniform, a kid no older than me. He was driving a 1957 Ford Fairlane like the one my brother and I drove to California in 1962. The seaman was stationed in Long Beach and heading home to Albuquerque on leave. He couldn't wait to ship out to Vietnam. We listened to country music on the radio. I helped pay for the gas and bought him dinner that night halfway across Arizona.

A couple of hours before dawn, he dropped me off at a nearly-empty, all-night, highway diner in Albuquerque where I had a small breakfast before walking across the parking lot to the shoulder of the road with the same hitchhiker's trepidation I'd felt the day before. Would I get a ride?

I wondered if the few cars and trucks that flew by in the dark even saw me.

The false dawn came, then the first morning light, and more cars, but no one stopped.

I peered through the windshields of approaching vehicles and tried to hypnotize the drivers into stopping. After each car or truck flew by, I made up stories about the occupants. The lone man was an ax murderer hurrying away from the scene of a crime. The car with the kids jumping up and down in the back seat was speeding home because the kids had to pee. The little boy with his face pressed against the side window was being kidnapped. The young man in the souped up car with the girl wrapped around him was about to learn that he was going to be a father.

Two hours after I had started hitching, an old, sunbaked Buick slowed down and pulled to the side of the highway only a few yards past me.

I ran to the car and jumped in. The driver was a grizzled old man who hadn't shaved in days and smelled badly. I was so excited about getting a ride, I forgot to ask him how far he was going until we were speeding along.

"Twenty miles out," he told me. "I got a ranch on the edge of town. You looking for work?"

"No, but thanks," I said as we got farther away from civilization. "I'm on my way to New York." New York sounded more important than New Jersey.

He dropped me on a barren stretch of highway before turning down a dirt road to his ranch. I watched the plume of dust trailing behind his car as it grew smaller and smaller before finally disappearing over a ridge. If there was a house on the property, I couldn't see it. I couldn't see any structures anywhere in any direction.

I'm screwed, I thought.

I was alone again with my imagination. A car or truck whipped by every five or ten minutes without even slowing.

I was also getting hungry and regretted not being near the diner any longer.

No one in the world knew where I was. I had mentioned only vaguely to my mother in recent letters home that I might try hitching, but I hadn't written or telephoned that I had started my trip. If I vanished off the face of the earth, the last known sighting of me by anyone who knew my full name would be Buddy and Teri, who had last seen me in Barstow. My parents had no idea who they were. Buddy and Teri had no reason to check on me. Ever.

CHAPTER 32

After another hour in the hot sun, I lost hope and was thinking about heading in the other direction to Albuquerque to get something to eat and hunt for the bus station.

As I was making up my mind, a light-colored van came toward me. I decided to give it one last shot. I stuck out my thumb as the vehicle drew closer.

The battered, old, gray van zoomed past me without stopping and then miraculously skidded to a stop along the side of the highway so far down the road that I wondered if it had even stopped for me.

Then, I could see it backing up slowly along the shoulder.

A ride.

Filled with optimism, I ran toward the van as fast as I could. I reached it half out of breath. Wary of being left in the middle of nowhere again, I pulled the door open and asked a weary looking, clean shaven, middle-aged male driver, "How far are you going?"

"Montreal."

His destination was so completely unexpected it took me a few moments to process it.

Canada, I thought. Montreal. McGill University. The East Coast. I would certainly be closer to home than I was in New Mexico.

"Are you getting in?" the driver asked impatiently. Tired, hooded eyes checked me out.

Why not? I thought. I jumped into the passenger seat and closed the door.

"Thanks," I said, feeling a great sense of relief.

He put the van in gear and returned to the road without a word.

"You live in Montreal?" I asked after we'd driven in silence for twenty or thirty miles.

"Northern Vermont. Faster to go through Montreal and then back down."

I asked what he did.

"Artificial insemination. Cattle and horses." He was moving his business from Vermont to Chandler, Arizona. He was returning to Vermont to collect his family and move the rest of his equipment and household effects.

I was too squeamish to ask him more about his business. Besides, Robert Brewster wasn't very talkative. He had picked me up to help drive, not to socialize.

We drove day and night, most often in silence, stopping only occasionally for coffee, sandwiches, and gas. Once in Missouri in the middle of the night, we pulled over at a roadside stop and slept in our seats for a couple of hours.

Later that afternoon, we went through the Detroit tunnel and emerged in Windsor, Ontario, Canada, which struck me as pristine clean and pleasant, nothing like the seedy border towns of Juarez and Tijuana, Mexico.

Ten years before I had had my only other sojourn into Canada. At Niagara Falls.

It had left me smelling like a skunk.

CHAPTER 33

I told Robert Brewster the story as we drove through the rich, green farmland of Southern Ontario.

My father, mother, sister, and I went to Niagara Falls in 1955. I was ten. The owners of the motel where we stayed had a baby pet skunk. They said it had been fixed so it wouldn't spray. I picked it up, and it sprayed me in the face and all over my clothes. I spent the next day—my skin scrubbed raw from a dozen baths and smelling of my mother's perfume— touring the popular sites around the falls and being given an extra wide berth by everyone who came near me. My parents didn't care. We went on the Canadian side and bought a big basket of cherries and drove along the Niagara River. My dad let me buy firecrackers and bring them back to New Jersey where they were illegal.

I hadn't been to Canada since, but I'd heard people talking about Canada over the past few months as a place to go to if the war got any hotter. Canada wasn't sending troops to the Vietnam War. And they didn't have a draft.

I heard Canada's Prime Minister, Lester B. Pearson, had won the Nobel Prize for Peace in 1957 for his role in preventing the 1956 Suez Canal crisis from escalating into a long, bloody war. Pearson had been the architect behind the creation of the United Nations Emergency Force, launching the beginning of the first modern-day, peacekeeping military institution.

Buffy Sainte-Marie was from Canada. Garry's family was from Canada.

I was in Canada. Was my trip a portent?

I breathed in the cool fresh air coming in through the van's windows.

Giant waterfalls, peacekeepers, and a country not at war. I liked the idea of Canada.

I heard somewhere that the Nazis called a section of Auschwitz "Canada," because it was supposed to be the land of plenty. At Auschwitz, Canada was where the possessions were sorted after the new arrivals had been stripped naked and gassed.

I had relatives somewhere in Canada.

My mother's father and her grandfather (my grandfather and great grandfather) had come to Canada and lived there for a few years in Glace Bay, Nova Scotia before settling with the rest of their family in New York City at the turn of the century.

We sped along the Trans-Canada Highway, a freeway that cut through southern Ontario. The landscape was filled with lush flatlands and rolling hills covered with farms and woodlands. The highway bypassed most of the towns and villages. The only glimpse I had of urban Ontario was a patch of new high-rises and housing developments bordering the highway when we passed through Toronto. The buildings gleamed in the pink light of the setting sun as we drove past. I imagined I was looking at the heart of the city. Canada seemed so clean and new. [24]

The freeway was still under construction east of Kingston, so, we drove along smaller provincial roads in the dark as we entered Quebec. By then, I was driving; Mr. Brewster was giving me directions, and soon we were hopelessly lost. We couldn't even decide which direction was north, south, east, or west. The little villages we passed through were closed tight for the night. We had a good laugh when we realized we had no idea which way to go.

We pulled into the parking lot of a closed-for-the-night log cabin restaurant and souvenir shop in the middle of nowhere and slept in our seats until the place opened early the next morning. Over breakfast, I found out Mr. Brewster's home in Vermont was in the middle of nowhere. Montreal was the last place we would be passing through that had a bus terminal.

I had enough money to get a bus ticket to New York, pay for a few meals in between and maybe enough to sleep over in Montreal. I decided to stay in Montreal and have a look around.

We arrived in the city during the morning rush hour and drove for a half hour to get downtown. We stopped to ask a policeman for directions to the bus terminal. Following the officer's directions, Mr. Brewster zigzagged through traffic, dropped me off on Craig Street in front of the terminal, and drove off a second later.

The terminal turned out to be the wrong one. It was for city busses, not long-haul busses. The station I wanted was on Dorchester Boulevard and Drummond Street. I took the mistake as a sign to slow down and have a look around.

I wandered up St. Lawrence Boulevard past secondhand furniture shops, Chinese restaurants, butcher shops, and seedy pool halls with indoor food stands selling steamed hotdogs in front, penny arcades in the middle, and pool tables in back.

St. Catherine Street at St. Lawrence Boulevard was a cross between Times Square, Coney Island, and Tijuana. The cross streets were lined with cheap restaurants, men's clothing stores, cafes, nightclubs, and bars with flashy neon signs and photos of near naked showgirls in the glass display cases in front.

A few establishments were already open.

A small man with an eye patch swept the sidewalk in front of one club as well-dressed men and women streamed past, heading to work.

I tried using the smattering of French I'd learned in high school. No one seemed to understand what I was saying, and I had no idea what they were saying to me in return.

I asked a young, smartly dressed woman how to find McGill University. She spoke English with a soft French accent, pointing me in the opposite direction, toward the mountain. She said McGill was less than a dozen blocks away.

Most of the women hurrying to work were beautiful and stylishly dressed. I fell in love a dozen times as I headed up the hill to Sherbrooke Street and walked west to the campus gates.

The campus was smaller than I imagined. Most of the buildings were crammed together on the side of a hill at the top of a long, grassy commons.

I wondered what my life might have been like if I had gone to McGill instead of USC. McGill was one of the schools I had briefly considered applying to. My mother mentioned a cousin of my grandfather had studied psychiatry at McGill. He was one of our distant Canadian relatives from Nova Scotia who now lived somewhere in New York.

I wandered into several of the fancy antique stores and art galleries along Sherbrooke Street. The street was lined with dozens of old stone mansions and a few modern buildings. It felt like a little slice of the Upper Eastside of Manhattan around the Metropolitan Museum of Fine Arts.

I like Montreal, I told myself. It felt so peaceful.

I knew nothing about the previous two years of sporadic bombs detonated by the Quebec separatist organization, the Front de Libération du Québec (FLQ), which wanted to take Quebec out of the Canadian confederation and form a separate French nation. I had no knowledge that a month before I arrived, a bomb had been detonated in Place Victoria a few blocks to the south of where I was walking, and another bomb had been detonated at the US Consulate, a few blocks north of Sherbrooke Street. Ten days before I arrived, violent street clashes had taken place between Quebec separatists and police during the annual Victoria Day celebration—celebrating the birthday of the late Queen Victoria. It had resulted in dozens of injuries and the arrest of over two hundred protesters.

I wandered through the downtown, trying to soak up the sounds and sights, trying to read the city vibes, not knowing very much about where I was. I felt like an outsider, and yet I was charmed by everything. On St. Catherine Street, I passed a large department store as big as New York's Macy's with a one-armed organ grinder out front. I passed by more women—beautiful, sexy women with intelligent, curious eyes, some who smiled back when they noticed me.

I could live here and be happy, I told myself. [25]

I thought about staying in a cheap hotel and spending a few days in the city, but I was bone tired by late afternoon. I had barely slept since California, and I had been walking around the city for hours without stopping.

I bought a ticket for the next bus to New York that evening but promised myself I'd come back one day. I fantasized that Montreal could be for me what Paris had been for writers like Ernest Hemingway and F. Scott Fitzgerald in the 1920s and Henry Miller in the 1930s.

If I came back and stayed, I could learn French, I told myself.

The bus ride to New York was easy. A flash of my driver's license was all that the US border and immigration officers required when we entered the States. It was dark for most of the ride through New York State. I slept off and on through the trip.

We arrived at the Port Authority Bus Terminal in New York City too early for me to catch the first bus to North Plainfield, so, I went for a walk along 42nd Street to Times Square as the sun came up, a walk I had made countless times. I soaked in the seediness of the facades of the dozens of old movie theaters playing triple bills; the all-night eateries serving the greasiest food imaginable; and the all-night drunks, some still wandering around, some lying curled on the sidewalk or in front of the gates to shops still closed for the night.

We have all this in Los Angeles, but it's more spread out, I thought. Here in New York, it felt like someone had shaken all the unfortunates in the city onto one spot.

Someone had left a bra and a pair of slacks draped over a fire hydrant.

How, I wondered, did someone lose a bra and a pair of slacks?

New York felt good. It oozed dirt and stories.

I promised myself I'd come back to soak up the grit when I had more time.

CHAPTER 34

As the bus bound for North Plainfield exited the Lincoln Tunnel, I caught my first real glimpse of the long, thick blue line across the horizon.

The Watchung Mountains. Home.

I lived a half mile through the woods behind Washington Rock, one of the most prominent points at the southern tip of the mountains, the first mountains west of Manhattan.

The land was considered holy by the Turtle and Wolf clans of the Lenape tribe that occupied the land to the south and north of the mountains when the first Europeans arrived in New Jersey. My mountains were sacred to George Washington and the Continental Army, too. The First Watchung Mountain was forty miles long with almost vertical cliffs rising several hundred feet from the plains to the south. The cliffs had acted like a castle wall, protecting the front lines of the American rebels from the British forces for much of the Revolution. Washington had camped in and around these mountains for four and a half years, longer than he spent anywhere else during America's War of Independence. Camp Middlebrook, where the first stars-and-stripes flag was raised over Washington's army, was five miles downstream from our house along the wetlands that fed the Middle Brook. John Johnston, founder of the New York Metropolitan Museum and head of the Jersey Central Railroad in the mid-1800s, had invented modern-day, middle-class tourism by promoting daytrips from Manhattan to Plainfield by train, then a carriage ride to the top of Washington Rock, where a tourist could see all the way to Manhattan as George Washington had. And a traveler could be back home in New York at the end of the day or stay in the hotel on the mountain ridge or in one of the fine hotels catering to tourists in Plainfield.

In 1938, the Watchung Mountains were mentioned three times in Orson Welles' radio play *The War of the Worlds*. An estimated two million radio listeners were convinced during the broadcast that the world was being invaded by Martians. [26]

The bus from the New York Port Authority dropped me off in North Plainfield, two miles from home.

I crossed the overpass to the north side of the highway and walked backwards, hitchhiking north through the Somerset Street Gap, along the Stony Brook and the quarry where a boy had fallen to his death ten years before.

I started planning ahead as I walked. It was a Tuesday morning, so, I might not find anyone home.

My brother Ray was teaching middle school in a nearby town. Classes were still in session. My sister Daisy was in the final weeks of her sophomore year at the high school on the other side of town. My father was at the shop. My mother might be at the shop, seeing buyers and jobbers in New York, at the high school tending to her board duties, or a dozen other places. If she wasn't there, I could let myself in with the key hanging on a hook in the garage.

I got a ride as I approached the Watchung Circle. We rode past the Watchung Lake and the golf course that my father had nearly bought with nine of his friends during his affluent Plainfield days when I was an infant. We rode by the gun shop and firing range where I bought most of my antique firearms and my Remington pump .22.

My ride dropped me off at the intersection of the county road and our little dead-end street. The rural setting was slowly being suburbanized.

I had picked wild asparagus with my mom in the field at the top of our road before I had started school. The field had been filled in with an Esso gas station a few years later. A year or so before my brother started university and I started high school, one of the underground gasoline tanks began to leak, and everyone on our street had to abandon their fifty-foot wells, seal them off, and drill new wells through the bluestone for more than two hundred feet to get drinkable water. Esso paid for our new well after my parents signed an agreement promising not to sue them.

As I walked down the hill past the gas station, the air was filled with the scent of hundreds of trees and flowers, many in full bloom.

I could see ahead to our house. My mother's car was in the driveway.

CHAPTER 35

I walked up the slate steps between the two Norway maple trees to the front door. The maples had been twigs when we first moved in. Now, they were big enough to throw a canopy of shade over the front lawn.

I rang the front doorbell, hoping my mother would answer so I could surprise her.

My mother opened the door a minute after I rang and looked right at me without a clue who I was.

"Can I help you?" she asked suspiciously. She didn't like people she didn't know at the door.

I stood there for a few seconds and grinned.

Her eyes narrowed.

"Don't you recognize me?" I asked.

She studied my face for a few seconds more before breaking into a warm laugh. "Oh, Joey, I didn't know it was you until I saw you smile. I recognized your teeth."

We had the same crooked front teeth. My moustache and clothes had done a good job of hiding my identity much more than I had imagined. Not quite the invisible man I had once hoped to be as a child but still effective.

We didn't hug or kiss. I didn't expect to. We weren't a hugging, kissing family. The only time my mother usually hugged me as a small child was when I fell or otherwise hurt myself, and even then, she was more likely to attend to the wound and simply tell me to stop crying.

My mother instinctively knew that too much affection would ruin me.

And yet, I never felt she didn't care. Communication was non-verbal, non-physical, conveyed through a smile or a sparkle in her eyes. She was happy to see me. Giddy, almost.

When I explained I had hitchhiked from California to Montreal and taken the bus from Montreal to New York, she beamed with pride. Before she learned to drive, she had regularly taken my six-year-old brother and two-year-old me hitchhiking the four miles between our house in the country and Plainfield, the closest city. My brother began hitchhiking around the township by himself when he was in first grade. From kindergarten on, I hitched across the township to school on rare occasions when I missed the bus. No one in my family had ever hitched as far as I had.

"You look taller and thinner," she said. "I bet you didn't eat." She led me into the kitchen and began fixing a new pot of coffee and asking me what I wanted to eat.

I was home and not home. The world I returned to had changed as much as I had in the past year.

My mother had grown older and gaunter; her face showed more stress.

"How long are you planning to stay?" she asked as I gobbled down a couple of sandwiches of day-old meatloaf, ketchup, and white bread.

"A couple of weeks."

She nodded without comment, but I could read her mind. She was glad to see me, but she didn't want anyone else to move back home.

I took my mother's car and drove to the factory. My father appeared noticeably sicker. He had lost more weight and become more stooped. I was afraid he would fall as he shuffled around the shop. His shaking was worse. I couldn't help asking myself: Is this my fate? Is his disease in my blood, too? How long can I expect to remain normal?

Dad said even less than Mom. At fifty-four, he was a physical wreck. His eyes told me how ashamed he felt at not only the loss of his strength and vitality but the decline of the glove company.

My father's glove business was draining my parents' savings. The debt they were carrying was staggering. The big buyers at the department stores increasingly wanted "imports and dollar items," my mother told me. The factory was unable to produce them at a profit. Had my father been healthier, he could have done what some other American leather goods manufacturers were starting to do. He could go to Asia, partner with a manufacturer there, and become an importer or overseas manufacturer.

It was difficult for me to understand how this minor captain of industry—the cofounder of the local Lions Club, United Way, and Little League, and the savior of the local Boy Scout Troop—was now having trouble dressing himself in the morning and undressing at night.

I wondered, too, whether he thought he had made a mistake by not going for the brain freezing operation a year and a half before. [27]

What an ugly choice my father had to make. He could choose to get an operation that could cure or kill him, or he could continue to fall apart without it and wait for a new medicine or new type of operation to be invented.

My brother Ray had reclaimed our old bedroom since he had moved home. I was now the guest in our house.

Ray was teaching in a nearby town for a few more weeks. When he wasn't teaching, he was spending all his time with his new bride-to-be, Linda, or studying for his master's degree so he could convince Linda's parents that he was worth marrying.

I barely saw him.

I saw even less of my sister. She was still in school, hanging out with her friends, singing and playing music with a couple of high school groups, and going through the final weeks of tests and papers of her sophomore year in high school.

It felt like home and it didn't.

I prowled the house, looking for traces of my old self.

My mother had entered the oil painting of the rooster I had done while still in high school into the local art show at the township municipal building the month before I arrived home. The painting had won first prize. It now sat in the cluttered dining room on the floor against the wall with a blue ribbon hanging from one corner. My mother was proud I had won. She was also a bit chagrined that her mixed-media bird entry hadn't won anything. I was, too. She was a real artist. I was a pretender. She had studied commercial art full time for four years in Brooklyn's best public technical school for business and commercial art. She had spent ten years on Seventh Avenue designing clothes. She should have won. [28]

I slipped into old sweaters and shirts I hadn't had on since high school. I told my mother to give them to charity. She insisted I save them. "You might want them someday." In her mind, nothing had changed.

I dug out the old boxes on the floor in my half of the closet in the boys' bedroom where my brother was living. I looked at my old photo collections of Civil War soldiers and Confederate and Union paper money; coins that went back a hundred years; and a cigar box of arrowheads and steel head pennies that had been made when copper was in short supply during World War II. In another box, I had a large, old, metal dump truck painted red, yellow, and green and a stack of old baseball cards from before the Dodgers and Giants moved to California. The small Teddy bear of cloth stuffed with cotton had been my constant companion for a few years before I went to school. The missing spots of nap came from the day I found my mother's sharp scissors and gave haircuts to my Teddy bear and me. My mother laughed hysterically when she saw me with half my hair chopped off. I kept the bear because it came from my father's factory right after the war when he had manufactured stuffed animals for a short time.

I checked out my collection of old guns and swords on the walls of the basement, most from the Civil War or a few years afterward. What fun it had been as a young teenager rooting around in old junk stores from upstate New York to Virginia collecting war junk with my brother while my mother hunted for art glass, old costume jewelry, antique clothing, old furniture, and anything she found attractive. I always thought of it as treasure hunting, like digging for pirate's gold. Once Mom had found some old nuggets wrapped in a ball of paper in a dresser she bought that turned out to be real gold.

My father stopped the car at every antique shop she pointed to but never once went inside to look around. He would stay in the car and listen to ball games or read the newspaper. He was happy if my mother was happy.

My grades trickled in on postcards during my visit home. I had received A's in all of my subjects, including statistics. I had scored another 4.0. My scholarship, which meant my future, was safe. [29]

I took the bus into New York several times over the next couple of weeks to bum around and also visit my forty-four-year-old Uncle Sam and my seventy-one-year-old Great Uncle Lew.

Uncle Sam, my mother's youngest brother, took me on his sales calls around the city to see art directors at advertising agencies to discuss photography assignments for George Elliott, his photographer partner. Uncle Sam and George had been partners for several years. Sam did all the selling and acted as George's producer. They split their sizeable income fifty-fifty. I had worked with George once while still in high school when he and Sam had photographed a herd of sheep on a local farm near our house for a Scandinavian Airlines System print advertisement. The ad had been in *Time* magazine and dozens of other major American periodicals. I was the sole photographer's assistant that day, herding sheep, helping with the lights and equipment, and performing other tasks as George snapped more than a thousand images with different cameras and lenses in order to get the one perfect shot for the ad.

I also had a few long lunches with Great Uncle Lew, who ran his real estate brokerage business out of an office building on East 42nd Street near Grand Central Station and the NY Public Library a block away from George Elliott's studio. Great Uncle Lew sold skyscrapers in cities around North America. He had made a lot of money over the years. My mother was his favorite niece, so he was quite fond of me.

Great Uncle Lew and I had exchanged letters for nearly a year. I had heard of him when I was young, but I only met him at family events a few times growing up, so I really didn't know him until he started writing to me after his wife, Fannie, died. Fannie was my grandfather's six sisters. Lew was lonely, my mother said.

He was cheerful and fun to write to. He was amused by all the women I had dated over the past year. He continuously counseled me to have fun. "Most of what you're going through is nothing more than hormones," he wrote.

He took me to lunch at one of his clubs where his fellow real estate brokers hung out. He introduced me to everyone as the "straight A student," and a man who was going somewhere.

Both Uncle Sam and Great Uncle Lew had strong opinions about the war. Both, I suppose, brought it up because they were war veterans. They were also tuned into what was happening because the news affected their businesses. Both were very aware that I was a good candidate for the draft. Each had a very different opinion of what I should do.

Uncle Sam was nearly thirty years younger than Uncle Lew. Sam had seen combat and been a POW in World War II. He thought the Vietnam War was "all bullshit."

"Stay in school and keep out of the war any way you can. If you get drafted, don't volunteer for anything. Keep your head down. This isn't the Boy Scouts." Uncle Sam was afraid the Army would grab me and put me on the front lines as a junior officer because I was an Eagle Scout. "You'll be the most likely candidate to come back in a box," he told me.

Uncle Lew served state-side in the Navy during World War I, guarding the Brooklyn Navy Yard. He also thought it would be a good idea if I stayed in school, but if a time came when I had to serve, he told me, "Let me know."

His friends in high places told him to expect a big escalation in the war soon.

"If you have to serve after graduating, join the Navy," Uncle Lew advised. He told me about connections he had with the War Department and the big banks. Uncle Lew had been pulled from the slums of Manhattan to be the star sprinter in the 50- and 100-yard dashes at Hotchkiss, the private prep school in Connecticut, which served as a feeder school for Yale bluebloods.

He explained that he once wanted to be a writer. He had sent off stories to literary magazines while at Hotchkiss. He had been the associate editor on the school newspaper and had been close friends with two others who had literary and publishing aspirations, Briton Hadden and Henry Luce. Luce was one of the few other poor boys at the school on scholarship. Luce and Hadden had both gone onto Yale and later founded *Time* magazine.

A few of Uncle Lew's long-ago stories had been published in literary magazines before World War I, but he gave up his dream of writing to speculate in gold in the Roaring Twenties before becoming an independent commercial real estate broker.

"Too bad," he had written me in one letter, "that your goal is writing. It's a tough way to make a decent living. On the other hand, writing out your ideas on paper will do you a heck of a lot of good in the future. Few people have the capacity to analyze their faults and good points except the very successful ones. If you fixed your goal on business, you could stand to make a lot of dough."

Great Uncle Lew had been an amateur bantam-weight boxer in the Navy who maintained his wiry physique and full head of dark wavy hair into his senior years. He had once been thrown in the brig in the Navy for slugging a sergeant who called him a dirty Jew. In the 1920s, he had a line of credit with one of New York's most famous bootleggers to sell booze by the case to his old friends from Hotchkiss who wanted reliable liquor for their high-society functions.

He had once confronted a famous theater producer with a pistol when the producer tried to cheat him out of a commission on the sale of the producer's property. The producer had paid him his commission on the spot.

I wasn't that tough. I would never be as tough as him. He knew I was soft. I had grown up in different times. For my own sake, he desperately wanted to see me go into something more forgiving and rewarding like medicine or even psychology.

"Here," he said, handing me ten dollars when we finished our lunch that day. "Take a nice girl out for dinner when you get back to California. I envy your energy and sex drive but be careful with the *Goya*"—his term for non-Jewish women, which conjured up images in my mind of a Latin lover.

"And give my best to your mother," Uncle Lew said as we said our goodbyes on the sidewalk. "She's got it pretty rough."

Yes, I knew my parents were having a tough time financially. I also understood that the longer I stayed in New Jersey, the more I could feel my mother silently urging me to get out, go back to California, go anywhere but New Jersey. If I stayed, their lives would suck me under like quicksand.

A day later I said my goodbyes to my family and headed into New York to catch a bus back home to Los Angeles. I didn't know it, but it was the last time I'd visit New Jersey for two years.

CHAPTER 36

My short, cigar-smoking, Italian Uncle Lou, the surviving younger brother of the two half-brothers who had started the nursery behind our house, had connections everywhere. Uncle Lou had pulled strings the previous year to get me the job as a short-order cook at the veterans hospital. During my most recent stay when he heard I was on my way back to California by bus, he made a phone call to one of his friends in the township who drove a bus for the company that had the concession from North Plainfield to the Port Authority. His friend Bob let me ride the bus to New York for free and then took me to the departure area for Greyhound. After a couple of words exchanged between bus driver Bob and the supervisor at the gate, I was given a seat without a ticket and rode for free to Chicago.

Unfortunately, Uncle Lou's influence ended when I switched busses in Chicago for Los Angeles. I paid for the rest of my trip myself, but the savings had knocked about a third off the full fare.

The rest of the ride was longer than it should have been because of several transfers and layovers. It took me five days to get to Los Angeles, slightly longer than it took me to make the trip from California to New Jersey.

Once back at my new apartment, I had to sit around for a few days, waiting to get the electricity, gas, and telephone hooked up. I also killed most of the ants, spiders, and cockroaches. The stench of the insecticide lingered for days.

Once settled, I bought oil paints and watercolors, big pads of watercolor paper, canvas boards, and brushes. I began to paint. I was delighted

I could do it without making anyone but myself sick from the oil and turpentine fumes.

I kept in touch with Buddy, Jeff, and Garry who were all living at home for the summer, so I had three places outside of the hot, sweaty basin of South Central Los Angeles to go to and eat a decent home-cooked meal.

Buddy's parents had moved to a new house on Gramercy Place in the Hollywood Hills. It had a spectacular view of the Los Angeles basin. Buddy was transferring to the University of California at Santa Barbara in the fall to save money and be close to his new girlfriend, another beautiful woman named Terri, who spelled her name with two r's instead of one. The tuition at USC was going up from $1,200 a year to $1,500, one of the highest rates in the nation. It only cost a few hundred a year in registration fees to attend UCSB. My scholarship was going up to match the costs or I might have considered transferring to the University of California system myself.

Jeff was in summer school at UCLA and getting ready to transfer full time to UC Riverside at the end of the summer.

Garry had given up his tiny, one-bedroom shack on Ellendale and moved home to Studio City for the summer.

Garry and Jeff both had swimming pools, so I could swim when I wanted to as long as I didn't mind the hour-long drive each way to their places.

If I had dinner at Garry's on a weekend, I would tag along afterward to his Uncle Sam and Aunt Hilda's house a block away to watch movies that Sam was screening for business. Sometimes when Sam and Hilda were out, Garry threw small film parties at their house.

Samuel Z. Arkoff and his partner James H. Nicholson had just appeared in a long article in *Life* magazine with a giant photo of Nicholson and Sam with his ever-present cigar. The article outlined American International Pictures' legendary formula for success. The formula was culled from years of experience from this small group of B-movie people, like Sam and Garry's father. They had come to Hollywood after the war and created a studio just as the old mega-studios were shrinking. The key to making a profitable film came down to understanding the Peter Pan Syndrome, said Sam. There were five rules: younger kids watched anything older kids watched; older kids never watched anything younger kids watched; girls watched anything boys watched; boys wouldn't watch anything girls wanted to watch, and the best way to catch the largest audience was to zero-in on the nineteen-year-old male.

Producers like Sam could get any movie they wanted at any time, including new films from the other major studios, and often before a title was released to the public. Garry could get any movies we wanted to see by using Sam's account. The movies were real 35mm prints that were shown in movie theaters. Sam had a professional projection booth between the dining room and the giant living room, so, he, his family, guests, and business associates could watch films while sitting comfortably on couches—something I thought was the height of luxury.

Garry earned extra money as a teenager operating the projection equipment. He pointed out to me the little dot at the corner of the screen that appeared during the showing of a film. The dot alerted the projectionist that the reel was running out. The dot signaled it was time to switch to the second projector with the next reel on it. In the old days, Garry explained, each film reel represented between ten and twelve minutes of viewing time, but the modern reels held two of the old reels and were called two-reelers. Each lasted about twenty minutes or a bit longer, so a two-hour movie was made up of six two-reelers or cans of film—the same cans I'd sometimes help Garry lug between Sam's car and the projection booth and back again.

I never knew what to expect when I showed up at his Uncle Sam's. One time Garry started the evening with a screening of the AIP picture *To Stuff a Wild Bikini* for Sam and a business associate, but Sam and his pal only stayed until the end of the first two-reeler and then left. Garry told me distributors rarely watched a film for more than twenty minutes. One two-reeler was long enough for them to decide whether or not to buy the film for distribution. As soon as the older men left, we switched to Michelangelo Antonioni's *Red Desert* and followed it with Federico Fellini's *8½*.

If Donna was around, she sat in the corner and quietly watched what we were viewing; the same with her older brother, Lou, who proved Uncle Sam's point—younger kids would watch anything older kids watched, and girls would watch whatever the boys were watching.

Garry's friend Mike Vosse told everyone at one movie night in the Arkoffs' living room about the most mind-blowing speech by Adlai Stevenson, the

US Ambassador to the United Nations. The speech was delivered in Switzerland to a UN convention where he compared the planet earth to a little spaceship. Stevenson pointed out that our safety and security depended on the love we give to the planet and our fellow space travelers. It perfectly captured the new reality, the goal everyone should be aiming for. Stevenson, the two-time presidential candidate, former Governor of Illinois, and peace advocate, died on July 14, five days after he delivered his earth-as-spaceship speech. [30]

Mike Vosse was the one who told us that Stevenson had been born only blocks from where we all lived on Ellendale when the neighborhood was one of the wealthiest in the city.

When I wasn't visiting friends, I enjoyed being alone.

As a full-time employee of the library, my salary of $350 a month was nearly $2.20 an hour, a fortune for me and much more than California's minimum wage of $1.30 an hour. My job for the summer was to sort through the boxes in the library annex and decide what to throw out and what to keep. Anything worth keeping, I re-boxed, labeled, and trucked to the decommissioned armory beside the Rose Garden in Exposition Park in my electric golf cart. If I wanted to discuss something that I found in the annex, I went to the main library to see Dr. Stieg or one of the Special Collections librarians. Otherwise, I worked alone.

A large number of boxes contained the bound scripts for hundreds of plays written by writers, like Clifford Odets and others, who worked for the Federal Theater Project. The theater project was one of the programs generally associated with the Works Progress Administration (WPA) that President Franklin Roosevelt put in place to support out-of-work artists, writers, and other creative types during the Great Depression. I kept two copies of each play for the library's collection and discarded the rest.

I helped the Special Collections librarians sort through gifts to the library. A box of old personal items included a very old locket with a tuft of George Washington's hair. Nobody seemed to know what to do with it, so, it was returned to the main library to be dealt with at some future time.

One of the Special Collections librarians told me to throw out an old baby grandfather clock that was in pieces. She said it would cost more to fix than it was worth. I took it home and painstakingly glued the wooden case back together, attached the pendulum, and got it ticking. Likewise, the library had no place to put a two-foot high statue of Moliere made of pot metal during the nineteenth or early twentieth century. I took it back to my place and set it beside the old clock and my growing collection of my own paintings.

Except for the occasional visits I made to the other library buildings, I often worked the entire day without seeing anyone, even while walking the half dozen blocks between the Annex and my garage apartment.

At night, I was often alone at my place, painting, writing, or reading. With no fan and no air conditioner, sleeping was a real challenge. My roof was flat, turning my place into an oven by day. At night, with the thick, grey-brown smog covering the basin, the air outside and inside rarely cooled off. Most nights I slept on top of the covers with the windows open and only the screen door barring any would-be intruders. I took some comfort from the married graduate students with two young children next door. They kept a large, unfriendly German shepherd in their fenced backyard. The dog barked at everyone who wandered along the driveway between the two houses.

Life is good, I told myself.

The music was awesome when I occasionally listened to the radio. The summer airwaves were filled with recent releases like the Rolling Stones' "(I Can't Get No) Satisfaction," Sonny and Cher's "I Got You Babe," The Four Tops' "It's the Same Old Song," The Beach Boys' "California Girls," and Bob Dylan's "Like a Rolling Stone." Anyone who thought the Beatles would be a flash in the pan only had to hear "Help!" and "Ticket to Ride" to be assured they were continuing to innovate, surprise, and delight.

Except for the war in Vietnam, I hadn't a worry in the world.

I was completely unaware that another war was brewing only a few miles away, and three thousand miles away, on a completely different battlefield, my parents were losing their own war.

CHAPTER 37

My mother's letter with the bombshell news inside arrived midway through July.

My parents had been forced to suspend operations at the shop at the beginning of July, a week after I left for Los Angeles. This was despite the orders my mother had gotten for gloves from Gimbels, Bloomingdale's, Alexander's, and their main customer in Chicago, the jobber Franklin Tru-fit. Even the publicity my mother had gotten earlier in the year from a small feature article in *Seventeen* magazine on a new line of suede gloves hadn't helped enough. My mother had designed the new gloves. They were lined with mouton that could be rolled over to create a cuff. She called it the Hi-Lo glove. Mom had been counting on the new design to save the business. It was very stylish and might have been the gimmick my mother had hoped for to revive the business, but it came too late.

My parents were only paying the salaries of the two cutters, Red and Johnny, afraid if those two left they would never be able to reopen.

I wasn't as surprised as I might have been. The business had been struggling for years.

My parents should have simply declared the business bankrupt at the start of the year, but they had gambled everything on one more season to turn the business around. Because they were already over their heads in debt to the banks, they had gone to loan sharks in New York for the $10,000 they needed to keep the factory running earlier in the spring. They had to pledge as collateral the company's assets, the house, the vacant lot beside our house, and the fifteen-acre Coddington property—a long thin parcel of wooded land near the ridge of the Second Watchung Mountain overlooking the town center.

By July when they decided to suspend operations for the summer, the ten grand they had borrowed from loan sharks had already been eaten up. They were nearly broke. They now had no money or collateral to reopen the shop without a miracle.

The business is "like a monster," my mother wrote. "It just gorges itself on money. What a pig. UGH!"

I tried to do my part by offering them the savings bonds I still had stashed away at home from baby gifts, childhood savings, and my bar mitzvah. I guessed it was probably about $500. My mother kept the bonds safe in a drawer in her dresser, so I never really looked at them.

I wrote to my mother that she could have my bonds and the money in my savings account.

My mother assured me she would continue to send the twenty-five a week, "but no extras" once school started. "And don't ship out to Viet Cong [sic]," she pleaded with me in one of her other letters.

Yes, the war. Always in the background.

With all her troubles, she was still concerned about me.

She also knew I had a habit of taking off on impulse.

I was planning a new trip, but it was not to Vietnam.

CHAPTER 38

Rumors spread in July that the monthly draft quotas would soon be increased again. The Vietnam War was still so new to most Americans that newspaper writers and letter writers like my mother and I weren't quite sure whether we were fighting in Vietnam, Viet-Nam, Viet Nam, or Viet-Namm.

Surely saner voices will prevail than those Americans who wanted all-out war, I continued to tell myself. Why weren't the United Nations Peacekeepers in Vietnam? What was there to win against a people determined to get foreigners out of their country and not turn it into a military testing ground?

On July 28, President Johnson announced he was sending forty-four combat battalions to Vietnam, more than doubling the U.S. military presence there, bringing the total to 125,000. He was also doubling the monthly draft to 35,000.

I buried myself in work at the library. I took the attitude that if I didn't think about the war, then it wasn't happening. I stopped listening to the radio. I had my mind set on exploring other, more important worlds at the moment.

I took my first acid trip on the last Saturday in July.

Michael Vosse was my guide—there to talk me back to earth in case I had a bad trip.

Mike Vosse was the only friend from Garry's circle of potheads and acid heads who I knew well and who, like me, had remained in the student ghetto over the summer. A pale, short, skinny, sickly, twenty-four-year-old Chicago native, he was already so prematurely bald that he almost always wore a brimmed hat, even indoors.

He had been in the theater department at USC and was close friends with both Garry and Carol, Garry's tall, dark-haired, dark-eyed, beautiful new girlfriend, who was also in the theater department.

Mike had quit the theater program and landed his first job in show business at a TV production company at the end of the school year. He hated it. He worked in a corporate office, fetching coffee and running mundane errands for the upcoming broadcast of the International Beauty Pageant. He was only sticking to it because he hoped it would lead to something better. I had run into him frequently at Garry's old apartment and more recently at movie nights at the Arkoffs' house. He followed the news and all the ins and outs in the movie, TV, and music businesses. He had been the one to bring to my attention the speech Adlai Stevenson made about earth being like a spaceship. He was like an antenna for events that I thought I should know more about.

He told me he was planning to drop acid over the weekend at his apartment on Ellendale across from Garry's old place, and he said I was welcome to trip with him.

I had been thinking about taking acid for months.

Garry had done it scores of times since his first trip two years before.

Like Garry, Mike had taken LSD many times and had been a guide for others in the theater department. I knew six or seven others who had taken their first or second acid trip with Michael, and all had talked favorably about their experience.

Everyone who had taken LSD told me something different in their own way, but it seemed to come down to the same things. It was a very personal experience—like grass but many times more intense. A person on acid could feel like they were going crazy at times, but they weren't. That's why they needed someone calm and experienced to be their guide. Some people said they saw God. No one had had any regrets or aftereffects. They all said they learned more about themselves and the universe than they had ever learned before. Of the dozen or so people I knew who had taken acid, all said they would take more.

Mike said I didn't need a guide. Some people do fine without it. He also said if I dropped acid on my own, I should remember, "If you get into trouble, the easiest way to get out is look for the humor."

Some said it was like taking a bath in magical waters, waking up, and seeing everything clearer than they ever had before. "You're just seeing what you have always been seeing, except without the filters," Garry had explained.

Why would anyone want to pass up a chance at a rebirth? In an era when the pharmaceutical industry was exploding, why not a drug that could make you see clearer, maybe end war, and bring world peace?

I wanted to try it before it became illegal. I wanted to know for myself whether I trusted the government to regulate LSD. I was already convinced that smoking grass hadn't done me any harm and had been enlightening.

I walked the half mile from my new place on University Avenue to Mike's on Ellendale so I wouldn't have to worry about driving home.

Mike lived in a newer apartment building on the west side of the street.

His apartment was on the side of the building with lots of light from the alley, but high enough up so no one could see in. The kitchen and living room were combined into one room. The ceiling was high, giving it an airy feeling.

Mike made tea, and while he was fixing it, he tossed me one of the little clear glass vials filled with acid. The transparent, sky blue liquid almost filled the inside of the vial. The vial was no more than an inch long with a black plastic screw top.

"That comes from a special batch Owsley just cooked up," Mike told me. "I took some last weekend. It's really mellow."

We settled on opposite sides of his small living room, me on the couch in front of the coffee table where I set out my notebook and felt pens, and Mike on the other side of the room near the kitchen where he sat in a stuffed chair. From there, he could easily change records on his stereo or pluck a magazine from the stack of magazines on the side table.

Mike put on a Ravi Shankar album.

We both drank the blue liquid at the same time. I tasted nothing. I washed it down with a sip of tea.

"It'll take about twenty minutes to start to kick in," Mike said. He rested his head on the back of his chair and closed his eyes.

I sat back and tried to relax, something I was never good at.

After a few minutes, I picked up my pen and paper and began to draw.

What I liked most about Ravi Shankar's music was the way it helped me create by pulling me more into the moment.

In twenty minutes, I began to feel a change in everything.

I saw colors I had never seen before. Objects around the room changed shape and size, melted away, and reformed. I saw molecules split. My felt-tip pen drew amazingly complex pictures, moving my hand around the drawing paper like a possessed planchette on a Ouija board.

Probably because I wished this to happen.

I could see my thoughts. They were tumbling through my head like they were going over a waterfall.

I laughed like crazy.

At nothing.

The only scary part of the experience was that I couldn't shake off the effects of the drug if I wanted to.

"Let it happen," Michael said, laughing as he placed a fresh cup of tea on the coffee table in front of me. I had no memory of him making tea a second time.

He turned into the joker walking off a playing card and appeared to float more than walk across the room and back to his own chair.

My mind jumped from thoughts of peace and sunshine to war.

Every image of war and savagery—documentaries of Auschwitz and the aftermath of the bombings at Hiroshima and Nagasaki; war movies in black and white and color; old Civil War photos I had seen of the battlefield dead and the starving and dead in prisoner-of-war camps—flashed through my mind. Paintings I had seen of martyrs with arrows sticking out of their bloodied bodies merged with images of Vietnamese monks and American citizens burning themselves alive in protest and soldiers being carried off the battlefield, some already dead, before becoming a bloody, carnal image of a neo-Hieronymus Bosch painting, which exploded and tumbled into rivers of random shapes of black and white and color, which turned into a red burst of blood in the patch of sky I could see through Mike's window.

Seconds later, images of fields filled with spring flowers, waterfalls, quiet lakes, fast running streams, images of the ocean slapping against the mountains in Big Sur, and a million other images flashed through my mind. My thoughts tumbled like this for hours. Each second turned into an hour. At times it was like being awake while dreaming.

Time was distorted and did not have the same meaning.

I could float to the ceiling and from there watch my every move from outside my body.

Most of the time, I was overwhelmed with thoughts of peace and good will for every living thing. I thought it possible that stones and inanimate objects had souls. Spaceship earth was real.

No violence could be allowed on the ship—it was the only way the planet would survive. That's what our times were about. We needed to change, and quickly, and win the peace, not the war, if we were to survive. Winning the peace by definition meant no more war. That was what winning the peace meant.

Everything was connected. Nothing mattered. I was nothing, a mere moment in the passage of time. I was an integral part of the universe. Everything mattered.

I wondered what Henry David Thoreau would have seen and felt on acid. Or President Kennedy. Or President Johnson. Or Ho Chi Minh.

Ho-Ho-Ho—I couldn't think of Ho's name without laughing hysterically.

I wanted to play my guitar with my teeth so I could taste the music. I regretted not bringing my guitar.

Everything was insanely funny.

And insanely serious. I was dying. My molecules were escaping. I felt like I was disintegrating into nothing.

Life is absurd, existential, transcendental, surreal, and transient. I am a tramp. I am whatever I imagine I am.

War mongers were aliens sent from outer space to erase the last vestigial memories of the Garden of Eden from our consciousness.

I was nothing and everything.

Somewhere around nine or ten at night after it had gotten dark, Mike drove us downtown in his sporty, new, red Corvair Monza Spyder convertible. We rode with the top down. It felt like we were riding in a spaceship. I was amazed he could drive. I could barely talk.

He showed me the gazebo in the center of Paseo de la Plaza that produced eerily haunting echoes of our voices.

He took me to my first Japanese restaurant. It was in Little Tokyo and somewhat oddly named the Atomic Café—oddly, considering the Japanese had borne the brunt of two atomic bombs. It was on East Front

Street and stayed open late into the night. I tasted tempura, miso soup, wasabi, and sticky rice for the first time.

Amazing.

Somewhere after midnight on the way back from supper, Mike dropped me off at my place where I spent the rest of the night and part of the next morning writing, drawing, and painting as I returned to earth.

I slept for several hours on Sunday morning and spent the rest of the day writing and playing my guitar. I went to bed after dinner, got up on Monday feeling perfectly normal, and returned to work with no lingering effects from the acid.

A few days later, I took my second acid trip, this time by myself at my place and spent the time writing, painting, and playing my guitar. I went to work the next day, satisfied that everything I had seen and thought on my first trip had really happened.

I finished a large painting with four standing female nudes that dominated one wall of my apartment.

I tried to start writing another novel. I wanted my characters in my writing to be intensely feeling life, but they remained dressed, it seemed, even when having sex.

I stayed up late into the night reading. I read Albert Camus's *The Plague*, Henry Miller's *Black Spring*, and James Baldwin's *Fire Next Time*, and found myself alternately intrigued and disturbed. *The Plague* made a great metaphor for my thoughts on Vietnam. War was like a plague, targeting teens and young men like me. War was a sickness that killed. I marveled at the freewheeling sex in Henry Miller's novel, but I was more impressed that he had the ability to let himself go as a writer and write about such personal, intimate moments. My writing was far too inhibited.

James Baldwin's writing was a different kind of letting go—angry, yet hopeful. Were the Black and white races in America on a collision course? My closest Black friend in the neighborhood was my dentist, Cato Robinson, a contemporary of my parents. Cato had his office near the pawnshops on Vermont Avenue. He was a graduate of the USC dental school and taught part-time at Cal State Long Beach. Besides students, celebrities like Ray Charles and Louis Lomax drove across town to see him. Cato had been on the frontlines in World War II and the Korean War. He walked with a limp from a wound he received in Korea. Like my Uncle

Sam, who had also seen action on the frontlines, Cato told me the war in Vietnam "is senseless. Don't go if you don't have to. We have enough issues to settle here in America."

The Black riots back East the year before—in Harlem, Rochester, Philadelphia, and elsewhere—were an aberration, I told myself.

The riots had mainly harmed the Black communities, destroying the businesses and jobs in their local neighborhoods, and scaring off others, making it harder for the local Blacks to buy groceries and everything else without leaving their neighborhoods. Local jobs were harder to find because small manufacturers moved to other suburbs.

The voices of cooler heads, like Martin Luther King, Jr., had to prevail. Civil disobedience, not armed conflict, was the answer.

James Baldwin was optimistic. Life for the American Black had been unquestionably awful, but things could and would change.

The peace and perseverance from the Black community's non-violent protests was a lesson for the world. With the 1964 Civil Rights legislation in place, I wanted to believe we were on the road to healing the rift, and the worst was finally behind us.

On Friday, August 6, 1965, President Johnson signed the Voting Rights Act. Discriminatory voting practices like poll and literacy taxes, used for years to keep Blacks from voting in the South, were made illegal. The drive to register Black voters had been the major focus of the civil rights movement for the past few years.

By the beginning of the second week of August, the days had begun to turn into a hot, smoggy blur. I had started a couple of new stories and was working on a new painting. I shut myself off from the world and was enjoying it, but I was also looking forward to the coming Friday night. Friday the thirteenth.

The television show Mike Vosse had been working on for the past few months—the International Beauty Pageant—was airing that night. Garry's mother had a color television, so we planned to meet at Garry's house in Studio City to watch the show.

I finished work as usual on Friday and locked the annex building. I cooked a quick meal at my apartment and headed to Garry's. On the way, I stopped at the Texaco station on Vermont to fill my gas tank.

The owner of the station was pumping gas. I had been buying gas there since I had driven my Volvo into the city almost a year before. We usually talked but that night he stayed beside the pump until the tank was full.

He seemed distracted when I handed him the money but leaned in the window while handing me my change and said, "You going to be all right tonight?"

The sun was just setting, and I was looking forward to an evening in Garry's air-conditioned place.

"I'm good. I'm heading to my friend's house. He has air-conditioning," I said, thinking he was talking about the heat. "And you?"

"I'll be okay," he told me. "I'm closing early. I sent everyone home already. Take care now."

He turned to deal with another car pulling into the station.

I took the freeway over the Hollywood Hills to Studio City. I drove with the radio off as I often did to let the battery charge after a week of not driving. I was late getting started but traffic was unusually light for a Friday night, so I arrived just on time.

Garry heard me as I drove up his driveway. He greeted me at the door and hustled me straight to the TV. The show started as I sat down. I was sitting next to Suzanne, Garry's mom. Garry was sitting on her other side. Beyond Garry was Mike and another of Garry's old friends, David Kent. David had been a Hollywood child actor, who now, as an adult, rarely got any acting roles and survived mainly by selling grass to his old Hollywood friends. David was a solemn character, always dressed in dark clothes, mostly black. I never saw him smile. Like Mike, he was short and skinny.

I wasn't a fan of beauty contests, but Mike Vosse made it fun with his running commentary on little production errors and his opinion of the hosts, guests, and contestants.

When the pageant finally wrapped up, the news came on. Suzanne left the room, and Garry looked away from me, listening to the conversation between Mike and David. I figured they were talking in a low voice because they didn't want Suzanne to hear. Garry already told me that Suzanne didn't care for Mike or David.

I kept watching the TV, not fully absorbing what I was seeing. The screen was filled with short scenes of police and Blacks fighting, storefronts on fire, and Blacks being arrested.

I wondered which Southern city had erupted this time. Or maybe it was a repeat of the Black riots back East.

The voice-overs by the commentators talked of numbers of dead, numbers of police on the street, the National Guard moving in.

I turned and asked Garry, "Where's that?"

"There." He pointed at the screen.

"Yeah, but where is that happening?" I asked again, trying to hear what the announcer was saying.

Mike, David, and Garry fell silent and stared at me.

Something terrible had happened again. I could feel it. These were the same looks I had seen on faces right after President Kennedy had been shot.

"What's happening? Where is that?" I gestured toward the TV, which was showing more quick-cut shots of location after location of fires, police arresting Blacks, Blacks fleeing from cops, and firemen huddled behind fire trucks as snipers shot at them.

"That's down by you," Garry said.

I nodded like I was brushing off a joke. "What's happening? Where is that?"

"Down by USC."

Mike and David nodded.

The narrator mentioned streets I recognized that ran close to USC. South Central was under fire.

Mike and I were the only ones who lived there. David lived in the Hollywood foothills in an apartment over a garage. Garry was living at home.

I was speechless.

"We were just discussing what to do," Mike said.

David planned to return to his place. He was out of the war zone.

"You two are welcome to stay here," Garry told Mike and me. "It's too dangerous for you to go home."

I was still trying to process my first impressions of the Watts Riots.

The riots had been going on for two days right in my backyard, and I had no idea.

CHAPTER 39

The Watts Riots started when a Black truck driver stopped a white motorcycle cop and told him about a car on the road ahead that was driving erratically. This was on Wednesday evening, August 11, 1965, one day before the full moon.

The motorcycle cop pulled the driver over in the middle of the sprawling Black ghetto of South Central Los Angeles on a hot smoggy night when a lot of people were out on the streets. A friendly crowd gathered to watch the obviously drunk twenty-one-year-old Black driver fail the sobriety tests. The officer had been super polite when putting the young man through the drills. Even the boy's mother seemed to be in support of the police.

If the intoxicated driver had been taken away immediately, the show would have ended. But the motorcycle cop had to call for a squad car to transfer the drunk driver to the drunk tank, giving the drunk time to gather his wits and begin yelling about police brutality, rousing the crowd to a heated pitch as more police were called in, and more arrests were made. The perceived and real violence on both sides escalated over the next two days into bottle throwing, pushing, fights, fires, looting, and shootings. Years of pent-up rage against police brutality, poverty, and de facto segregation in Los Angeles quickly spun out of control and erupted into chaos and unprecedented and unpredictable violence. [31 32 33 34 35 36]

By Friday morning, August 13, before I went to Garry's, the police had already lost count of the number of injured officers and civilians. One of the gunshot victims was popular Black comedian and civil rights activist Dick Gregory, who had entered the war zone with police permission to try to pacify the crowds. He received a flesh wound from a bullet hitting his leg.

Rioters and police continued to clash. Looting spread from one commercial strip to another. Stores and vehicles continued to be torched all morning. Los Angeles Police Chief William Parker III formally requested the National Guard just before eleven o'clock on Friday morning. Lieutenant Governor Glenn Anderson, who was in charge of the state while Governor Pat Brown was vacationing in Greece, sat on the request as the rioting and attacks on whites continued to spread to new neighborhoods.

The arrests of adult offenders were running at seven times that of juveniles, but the statistics were deceptive. The police were quick to admit that the teenagers could simply outrun and out-dodge them.

The fires, looting, and battles between police and Black rioters grew more intense on Friday night under the cover of darkness.

The sensible thing to do would have been to stay the night at Garry's and wait until it was light before driving home.

I wasn't feeling sensible. Mike wanted to go back to his place to pick up a stash of LSD, pot, and cash to hold him over until things settled down, but he was afraid his new convertible would draw too much attention. So, I offered to drive.

David Kent left Garry's, and Mike and I headed into the unknown.

Mike and I took the Hollywood Freeway back and listened to the news on the radio.

A fireman had been killed earlier in the evening when a wall of a burning building had collapsed on him. Police, responding to a liquor store fire, were shot at from all directions. During the arrest of three Blacks at the scene, one suspect grabbed the barrel of a policeman's gun, and it discharged into the stomach of a second officer who was pronounced dead on arrival at the hospital.

A Black bystander was shot when police returned fire from snipers.

At ten that night, as we drove south, the first troops were being deployed on the streets. They had orders not to fire. [37][38]

Black youths tried to storm the Oak Park Community Hospital at Manchester and Broadway.

Some cops lost control and arrested and beat bystanders. Women and children were manhandled.

Two hundred fires were burning simultaneously, many of them visible from the freeway as we headed over the Hollywood Hills and into the basin.

The landscape looked like a vision of hell. Some fires were giant red balls of flames in the distance. Others appeared as smaller yellow balls.

The radio reported looting at Vermont and Jefferson, only a few blocks away from our apartments.

Very few cars were on the freeway going south. The ones we crossed paths with were driven by Blacks with one or two Black passengers. Their inside lights were on. We appeared to be the only whites on the freeway driving into the war zone that night.

Our intentions didn't matter. Our thoughts on civil rights didn't matter. The violence had reduced the world to skin color. I felt scared enough that my legs shook. I was having trouble holding my foot steady on the gas pedal.

"Don't look, don't speed up," Mike ordered me as a car pulled alongside us. From the corner of my eye, I could see the young Black man in the passenger seat, staring straight into our car with eyes narrowed, lips drawn tight. Holding my breath, keeping a steady speed, I wondered if he was as worried about me as I was about him. I focused on the road ahead until the other car went past without incident.

Mike let out a nervous laugh.

All the homes and businesses we could see on either side of the freeway were blacked out. "So, no one will shoot at them," Mike concluded.

Near the end of the Hollywood Freeway, we caught up with a small convoy of National Guard vehicles traveling slower than we were. I decided not to pass them. I followed behind at fifty miles an hour, taking some comfort in the soldiers in battle gear holding rifles, staring grimly back at us.

"I hope they know we're not looking for trouble," I said, as we followed them to the Harbor Freeway and down the Adams Boulevard ramp.

They headed along Figueroa in the direction of the USC campus ten blocks away. I turned onto Adams and headed toward Mike's. We drove past Hoover Street and then Monmouth Avenue, where the late UN

Ambassador Adlai Stevenson had been born. I wondered what he would think of the rioting in our little corner of our spaceship.

Even with the windows rolled up, we could hear sirens screaming everywhere in the night.

The streets were completely deserted—no lights in the houses, no cars driving by, and no cars parked on the streets.

I drove at a modest speed but went right through red lights and stop signs without slowing down. The absence of life stepped up my fear.

What the hell are we doing here? I asked myself as I pulled in front of Mike's apartment on Ellendale. Sirens screamed from the direction of Vermont and Jefferson two blocks away.

"Come right back as fast as you can," Mike whispered as if worried someone might hear him even though the street was completely deserted. A second later, he was sprinting for the door of his building, holding one hand down on his hat so it wouldn't fly off.

I was suddenly alone on the street for the first time. I had a tingling sensation down the back of my neck as I pulled away from the curb. I drove along the deserted streets toward my place on University Avenue. My heart raced. My eyes dashed everywhere, looking for signs of trouble.

The houses and buildings along the way were blacked out.

I parked in my driveway and got out. I became more aware of the acrid smell of smoke mixed in with the usual thick smog of the basin. The city was burning.

The German shepherd was not in the backyard of my neighbors' house. I peered at the dark windows at the back of their house but saw no signs of the grad students or their two young toddlers.

Were they at home? Had they fled?

Oddly, I could hear the sound of crickets in the yard mixed with the sound of sirens.

I climbed the stairs to my apartment and unlocked the door.

I didn't dare turn on the lights, fearing I'd make myself a target. I used the ambient light coming through the open door to navigate.

Nothing inside had changed. It was exactly as I had left it earlier in the evening.

I grabbed my guitar, typewriter, and checkbook, and left.

I returned to Mike's and rang his buzzer. He came out wearing a different fedora and carrying his briefcase.

"I found us a place to stay in Silver Lake. We're going with some other friends of mine. We have to hurry. They're waiting for us," he said.

Mike's friends were graduate students who lived a block away. They were already outside in their car.

"We're going to travel in a two-car caravan so we can provide each other with assistance if one car gets in trouble," Mike explained just as we pulled up beside the other car.

Seconds later, everyone jumped when we heard shots coming from the direction of Vermont and Jefferson.

The other car pulled away from the curb.

I followed behind the other car through the deserted surface streets. Silver Lake was several miles away.

During the ride, Mike kept fiddling with the radio, tuning it from station to station, listening to the reports of the violence spreading over a rapidly widening area.

From the speed at which the violence was spreading, I wondered how long we would be safe in Silver Lake.

CHAPTER 40

We arrived without incident at an old, detached, two-story, wood frame house between the Hollywood Freeway and Sunset Boulevard in Silver Lake. A dozen people were already inside. The gathering felt more like a frat-house beer party than a refugee camp. Friends stopped by to drink, smoke pot, hover around the radio in the kitchen, or listen to loud rock music in the living room. I was never quite sure who lived there and who was crashing for the night. Anyone who wanted to sleep found a free bed upstairs and conked out.

I was bone tired. We all were, but hardly anyone slept. I spent much of my time listening to the news on the radio. Neither the police, National Guard, firemen, city hall, nor the media seemed to have a clear picture of what was happening. The size and intensity of the riots were unprecedented. Conflicting stories came and went from different sources. It was chaotic and frightening. The reported and rumored body count, injuries, and fires continued to rise, seemingly with no end in sight.

By morning, the only edibles left in the house were a couple of heels of white bread and a half dozen cans of Coors. With the three-hour difference in time, I called home collect. I woke my father. My mother was out. My father hadn't heard a thing about the riots. He scolded me for calling on a Saturday morning and told me to get off the phone and call back when rates were cheaper.

I told him I'd call back another time.

I was angry, but I also realized he couldn't possibly comprehend what I was witnessing. If he did, what could he do?

Nothing.

I was on my own in the middle of an insurrection. It was fruitless calling New Jersey.

Except for Mike, the others at the old house in Silver Lake were strangers to me. They were Mike's friends, not mine. They were all several years older than me. No one was in the mood to make new friends.

Growing increasingly hungry and restless I tried calling Garry in Studio City. His line was busy. No one answered at Jeff's in Tarzana. I wondered if they were outside at the pool enjoying a morning swim.

The first friendly voice I reached that morning was Buddy.

"I was wondering what happened to you," he said. "I've been calling your place since yesterday."

I gave Buddy a brief rundown of the past day, and he invited me over.

I gave Buddy's phone number to Mike and told him to call me there later if he felt like it. "Here," Mike chuckled, handing me a joint and a hit of Owsley's acid he'd rescued from his apartment. "In case you want to get high."

I took a hit from the joint he was holding, pocketed the rest of the psychedelics, and headed to Buddy's place.

Buddy's house was a good choice. It was only about a mile away and had a 180-degree view of the Los Angeles basin. I could see my neighborhood in the distance under all the smog and smoke. I felt as if I could keep a better eye on things from Buddy's.

Buddy also had a well-stocked refrigerator. His mother and father were very welcoming. His mother sat me down right after I arrived and fed me a big breakfast of orange juice, toast, and scrambled eggs.

They had the television on in the living room and the radio on in the kitchen. By mid-morning, between four and five thousand National Guard troops were on the streets of the war zone,

The rioting continued. The death toll, including the dead policeman, fireman, bystanders, and looters had reached ten by dawn and was expected to go up. New fires were being set across a vast area roughly bordered by Washington Boulevard on the north, Crenshaw Boulevard on the west, Rosecrans Avenue on the south, and Alameda Street on the east. My little shack was well inside the riot zone. Fire and smoke were visible across the field of combat below us. Sirens wailed in the distance.

A friend of Buddy's called later in the morning. He'd heard white, commercial areas would be targeted that night outside the Black communities because most of the commercial strips in South Central had already been looted and torched. Police and sheriffs' stations were preparing for attacks. Buddy's friend said he was going out to buy a gun and wanted to know if Buddy wanted to go with him. Buddy turned him down, but his friend got both Buddy and I thinking.

The newscasters on TV and radio said everyone was bracing for the worst on Saturday night.

Lieutenant Governor Anderson signed a curfew order for the riot zone later that afternoon, giving the police and Guardsmen the power of martial law to arrest or shoot anyone on the streets in the curfew zone between eight at night and dawn.

What about outside the zone? Was it even possible that anyone would show up at Buddy's house?

The Harlem, Rochester, and Philadelphia riots of the summer of 1964 had been confined to a relatively few blocks in Black ghettos. The official curfew area of the Watts Riots covered an area of 46.5 square miles, nearly a tenth of the city limits and more than twice the size of Manhattan.

The Watts Riots war zone covered Black and mixed neighborhoods. White, Jewish, and Asian-owned businesses were specifically targeted.

No one in Los Angeles knew how long the violence would last or how far it would spread.

Another friend of Buddy's phoned. He'd heard that young Black militants with guns were gathering far outside the curfew area at friends' houses and were planning to extend the war zone into Beverly Hills and the Hollywood Hills that night.

Buddy and I talked about how difficult it would be for police and Guardsmen to get quickly to trouble spots on the winding roads that crisscrossed the hills.

We heard over the radio that the sporting goods stores and surplus stores were running short of guns. On a whim, we decided to head into Hollywood and see if we could buy some guns.

I was twenty. Buddy was nineteen. We couldn't buy guns on our own, so, we talked his father into accompanying us. He drove us down the hill to the Hollywood Gun Shop on Hollywood Boulevard and Gower. We found a line stretching for a half block. With nothing else to do and curious about what was going on inside, we joined the line. Another customer told us the Hollywood Gun Shop was one of the only stores left in the county that still had guns. He had been to two others. Another man with a thick foreign accent exited the store and told everyone he hadn't been able to produce the right papers to purchase a gun. He was frantic and asked everyone in line to buy one for him. No one wanted to get involved.

The craziest rumor spread among those in line was that armed Black radicals planned to invade white areas that night to loot and kill. They would be coming in garbage trucks, using them as de facto armored vehicles.

By the time we finally entered the store twenty minutes later, the selection of firearms was slim. The only guns left were a few surplus weapons. The skinny young clerk, who looked like he'd been up all night, showed us two bolt-action Berthier Fusil mle 1907-1915 M34s for fifteen dollars each. Each gun came with a five-shot clip, and that was it. The shells showed some oxidation. No additional shells were available. The clerk told us we would probably have trouble finding more ammunition anywhere. The next to last guns with ammunition in the store were sold while we were trying to make up our minds. [39]

Buddy had never owned a gun. We discussed our options and almost ran out of time when someone else offered to buy the guns we were holding. We made up our minds quickly. Minutes later, we had paid for the last two guns with ammo in the shop and were on our way back to his place like two kids who had gone fishing in the pond and arrived home with a half dozen fish too small to eat.

I showed Buddy how to take the guns apart and check the barrels to make sure they were clean. The guns were in good shape, but it was unclear whether the somewhat corroded shells would fire.

Shortly after we had the guns reassembled, I received a phone call from Mike.

"What have you been up to?" he asked.

"Not much. You?"

He explained that he was at the new place near the Hollywood Bowl that David and Sherril Anderle had just rented. David and Sherril had been frequent visitors to Garry's during the spring and they had married at the end of July. They had lived in the new apartment building across from me on Ellendale. So, I knew them fairly well.

"You're not that far from here. Why don't you come over?" Mike suggested.

The house David and Sherril were renting was only two miles away or a six or seven-minute drive from North Gramercy Place to there. I went alone. I knew there'd be plenty of pot and acid, and Buddy wasn't into drugs.

David, Sherril, and Mike were the only people I knew at the house. David, a tall handsome, clean shaven, dark-haired man, had been a professor in the USC theater department before landing work on the production side of the music business as a talent scout at the beginning of the summer. He was in his late twenties. Sherril, a tall, beautiful redhead with an infectious smile, was closer in age to me. She had been in one of my psychology classes.

The other half dozen people were friends of David's and Sherril's. They were listening to music and passing around a joint when I arrived. I found a comfortable spot in the corner of the living room and listened to the music and conversations.

A few more people arrived soon after me, and then a few more. Mike explained the grand plan for the evening. He had enough LSD for everyone. The plan was to take acid at sunset, hike into the hills behind David and Sherril's house, and trip while wandering around the top of the Hollywood Hills.

"We'll get arrested," someone said.

"No way," Mike insisted. "Think about it. What would you do if you were the police, and someone in the Hollywood Hills called to report a bunch of white freaks wandering around acting strange? They're not going to give a shit."

Sherril and David were planning on taking acid. Everyone seemed to think it was a good idea.

More people arrived, including a young woman with long, straight blond hair halfway down her back. After a while, she headed to the other side of the room and turned on the TV but left the sound off. A few people moved closer to the TV to watch the latest black-and-white images of the riots.

The woman turned the dial on the set, changing the channel to an old gangster movie.

The gangster movie played for a minute before the woman changed the channel again to another station with helicopters flying over rice paddies. Vietnam.

A beer commercial interrupted the war.

She was beaming as she glanced around the room at those who were watching her change channels.

She was tripping.

I was tripping.

Television. We were the first generation of humans on the planet to grow up on TV. For the first time in history, we had access to a crude, personal time machine and spaceship wrapped in one. We could change channels. We could travel back and forth through history. We could visit outer space and TV-and-movie versions of what the future would look like. We could see what was happening on the other side of town or on the other side of the planet in real time. We could see wars and quiz shows. TV gave us the visual proof for the first time in history that everything is interconnected. Here we were at a time when we could blow up the planet or speak to everyone on the planet and say, hey, let's love one another, and we were still hesitating, still wrestling with which to choose.

The young woman changed the channel again to a baseball game in progress somewhere in the country. I wondered if my dad was watching the same game in the cool basement of our house in New Jersey.

The woman looked around to see if anyone was still watching. She glanced at me for a second and smiled before changing the channel again back to the rioting.

I thought about staying.

Dropping acid and taking off to another world sounded tempting, but another couple arrived a few minutes later and said they'd heard the body count from the riots had reached into the teens, and it wasn't even dark yet.

I didn't feel in the mood to get high on acid.

I wanted some quiet time to think about what was happening around me.

"You're going to miss out on a good time," Mike said, handing me a joint to take with me.

I said goodbye to everyone and returned to Buddy's place.

Buddy and I ate dinner with his parents. After they went to bed, Buddy and I sat on the outdoor patio with our rifles leaning against the wall behind us, watching the fires spread out for miles below. We paid extra attention to the very infrequent headlights of vehicles moving slowly along the roads beneath his house.

Saturday night was also when the Guardsmen were ordered to load their weapons.

CHAPTER 41

Saturday night, August 14, 1965

After Buddy crashed, I sat alone on the patio with my gun leaning against the wall. Buddy had taken his rifle inside.

Strange what goes through your mind when you're trying to decide what to do in the middle of chaos.

I thought of my father and how everything about his growing up and coming of age had been so much different from my experiences.

My father hated guns.

He loathed fighting and war.

I could understand why. He was naturally brave. He came from the mean streets of Brooklyn and lost his mother when he was nine in the last years of the Spanish flu. He had lived through poverty that I couldn't even imagine. He rarely talked about growing up. He had little nostalgia for his past.

I could never step into his shoes. People didn't inherit or earn that kind of strength.

He was the type of man who other men followed without being asked. Why? Because he was handsome, strong, and a good listener. People were drawn to him.

At family picnics, Dad would always be one of the captains or the first picked no matter what the sport.

He didn't have to fight because he wasn't afraid to fight if he had to. I witnessed this firsthand when I was twelve, I stood on the side of the road in a then-heavily wooded part of the township with my mother, waiting for the state troopers to arrive. A man in one of the shacks deep in the woods was holding three Scouts hostage with a shotgun because the kids had wandered onto his property. As president of the local Boy Scout Committee, my father had been called first by the panic-stricken Scoutmaster. My father arrived on the scene before my mother and me. Dad had gone into the woods by himself and talked the man into letting the Scouts go in exchange for himself. I watched the three freed Scouts come out of the woods. My father still hadn't come out by the time the two young state troopers arrived in two different police cars twenty minutes later. They entered the woods after assuring themselves that all the Scouts were out of harm's way.

The state police officers and my father talked the man into putting down the shotgun after it was agreed that the Scouts would never go on his property again. No charges were laid, and it never made the newspapers—typical in such a small rural community.

Despite what my father felt about guns, he let my brother buy his first shotgun at thirteen after Ray passed a firearms course given by a neighbor who hunted the fields for deer, pheasant, and rabbits to put extra meat on his family's table.

My father never said anything more about guns. He left the enforcement of rules at home to my mother.

After living through the agonizing war years where two of her brothers and an uncle her age fought through the war, my mother wanted her own boys to know how to use guns in anticipation of the next war. So, she encouraged it as long as we showed an interest.

I followed my brother into gun ownership when I was thirteen, buying a Remington pump .22 and a Marlin bolt action .22, but I didn't share the passion my brother had for hunting. He and his friends seemed to have no qualms about shooting and killing animals. I tried and tried, but I always had qualms and remorse. I thought if I killed enough, I would toughen up and get used to it, but I never had. The last time I had shot an animal was off the rear of a pickup truck when I had been with my brother in the summer of 1962. He had taken me to the ranch outside Silver City, New Mexico where he had ridden in cattle roundups. There, my brother, the rancher's son, and I drove out to the range in the pickup at dusk to hunt jackrabbits with .22s off the back of the truck. The rabbits were a nuisance because they dug holes in the range land that could break the legs of horses and cattle. We were doing a service, and of course I had to show off and outdo my brother and the rancher's son, beating them in the number of rabbits I'd slaughtered that night. I was a natural shooter. My brother was proud of me, but all I felt was disgust, and I swore to myself I would never do it again.

Now, here I was, armed, and not very ready to bear arms.

The fires across the basin continued to glow. The gunshots and sirens continued into the night.

There has to be a better way, I told myself.

CHAPTER 42

Over breakfast the next morning, Buddy, his parents, and I heard on the radio that the official death toll had climbed to twenty-three. Three thousand more Guardsmen arrived to relieve the 12,000 already in place. The radio said grocery stores in the curfew area had either been looted or were running out of food.

After breakfast, Rick called. Rick was Buddy's pal from high school. The three of us had worked at the library the previous summer. Rick had transferred to another school but still kept in touch with both of us. Rick wanted to take a drive along the freeway through the war zone, but he didn't want to go alone.

Buddy and I were eager to go. We went in Rick's five-year-old white Valiant, the most road-worthy of the three cars among us. We left the guns behind. The novelty of buying the guns had already worn off.

The traffic thinned to a trickle as we headed south along the Hollywood Freeway to the Harbor Freeway, which cut straight across South Central and Watts.

The freeway was nearly empty. No one was breaking the speed limit. Everyone was keeping a respectful distance from cars ahead of them. Most drivers and passengers were Black. Most were older couples or families with children. We speculated that some were making a run out of town to the south, hoping to stay with relatives or friends out of the war zone. I wondered how Cato, my Black dentist, and his family were weathering the storm. He lived at the western edge of the war zone. I wondered how my Black friend at the Texaco station was doing. I had no idea where he lived. I now realized his nervousness on Friday night had been about the riots.

We caught up with a convoy of military trucks carrying Guardsmen in full combat gear. They stared grimly at us from the back of the vehicles. White, black, and brown faces. A totally integrated fighting unit.

The raised freeway gave us a good view of the city below. We could see more military vehicles moving around on the smoggy streets. We spotted a few smoldering fires in the distance. Most of the businesses and houses we could see looked untouched.

We drove to the intersection of the Harbor and San Diego Freeways, turned around, and headed back.

We drove home in silence as if coming from a funeral. None of us felt like taking the exit to USC to see what had happened there.

From Buddy's house that night, we could see a few more small fires, one near Sunset Boulevard not far from us. We heard fewer sirens.

The utter fear of Friday and Saturday nights had given way to indifference.

It bothered me that I could get used to war-like conditions so quickly.

I called home on Sunday night. My parents had been worried sick. My father had not realized how bad the riots were when I called on Saturday morning. My mother had been calling my apartment for two days.

Ironically, Cato, my dentist, had also been calling my place as well. When he hadn't reached me, he had phoned my mother in New Jersey. Mom told me Cato and his family were fine. He had worried about young Blacks breaking into his dental office and stealing equipment and pharmaceuticals, but he had heard from the police that his office remained untouched. I phoned him to thank him for his concern. He told me his family was safe, but he was worried the rioting would set the Black community back a generation. He told me not to go back to my place until things settled down.

The riots and their aftermath continued to fill the local news that night on TV. The national news showed clips of the Beatles and their hysterical fans at their Shea Stadium concert in New York, the first large record-breaking pop concert of its kind. I wondered if any of the Beatles or their screaming fans even knew or cared about the riots in Southern California. It probably had as much impact on them as the Vietnam War was having on the majority of Americans at that moment, which wasn't much.

All anyone had to do to skip the horrors was turn the channel and tune into something else.

My firsthand taste of large scale street violence had profoundly saddened me. The death toll was thirty-two by Monday. The police and Guardsmen were still fully deployed in the curfew zone, which included my neighborhood.

The daylight gave me courage. I drove into the riot area by myself early Monday morning a few hours after the overnight curfew was lifted.

On Friday night when I had last been there—two and a half days before—the looting and gunfire had reached Vermont and Jefferson, a ten-minute walk from my place and steps from Cato's office. With the violence lapping at the edge of my neighborhood, I half expected to see signs of break-ins and fires, but none of the buildings in my neighborhood appeared to have been touched.

Every third vehicle that I crossed paths with on the near-empty streets was either a cop car or a National Guard vehicle.

My tiny apartment, perched on the top of its garage, appeared unharmed.

I parked in front of the building, took my belongings from my car, walked up the stairs, and went through the door.

The heat inside was stifling, but it was always like that.

I put the typewriter back on my desk and shoved my guitar and gun under my bed.

A quart of milk in the refrigerator had spoiled and a peach had grown blue mold. I noticed the window in the kitchen was open—not because anyone had tried to break in but because I had forgotten to close it when I left for Garry's three days before. It seemed like years.

I took a bath and changed clothes for the first time in three days. I went outside and ran into my neighbor, the pretty, blond, grad student with her two blond toddlers and their German shepherd. She told me they had been living in their house throughout the riots. They had heard a car drive in late Friday night, but by the time they realized it was me, I was on my way out.

"There was a sniper across the street on Saturday," she told me. "The soldiers were all over the place. Most of the houses around here were deserted. We were worried about people trying to break in. We were okay here," she assured me, patting her dog on the head. It had been giving me menacing growls throughout our conversation.

I walked a couple of blocks to the 32nd Street Market, a general grocery and liquor store owned and run by a guy named Morrie, who had a worse five o'clock shadow than Richard Nixon. I expected to see the store burned or at least boarded up. It was untouched and open for business though no one was inside shopping. I bought a prepackaged ice cream cone. Morrie told me he heard there would be more trouble that night.

I headed toward the campus on foot eating the ice cream cone.

I was surprised to see the stores around the gates of the university were apparently untouched.

Over the years since the riots, I've heard numerous theories about why this particular pocket, and indeed the entire campus of the University of Southern California, went untouched during the mayhem. I've heard theories that the rioters held schools in high regard and that little of value would be found in school buildings. Few public buildings citywide were in fact damaged, but two additional, more sobering reasons explained to me why USC went unharmed.

First, the rioting didn't reach the vicinity of the university until after dark on Friday night.

Second, as the sun set over the city that night, the first thousand National Guardsmen were arriving at staging areas in the riot zone. The USC campus was a staging area along with the old, deactivated armory across the street at Exposition Park. The USC campus was one of the first locations the troops made secure when they first arrived in the war zone that night. They reached the neighborhood *before* the rioters.

How intimidating was their presence at the school? Besides the military vehicles with armed troops cruising the streets while I was there on Monday, I was startled to see a squad of Guardsmen in full battle gear behind sandbags with a machine gun on a tripod at the north entrance to the campus grounds.

I was stopped by a couple of Guardsmen at the campus gates, who asked me for ID. I produced my student ID card and explained that I wanted to check the annex building, which I was in charge of.

They let me pass, and I walked onto the campus.

The smog brought the visibility down to a few blocks. I felt undersized in my T-shirt and jeans as I passed several more Guardsmen in battle gear and unsmiling, tired faces.

A block away, I saw a lone young woman, the only other civilian in sight, walking in front of Doheny Library, crossing my path in the distance as I headed east toward the annex.

Even from far off, I could see she was attractive, trim, and blond. She was walking quickly, head held high, shoulders back, seemingly deep in thought, and going in the same general direction I was heading. She glanced quickly at me for a few seconds—I guessed she was checking to see if I was a menace or not. I raised my hand and gave her the peace sign, but she had already turned away, eyes straight ahead as she crossed my path, acting like she hadn't seen me or didn't want to.

We both continued in the same direction for another block before she veered off toward the women's dorm and disappeared through the front door.

Was she a summer school student?

For a second, I found myself wondering if I would see her again. My thoughts of sex and love seemed incongruous and yet somehow comforting and life affirming in the middle of a city turned upside down.

I crossed the empty parking lot to the annex building.

It was locked just as I left it on Friday. The air inside was hot and stuffy, the kind of stuffiness that came from old books. There was nothing new to see. I locked up.

I meandered south through the campus past more armed Guardsmen and crossed the normally busy Exposition Boulevard. A few military vehicles passed by. They were the only traffic on the street.

As I approached the armory gate, I noticed the grounds had been turned into an armed camp. I tried to bluff my way through the gate just to get an inside view of the encampment, explaining, "We have some medieval and Renaissance books in the storage area in the basement. I need to check on them."

The young Guardsmen protecting the gates of the fortress didn't buy it and sent me away.

Doheny Library and all the other campus buildings were locked tight.

I toyed with the idea of putting in a half day at the annex, but since the school was officially closed and I was on salary, I figured I should take the day off like everyone else.

I intended to stay the night in the curfew zone, but Jeff phoned me, worried sick that I had been burned out. I explained what I had been through. He suggested I drive to Tarzana.

"You can stay overnight."

Good idea. He had a nice pool.

Before driving out of the war zone, I made a detour and headed south on Vermont toward Watts, feeling safe in the daylight.

It took me only a few blocks along the commercial strip to get my fill of boarded-up stores. Many of the businesses had been burned or had their doors and windows covered with plywood. An old burned-out Studebaker like the one my brother drove in high school sat beside the curb on Vermont south of Jefferson.

What a waste, I thought as I turned around and headed toward the freeway and out of the war zone.

CHAPTER 43

I spent a quiet afternoon with Jeff, sitting in their beautifully landscaped backyard and swimming in their pool surrounded by tall, perfectly trimmed cedar trees.

I had become good friends with both of Jeff's parents and enjoyed visiting them. His mother, Dorothy, a short, dark haired, intense woman, had been a concert pianist in Chicago. She continued to teach classical music to a few private students and sometimes entertained us with a few tunes on her grand piano in the living room. Jeff's father, Sidney, a tall, balding, powerfully built, easy-going man, had grown up poor in Chicago and had worked his way through university and law school playing the saxophone in Chicago brothels and later on the radio during the Depression. Instead of practicing law, he learned how to fix automobile transmissions and operated a transmission repair business before moving the family to Los Angeles where he started a scrap metal business in Torrance. Sidney was doing well. Besides the new house in Tarzana, he recently had purchased a giant 600cc BMW motorcycle and started taking classes at UCLA in psychology for fun. One time he told Jeff and me about sitting around with a few of his wealthy friends. They were talking about how they made their money. Sid told us, "Every single one of them thought they knew how they did it. They thought they were geniuses. You listen to them, and you realize they only think they know how they made their money. No one knows how life is going to turn out. Some people have all the luck. That means a lot of people don't have as much. Two people could do the very same thing and for the same amount of time. One could be successful. The other a failure. Or both could be failures or succeed. Nobody knows."

I sometimes thought he was telling us stories like this to make it easier on Jeff, who had a very tense relationship with his mother. Jeff's older brother Noel was at Stanford in medical school, fulfilling the dream that his mother had for him. Jeff had given up on being a doctor and had his sights set on becoming a psychologist instead. Jeff was brilliant but impatient and also still dependent on his parents, which made him uneasy. He had abandoned his plans to go to UC Riverside. He had decided to return to USC in the fall and get a place of his own. If all went well, he was hoping to graduate at the end of the year and head to graduate school somewhere far away from home.

Before we went to bed, we caught up on the news on TV. Monday had been relatively calm.

No major incidents were reported on the news that night or the next morning. Governor Pat Brown, back from his vacation, lifted the curfew for Tuesday night, and plans were underway to begin withdrawing the state militia.

Jeff and I spent the morning soaking up the sun and swimming in the pool.

After lunch, I drove to my apartment, replaced my spoiled food, and cooked dinner. Afterward, I wrote a letter to my family with a brief day-by-day account of my experiences.

I washed up and then slipped under my own covers for the first time in five nights.

It felt good to be home.

On Wednesday, one newspaper removed the score box of deaths, arrests, and injuries "at a glance."

Another paper made the war in Vietnam the lead story again.

Rioters and looters were already beginning to make their way through the court system. The police were soon riding around with their helmets unbuckled.

The Congress of Racial Equality was picketing against Police Chief William Parker III over brutality.

My local Black-owned Texaco station was untouched. The owner told me he had been worried it would be hit, but no gas stations in the city, Black-owned or white-owned, had been attacked.

By the weekend, only a few hundred Guardsmen remained in the riot zone.

No one was a hundred percent sure the rioting might not flare up again. Most people were hoping it wouldn't. The Black community had suffered the most.

In the chapter of the McCone Commission report called "144 Hours in August 1965," the final statistics reported for the six days of rioting were staggering. Thirty-four people had been killed, twenty-five of them Black. The 1,032 reported injuries included 773 civilians, 90 Los Angeles police officers, 136 firemen, 10 National Guardsmen, and 23 from other government agencies. One hundred and eighteen injuries were gunshot wounds. The dead included a fireman, a deputy sheriff, and a Long Beach police officer.

Property losses were estimated at $40 million, including 600 buildings damaged by burning and looting. Between 2,000 and 3,000 fire alarms had been recorded, a thousand of them between seven on Friday morning and seven Saturday morning when Mike and I drove into the war zone from Garry's.

Of the 3,438 adults arrested, 71 percent were for burglary and theft. Eighty-one percent of the 514 juveniles arrested were also charged with burglary and theft. Two thousand and fifty-seven of the adults arrested (about 60%) had been born in sixteen Southern states, while 131 of the juveniles arrested (about 25%) had been born in the same Southern states.

A substantial number of weapons used in the riots were stolen from local pawn shops during the riots and were never recovered. [40]

My brother took my firsthand account of the riots to the Plainfield *Courier News*, a Gannett newspaper. I had been one of their paperboys when I was in eighth grade. They published my story the next day, calling it an impressionistic and graphic description of the rioting.

I had no special insight. I simply recounted the insanity, fear, and finally, the indifference I felt as the riots unfolded.

I was poor and lived in South Central Los Angeles in the combat zone, but I was also white. I had been able to escape to the suburbs. I couldn't help wondering what it must have felt like for ordinary Blacks living in

South Central who had experienced the same fear, the same disorientation, and couldn't even leave the house for a quart of milk because their local stores had been looted or burned.

Unquestionably in my mind, the Blacks living in South Central had suffered the most.

My mother bought dozens of copies of the paper with my article in it and sent clippings to our relatives and family friends.

Several sent me letters. The opinions were quite diverse. My cousin Barney Plotkin, the New York graphic artist already famous for cigarette illustrations and book covers, wrote me that if there was one thing we could all agree on it was that the white community must be a lot more forthcoming before all mankind could really enjoy this "wonderful thing called life."

Great Uncle Lew was happy to hear that I hadn't been "shot at" or "hit on the head with a blackjack." He counseled me to get a place outside of the area, warning me a second round of rioting would surely occur, and suggesting the driving force behind the first riots had been the Black Muslims. He thought Police Chief Parker was the best top cop in the country, because he had driven the Mafia out of Los Angeles. Great Uncle Lew also told me about two multimillion dollar deals he had in the works and sent me a check for ten dollars as a token of "my esteem for you."

The lessons of Watts were mixed. Martin Luther King, Jr. was roundly dismissed by most of the young and radical Black leaders because he had publicly condoned the use of force by the government to put down the riots. For the past two years, his non-violence movement had been under attack by a growing number of Blacks who believed that African Americans should take up arms like the Deacons for Defense and Justice. Deacon founders and members were Black World War II and Korean War veterans, who had formed an armed civil rights group in Louisiana the previous year to protect civil rights workers. A month before the Watts Riots, the Deacons had repelled a Ku Klux Klan mob.[41]

Other Black radicals, many of them young and university educated, began talking about taking up arms against the government and becoming part of the growing worldwide Marxist-Leninist revolutionary movements in South America, Africa, Asia, and the Middle East.

The much needed aid and attention to poverty and unemployment in the sprawling ghetto of South Central Los Angeles never materialized. The radicals took over more Black organizations, started new ones, and began sending increasingly loud signals that they didn't want white liberals in their midst. The warm camaraderie and common cause that had been built between the white and Black student populations of the short-lived sit-in and freedom-rider era of the early 1960s were melting away.

The damned war, I thought to myself. Everything is turning violent because of it.

A local reporter from our small-town community weekly in New Jersey called my mother to say how much she enjoyed my article on the riots and wanted me to write another piece for them.

I penned a longer version of the original article and sent it off.

They rejected it.

By then the story was old, she told my mother.

I hadn't been able to add anything new.

I had no way of knowing whether I could make it as a writer.

I struggled to read in first grade as soon as I began to learn the alphabet and had trouble telling the lower case b from d.

At my best, I could read only one word at a time. I was sent to remedial reading in high school to learn speed reading.

The reading teacher thought I was cured because we read novels in the remedial class. Instead of speed reading, I taught myself skip-reading. I read one or two sentences a page, enough to get the gist of what was happening, and then, I filled in the rest with my imagination, something much more difficult to do with science, languages, and math. With those, I simply put in more time in order to read every word.

My hopes of winning a scholarship to a top Ivy League school were dashed by my poor performances on the verbal half of the Scholastic Aptitude Test. The school guidance counselor was so puzzled by my poor test results that he had my mother take me to a psychologist for further testing. The doctor said I was dyslexic. The words jumbled up if read too fast. There was no cure.

I had only been keeping up with the other students by outworking almost everyone. I was too afraid of failure to give up. I continued to put in the extra time. What else could I do?

Ironically, reading slowly combined with a good memory and a determination to learn how to write worked in my favor. I could see how a writer used sentences to build paragraphs as clear as simple math. Sentences, not words, were the building blocks of writing. Some aspects of style were quantifiable. Short sentences versus long sentences. Simple sentences versus complex sentences. Short paragraphs versus long paragraphs. Short chapters versus long chapters. Slang versus conventional speech. Lots of description versus little description. Lots of dialog versus little dialog. Choosing between first, second, or third person. I could hear the rhythms of a writer in my head as if they were tunes on the radio.

I could forge almost any style just as my mother could hear a tune once and play it on the piano or sit through a fashion show in the morning and be able to draw all the dresses later in the afternoon without taking a single note during the show.

I could write like JD Salinger, Ernest Hemingway, F. Scott Fitzgerald, Alan Sillitoe, Christopher Isherwood, John Steinbeck, or any of a dozen other writers for a few pages. I copied the themes and sentiments of other writers as well. I hated the sense of copying, but I had no profound thoughts, no original ideas, no experiences worth retelling, and no real commitments or beliefs.

What gave me hope was all my fellow high school students, who were better than me at writing and who bragged of the novels they would write, spent all their time talking about writing while I was simply writing.

What I liked most about writing was the hypnotic effect it had as I struggled to assemble sentences in my head and write them down. It helped that I could write or type almost as fast as I could read, almost as fast as I could think.

I thought nothing of spending ten or twenty hours writing and rewriting a one, two, or three page paper, looking up every word to make sure it was spelled correctly and committing it to memory; writing lists of sentences; and moving them around until they were in the right order, and only then creating paragraphs. By the end of high school, I had mastered the basic mechanics of writing though I had nothing to say that ever won

me special notice or praise from anyone. But I knew I was a good crafts-
man. I taught myself closure. I learned to change what made the story
better, not just different.

Just write. Copy. Make up things. Write.

The one thing I was sure of was that a novel was not just a bunch of
short stories strung together.

Did I have a whole book somewhere inside me? What came out when
I wrote was more of a scrapbook. Everything from tying my shoes to
headline news. Could my thoughts, prejudices, naivety, bravado, hopes,
fears, truths, and lies ever turn into a book worth reading?

I was annoyed at myself that another summer had passed and I still
had not made any progress on writing a novel.

The Beatles hung out in Benedict Canyon near Mulholland Drive in Los
Angeles for a few days rest on the last leg of their American tour. John and
George took LSD for the second time. Ringo took it for the first time. Paul
passed it up but would get into acid at a future date. During this last leg
of their tour, the Beatles met their childhood idol Elvis Presley (August
27), played a concert in San Diego (August 28), and played two concerts
at the Hollywood Bowl (August 29 and 30) where I had been in the musical
with Leslie the previous year.

A couple of weeks later, Rick asked Buddy and me if we wanted to go for
a drive on the weekend. The three of us had taken a few driving trips up
the coast to Santa Barbara and Solvang, a Danish village north of Santa
Barbara, over the summer. We usually took three cars in a caravan so we
could each drive the Coast Highway. Buddy couldn't go this time, so Rick
and I decided to save on gas, take one car, and camp somewhere around
Big Sur. My car was in good shape. I just had it tuned up, so we took my
Volvo.

I had always wanted to drive the Coast Highway through Big Sur. I
had seen it two times in the past, both times when other people were driving. This time I wanted to not just see the majestic mountains but wrestle
with them as I drove the seventy-five miles over the hairpin two-lane road
from north of the Hearst Castle to Carmel. The drive was everything I
hoped it would be as we twisted and turned along the coast. We stopped

several times, parked, and got out of the car to just gaze down at the ocean many hundreds of feet below or stare at the mountain range that seemed to go on forever.

I thought, if I ever painted a picture of California, it would be a picture of the mountains rising out of the sea so high they rose higher than the clouds.

We drove around Monterey and tried to pick up a couple of girls in Carmel but didn't have much luck. We did meet a couple of young recent recruits in civilian clothes from Fort Ord who had also tried and failed to pick up the same girls. They said they were camping south of town. We followed them to a deserted spot off the Pacific Coast Highway and hiked down a trail to the beach where they were bunking down. They were on leave for a few days and expecting to ship out soon, most likely for Vietnam. They wanted to know if we had any grass. We didn't. Rick had never smoked pot, and I didn't let on that I had. The soldiers said they hated the military, but there was nothing they could do now that they were in. One of them told a story he heard from another soldier about how Special Forces trainees were assigned a dog and put through a month-long survival course with incredible hardships with the dog as their only friend, and then, they were told to kill the dog at the end of their training to complete the course. None of us, including the soldier who told it, knew whether the story was true.

On the other side of the world at the same time in late August, the US Marines launched Operation Starlite, a major preemptive strike against an estimated 1,500 Viet Cong, who were planning to attack the Chu Lai airfield. The US preemptive strike was the first decisive US victory. It increased morale among the US troops. It also set fire to the anti-war activists as students across the country returned to their campuses for the fall term.

In another preemptive strike on the last day of August, President Johnson signed the law making it a criminal offense to burn a draft card, punishable by a $1,000 fine and five years in prison.

The idea of resisting the draft continued to grow in my mind.

Ironically, I was about to meet my very first draft dodger, and she was a woman.

CHAPTER 44

Just weeks after the Watts Riots, Columbia Records released Bob Dylan's album, *Highway 61 Revisited*, his first full album backed by a rock 'n' roll band. It was released five months after his half-rock, half-folk album, *Bringing It All Back Home*. Dylan's commitment to rock was total this time.[42]

David Anderle in his new job as a talent scout discovered Frank Zappa and the Mothers of Invention at a Sunset Strip club and was trying to get them in the door at MGM's record company Verve.

The Beatles' hauntingly beautiful "Yesterday" came out as a single on September 13, 1965. The Stones' single "Get Off of My Cloud" came out twelve days later. Simon and Garfunkel's single "Sound of Silence" was also released in September.

President Johnson signed an executive order on September 24 directing all government purchases to be made only from suppliers who didn't discriminate against employees because of race, religion, color, or nationality.

I felt conflicted. Johnson was doing the right thing regarding civil rights, which was good, but at the same time, he was sinking us deeper in the war in Vietnam.

CHAPTER 45

Anna was attractive, intelligent, and full of energy.

She was the woman I had seen twice before on campus and found charismatic. The first time I saw her was when I returned to the campus during the Watts Riots. She was walking near the library with her head held high. The second time was the day before classes started while driving my electric cart through the sea of students returning to campus. She had disappeared through the doors of the registrar's office, walking with what I could only describe as attitude.

Weeks later, our paths crossed a third time when I saw her late one evening after my night class when I ventured into the main reading room of Doheny Library. She was sitting by herself. The library was nearly empty. I sat down at the far end of her table and smiled when she glanced over at me. To my surprise and delight, she smiled back and said, hello. I asked her what she was studying.

"English," she said in a heavy accent.

I moved to the seat opposite her. We introduced ourselves and began to talk quietly.

Anna was a freshman, a foreign student, from Mexico City.

I told her I had seen her during the riots. She remembered crossing paths with me. She had been studying English at summer school. Now, she was taking a full load of courses in the fall semester.

She boasted that she hadn't been scared at all during the days of violence and curfews. She thought it was silly that the woman overseeing the dorm had made all the girls stay in the dormitory for the first few days. The first time Anna had gone out was the day I saw her walking across the campus. She was the only one from the dorm who had ventured outside. She went to see for herself what was happening.

"How could anyone be afraid?" she asked. "There were soldiers everywhere."

After an hour of reading, we went outside in the cool night air, sat on the front steps of the library, and talked about nothing and everything.

I was surprised when she told me she was Jewish.

"I'm Jewish, too," I said, expecting to surprise her.

"I know you are Jewish before you tell me," she said.

"Really?" I grew up among Protestants and went to YMCA camps. According to my mother I was the only person in our family who could "pass"—by that she meant I could appear as a secular white Anglo-Saxon Protestant.

"It's not how you look. It's just a feel," she said.

She told me she was born in Israel, a Sabra. She explained that the Sabra was a Mediterranean cactus, prickly on the outside, sweet on the inside.

Her parents were Polish and German. Anna's German father had emigrated to Palestine before World War II. He had moved the family to Mexico in the early 1950s where he owned a sweater factory in Mexico City. Her Polish mother was a survivor of the Bergen-Belsen Concentration Camp, the same hell hole where Anne Frank died. Anna's mother had met Anna's father in Palestine after the war and witnessed the birth of Israel.

Anna asked me why I had long hair and a beard; she called it a "bard" and told me about how she thought I would look better with it shaved off. She wanted to know if I liked Bob Dylan, took drugs, and what I thought of the war in Vietnam.

I told her I loved Bob Dylan, Joan Baez, the Beatles, and Buffy Sainte-Marie. I said nothing about drugs or my beard.

About the war, I told her I thought America was wrong to be fighting in Vietnam. I had no interest in going there. Most of the Vietnamese didn't want us there.

"Are you afraid to fight?" she asked. She was the first person who had asked me that so pointedly.

"I can't imagine going to war and not being scared," I told her, remembering how my uncles, who had seen combat, talked about everyone being scared or crazy on the frontlines. "I don't believe we should be fighting in their civil war. It doesn't make any sense."

"Would you fight if your life depend on it? Like in Israel?"

"I don't think I'd want to. But I guess I would if I lived there. It's not the same as the US fighting in Vietnam."

"How can you know?"

I told her what friends of mine told me, what young writers and journalists were telling us in the underground press, and what I had learned from the few professors who had talked about Vietnam.

"Why do you believe them?"

"Because they make more sense than the war mongers. I don't want to be a mercenary or a Hessian."

"Ashens?"

"Hessians. The American Revolution? George Washington? Independence Day?"

"American Revolution, yes. George Washington, yes. Independence Day, yes. I am already here on Fourth of July. Some girls from dorm take me to big celebration in a park. Lots of fireworks. We read American history in high school. But not Hessians."

"I'm surprised you know as much as you do. Hessians were German soldiers hired by the British forces to fight the Americans during the Revolution. People are calling Ho Chi Minh the George Washington of Vietnam. This is Vietnam's war of independence. They're calling the Americans *Hessians*—hired mercenaries brought in to prop up a failed government. I don't want to be a Hessian."

I explained that I thought I could do more for the world in the Peace Corps, which I was thinking of joining. I was also thinking about going to the Canadian consulate in Los Angeles to find out how to immigrate there. My trip through Montreal earlier in the summer had heightened my interest.

I told her what little I knew about Canada and pointed out that Canada had a Prime Minister who had won a Nobel Peace Prize. "They don't see the need to fight anyone in Vietnam."

"When do you go to Canada?"

"I don't know. You want to go with me?" I joked.

"I tell you something now, maybe a little funny, maybe a little sad. I leave Mexico and go live in Israel by myself last year. I was seventeen. I would have stay there," Anna told me in her choppy English, "but my mother make me come home when I turn eighteen. If I stay, they draft me because I am Israeli. I cannot go back there right now."

Drafted? Far out, I thought. The very first draft resister I meet is a woman.

I tried to think of ways to keep talking all night, but it was late. She had to return to her dorm. I walked her to her door and told her I'd like to see her again.

"Maybe I see you in the library tomorrow night."

Her voice was soft and promising. I walked away feeling good.

CHAPTER 46

The Byrds' single "Turn, Turn, Turn" was released in late October. The first Loving Spoonful album, featuring the already released "Do You Believe in Magic," was released in November. The second single by the Mamas & Papas, "California Dreamin'," was also released in November. It caused an instant sensation after their first single "Go Where You Want to Go" had failed to make much headway on the charts.

Anna and I saw each other erratically. We had all the usual things in common for curious college students in 1965—books, poetry, paintings, museums, making out, the rapidly escalating war, and sex.

She loved not only Dylan and the Beatles but the scratchy classical albums of Mozart, Bach, and the others I had bought for eighty-eight cents at the discount bin at the local Ralph's supermarket. She listened to my records in my tiny apartment by candlelight on my terrible second-hand record player that only took one record at a time.

We made out whenever we saw each other, and I was sure we would sleep together, but I wasn't so sure how we'd get past some other serious and worldly differences.

She was a self-styled Communist.

I was skeptical. I told her, "The idea of permanent revolution is insane. It's a recipe for ongoing violence and leads to strongmen and authoritarian regimes with no democracy, rigged succession, and no checks and balances."

"That's because you don't know true Communism yet." She was infatuated with the idea of revolution, particularly the Latin revolutionaries though she said war was wrong. "If enough people know about Communism, they would want to do it," she insisted.

She saw no irony in the fact that the money from her capitalist father's factory was paying for her room, board, and tuition at USC.

I didn't know if Anna's father was exploiting his workers, but I had seen how my father ran his business. I had worked on the payrolls, stuffing coins and bills into the weekly envelopes before my father began issuing weekly checks. His draw was never more than twice his top workers or three times his lowest paid workers. He put in almost twice as much time at the factory as anyone else. He had skills that none of his workers had. He had the charm to convince department store buyers and jobbers to purchase his gloves. He had the organizational skills to pull together a team of people to make the gloves. He had the skills to convince the bankers to lend him money, and he took all the risks, borrowing the money for equipment and rent and loans each year at the start of the season to pay for salaries, leather, fur, and other supplies like a farmer paid for the seeds on money borrowed from the bank and hoped his crop would turn a profit at the end of the year.

Dad paid his workers higher wages than the union. Employee turnover was incredibly low. I had no trouble sympathizing with the exploited workers in Steinbeck's *In Dubious Battle* or *Grapes of Wrath*, but the Plainfield Glove Company wasn't that kind of story. It was an honest business. The employees worked together to get the product out the door each week and on time.

I had worked on the shop floor. I had none of the innate skills that my father had for leading other men. He deserved more pay than me or anyone else in the factory. The Beatles and Dylan deserved more money than me because they wrote and sang better. I didn't believe you could be a good socialist without recognizing that individual achievement was worth something.

Whatever I told Anna fell on deaf ears, but it did nothing to shake my attraction for her.

Garry spent the first few weeks of the fall semester in traction. His old back injury had flared up again. He was still walking like a frog weeks after he had gotten out of traction. When he returned to school, he and Mike Vosse moved into a house on 32nd Street across from the Shrine

Auditorium. Carol was there so often that she and Garry were practically living together.

One day in the middle of the semester and a few weeks after I met Anna, Garry and I were crossing the campus between classes when I spotted Anna and Donald coming toward us. Donald was a tall, handsome graduate student with dirty blond hair and narrow, condescending eyes. His younger brother, who was nothing like him, had been in a couple of my classes, so I knew the two brothers were loaded. Their father was a doctor who owned a string of private medical facilities. Like Anna, Donald was a self-styled Communist.

Anna stopped laughing as soon as she saw me. She suddenly looked more uncomfortable than happy. I would have to be blind *and* stupid not to know something was going on between Anna and Donald.

They stopped in front of us, and she introduced me as "Joe, my friend," and Donald to me as "Donald, my friend."

Donald looked like he was greeting lepers when he shook hands with us. As soon as the introductions were over, Donald said he had to go. Anna followed after him with only a quick, indecipherable glance back at me.

"Is that the girl you've been telling me about?" Garry asked.

"Yeah."

"Oh, man, you're in deep trouble. What are you going to do about it?" he asked laughing.

I felt like a fool. I hadn't a clue what to do. Maybe, I should forget about her, I told myself.

That was impossible. I couldn't stop thinking about her.

CHAPTER 47

Mike Vosse had located the old, two-story house on 32nd Street that he was renting with Garry. I could walk along the alley behind my place to their front door in a couple of minutes.

Garry and Mike's new house was a dump, but it was very spacious. It had an open-air front porch, a large living room, dining room, kitchen, and two-piece bathroom on the ground floor, and four bedrooms and a full bathroom upstairs. It immediately became psychedelic central. Mike was still working in television on some new crappy production and hating it. In his free time, he was trying to make inroads into the record business like David Anderle. Mike was trying to establish himself by searching the clubs in Hollywood and on Sunset Strip for new raw talent worth signing.

The house on 32nd Street was a drop-in center for a strange assortment of characters in and outside the arts, some attached to USC like Garry, Garry's girlfriend Carol, and budding theater directors Steven Kent, Jack Rowe, and Tom Costello from USC's theater department, and some outsiders like Crazy Bob and Paul X.

The most unusual character was Crazy Bob, a brilliant former chemistry major who had dropped out of school to dedicate himself totally to taking drugs. Dressed like a preppy student—clean shaven with short dark hair and glasses with black plastic frames—he was about my height and weight and always smiling, always pleasant and usually quiet. He lived in a garage—not a garage apartment, but a garage—across town near UCLA. He spent his days following mailmen through the richer neighborhoods as they delivered mail to some of the most prosperous physicians in the city. In the Golden Age of new miracle drugs, the pharmacies were constantly sending samples of every kind of pharmaceutical on the market to doctors. Bob would wait a respectable time after the postman had delivered the mail, then steal the samples that had been pushed through the mail slot to the doctors' office or left in their unlocked mailboxes. Bob sold some of the drugs to UCLA students and kept the rest for himself. He carried these in a pouch and munched on them regularly like he was eating candy with seemingly no cares as to which pills he popped in his mouth. He held out the sack to me on several occasions and told me to help myself. I always declined. I asked how he knew what he was taking. He said, he never knew, and it didn't matter. "The only reality is what you see right now in front of you," he said philosophically. "The rest is just something you make up."

Another unusual outsider who frequently visited the house was Garry's friend, Paul X, a thin, bedraggled beatnik-freak, and street poet with a Fu Manchu moustache and sad eyes. Paul X almost always wore black shirts and pants. He was the first person who told me stories about the government refurbishing the old internment camps around the country that had held Japanese Americans during World War II. According to Paul, President Johnson was planning a massive crackdown on freaks and anti-war protesters. Those rounded up would be sent to these concentration camps. If I weren't such a skeptic, I would have been more worried. I thought the story was likely just another scare story that someone had made up.

"The government has a list of everyone who smokes grass and drops acid," Paul X insisted. He himself never stayed in one place very long, moving from apartment to apartment in Los Angeles, Berkeley, and San Francisco.

At the beginning of October, Rick Smith, a talented musician, showed up in Los Angeles after a gig playing blues harp in Greenwich Village over the summer. Rick had been the previous boyfriend of Garry's girlfriend Carol when she had been studying at Bard College in New York. Rick came to Los Angeles hoping to renew his relationship with Carol. But Carol and Garry were too much in love for Rick to stand a chance. Nevertheless, Rick's arrival did have consequences.

Rick drove across the country in a drive-away car with Jan Ward, an underage seventeen-year-old troubadour, who had been playing professionally in coffeehouses on the East Coast and in Europe for several years. This was Jan's first taste of California.

Jan immediately took off for Sunset Strip where he made his own musical and drug connections. Not yet eighteen, he couldn't legally perform in the clubs that served alcohol. Still, he managed to get a few gigs and became part of a small group of budding, underage musicians on the Strip, who played together, formed bands for a week or two, performed illegally whenever they could get a gig at one of the lesser-known clubs, and became small-time pot dealers to maintain their precarious existence.

Jan was a godsend for Mike Vosse.

Mike took Jan under his tutelage. Mike saw Jan as his big break. I saw Jan perform in clubs a few times. Mike thought Jan could be the next Bob Dylan. Garry, Carol, and half of the people hanging around the 32nd Street house were taken by the young, blond-haired kid with the guitar and notebooks full of songs. Jan had already developed the hardened attitude of someone out to prove he was a star.

Jan's drug dealing a few months later almost landed me in jail. Others weren't so lucky.

CHAPTER 48

I stopped phoning Anna after seeing her with Donald again. They were walking across the campus together. I didn't think she saw me.

She called me a few nights later just as I got back from the 32nd Street house. She was angry that I had stopped calling her. She said she'd been calling me for over an hour. She didn't believe that I hadn't been at home. She became even angrier when I told her, "What do you care where I am? You're with Donald."

"You're a fool. You think I like him like I like you?"

"Yes. And more."

She hung up but called right back. "I defend you. He call you a fog. Why do I defend you if I don't love you?"

"A fog?"

"A fog. Donald say you and your friend are fogs."

Finally, I thought I understood what she was trying to say. Donald thought Garry and I were fags.

"Fags?"

"Fogs. Fairies."

"And you believe him?"

"Of course not. I defend you. You are a good lover."

I wondered how she could possibly know that since we still hadn't made love. "Are you sleeping with him?"

"Are you stupid?"

Am I stupid? I wondered.

"I meet him before you."

"I saw you before he did," I reminded her.

"And you take a long time to find me again."

"You should have told me you were seeing someone else."

"I don't tell you because I know you will be jealous. I don't love him. His politics interest me. He takes me to the theater and concerts."

"I'll take you to the theater and concerts," I said lamely. "When do you want to go?"

"It's nothing important. You should not be so jealous." In a flash, she had turned soft and sweet. Her voice was soothing, loving. "With you, I don't care if we go out. I like being with you at your place. I love you."

She knew exactly the right words to lure me in. My problem was I couldn't quite figure out if she meant anything she said. I was swimming in quicksand. I wanted to run away as fast as I could; I wanted to wrap my arms around her and never let go. "You can come over on Friday," I said, trying not to sound desperate.

"Donald already ask me to a play."

"Tell him you can't go."

"He already buys tickets. I already promise."

I felt too jealous and hurt to say anything.

"Please don't be jealous."

"I'm not jealous."

"I come afterward." She hesitated a moment, then added. "I stay the night if that's what you want."

"Is that what you want?"

"Of course."

Of course, I only half believed her, afraid to let myself hope too much.

Of course, she didn't come to my place on Friday night after the play or any time that night. Like a fool, I waited around all night, not even daring to leave for a few minutes to head down the alley to the house on 32nd Street to check out what was going on there.

My phone started ringing at seven the next morning. I knew it was her. I didn't answer it.

I have to break the addiction I have for her, I told myself. She was taking up too much space in my head. I was afraid of more disappointments, and I was angry at myself for becoming so entangled with someone so unpredictable.

My phone kept ringing, ten, fifteen rings, and then it stopped for a few minutes and started again. I headed to Garry and Mike's. I had never taken Anna there since she didn't approve of drugs. I wondered what she would think if she knew she was more addicting than anything I had ever smoked or ingested.

At the house on 32nd Street, I found a few people awake, including Mike and two art students from Germany who Mike had met at one of the clubs. They had dropped acid around two or three in the morning and were still tripping. I hung around with them for a few hours and then headed home.

I had mixed feelings when I heard my phone ringing as I climbed my stairs and entered my place. I used all my willpower to resist answering it. I was certain it was Anna. I feared getting caught in her web again.

The ringing stopped but started again five minutes later.

I put on my swim trunks, grabbed some books, and headed to Venice Beach where I could get free street parking close to the ocean. I parked and walked toward the beach. Halfway there, I stopped as I sometimes did, at the ratty little house where one of my old friends from the freshman dorm had moved.

Rick Kaplan was already up when I arrived, and we were soon drinking coffee. Rick was a short, hairy guy with a huge black beard, who had been a science student like me but had drifted into the arts and spent most of his time playing his guitar, listening to music, smoking grass, and collecting antique Chinese opium pipes.

He showed me the latest addition to his pipe collection. He had nearly a hundred antique hookahs and pipes which he used for tobacco and pot. The water pipes were mainly made of brass or bronze. He bought them in junk shops for next to nothing. A few pipes, like his latest find, were made of silver. An elaborate dragon was etched in the metal.

"I'm going sailing with my father and his new girlfriend in an hour. You want to come?" Rick asked.

I thought about Anna. I imagined her sitting on my steps waiting for me. Half of me wanted to go back and see her. Half of me said that was the last thing I needed.

"I have to study. I probably shouldn't be gone that long," I told Rick.

"Come on. It'll be fun. Like last time."

Rick's parents were divorced. His father owned a big yacht. We were supposed to help sail the boat, but Rick acted crazy the first time we went sailing, and his father let Rick and me ride along without doing any of the work. Rick pulled the same stunt again on our second outing, and almost immediately, his father stopped asking us to help with the sailing chores, which was fine with me.

Rick told me, "There's two ways of owning things in this world. One, you have the paper that says you own it, and in the case of my father's yacht, that means all the original cost of the boat, the upkeep, and the obligation of having to use it on weekends to justify owning it. Or, two, you can have the right to use it whenever you want without any of the responsibilities, like me."

The views of the sea and the mountains along the Malibu coast rising up to the sky were stupendous, but the water was rough. I felt pretty wobbly the whole time and was happy when we finally turned back and motored the rest of the way to the dock. Despite covering myself with gobs of suntan lotion, I got badly sunburned. I felt achy on the drive home.

Anna wasn't there, but she had been at my place and left a copy of *The Little Prince* at my door.

Anna had mentioned *The Little Prince* to me on several occasions and said I should read it. I had only been half listening when she first told me about the book. I mixed up the title with *The Prince* by Niccolo Machiavelli, which was a book I also had heard about but hadn't read. [43]

I called Anna's dorm to thank her, but she wasn't there.

I stayed up late and read the book twice, half believing that if I kept reading, she might show up at my door. It was a simple story of feelings and love. That's what I wanted to happen—I wanted to be in love. [44]

Anna and I got back together. We made love. We broke up. She went back with Donald. They broke up. She and I got back together. I shaved off my beard and moustache to please her. Nothing pleased her. She left me and went back to Donald. A few days later, she walked out on him and came back to me.

My spirits soared and sank, sometimes at the same time. Could we find peace together or would we always be in turmoil? Was turmoil what real love was about?

Senator Robert Kennedy visited the campus on November 5 and viewed the plaque dedicated to his brother, President Kennedy, at the front of the library. A small gathering of students and bigwigs followed him as he walked from the library toward Bovard Auditorium. I was driving by in my electric cart on University Avenue. I parked at the edge of the sidewalk to let Kennedy, California's Assembly Speaker Jesse Unruh, USC president Norman Topping, and a small group of students pass by on their way to the auditorium across the street. Kennedy looked toward me as he crossed University Avenue. It felt like we made eye contact. I wanted to flash him the peace sign, but I let it pass. He had come out in previous statements defending the right of students to protest, but he was against students who shouted down opposition speakers, turned to violence, or burned their draft cards, claiming they were doing more harm than good. He had not spoken out against the war in Vietnam. Few national politicians in either party had. I couldn't help wondering if we would be in the mess we were in if President Kennedy was still alive.

Anna believed that life was about fighting, about a constant struggle.

Anna told me a strange story about her willfulness.

When she was in her early teens, she had been in love with a boy in school who wouldn't pay attention to her. So, she set out to learn everything she could about appendicitis from a girlfriend who had had an emergency operation. Anna faked an appendicitis attack so convincingly with all the accompanying agony that she had her appendix removed in an emergency operation, and then she was happy for a minute or two because the boy came to visit her in the hospital.

"Afterward, I don't even remember why I want him in the first place," she told me.

I had seen the scar on her stomach. Whether the story was true or not, I was in love with Anna because she wanted to live her life as a character in a novel. Her hero was a Mexican woman Communist artist Freda Kahlo.

Anna stopped by at odd hours and asked me to go places with her—a movie in the afternoon, a restaurant, a park, sometimes just a drive to the beach.

One time she needed something downtown at the Mexican consulate, so I drove her. When she was done, she took me to the market area with outdoor Mexican food stalls that catered to Mexicans. She went from stall to stall, speaking in Spanish to the vendors, asking for samples before she found the perfect pork taco and ordered one for each of us.

While we were eating our tacos, she told me another story. "I want to bring you here to share a story about how I stop being afraid of God. I was nine. It was Yom Kippur. I was dressed in my best clothes, playing outside the synagogue in Mexico City. My parents were inside praying and fasting. I talk my girlfriend to go with me to buy a pork taco from a street vendor."

"Let's eat it," I said, "and if God exists, something will happen to us."

Unlike me, Anna had been brought up in an orthodox household where her parents were strict about the dietary laws.

The girlfriend was too scared to try, but Anna devoured the taco in a few bites, telling her friend how delicious it was. When nothing happened, she told her friend, "See? Nothing happens to you when you eat it. God is a fake."

The girlfriend warned her something might happen later on, but Anna said she didn't believe in superstition.

She brought out stories in me and helped me consolidate ideas.

"I have a different view of God," I told her. "I don't know if God exists, but if so, I think God would be saying. 'Don't try to understand me. Don't think about what I do. Don't try to draw a picture of what I look like. You're wasting your time. I want you to stop trying to figure me out. I don't even want you to give me a name.' My god would disapprove of religion and say, 'You stupid people, stop pretending you can speak for me. Literally, mind your own business. Think for yourselves. Use what I gave you to come to your senses or your spaceship will crash and you will destroy yourselves.'"

"You are a Communist," she insisted. "You don't believe in religion."

"Communism doesn't work because it's just another religion with its own saints, high priests, hierarchies, prejudices, and scripture. It's just another minority telling the majority: 'Do it my way and everything will be perfect.' The trouble is people are contrary by nature. The only way anyone can get everyone thinking and acting like everyone else is through violence and oppression. That never works in the long run. It breaks down."

"What is your answer?"

"I don't know. I'm still looking, but I'm guessing we have to find a way to make democracy and the rule of law work better. Some people will always want to be part of a group and some would prefer to be loners. Nonviolent socialism, social programs, good government, and activities that help people live better lives, and individual initiative, entrepreneurs, artists, writers, musicians, and others who want to express their individuality without belonging to a group aren't enemies. They're just different parts of the human condition."

"Sometimes I think you are a worse idealist than me," she said.

Her eyes sparkled when she smiled.

Anna sent her mother a few of my drawings. She insisted I write to her mother. I wrote in German since her mother spoke German and my Spanish was negligible. Her mother wrote back a very warm, funny letter in English, thanking me for the drawings but pointing out gently that my German was so bad she didn't understand much of what I had written.

The familial side of Anna made me feel good, even special. The family ties and the intimacy felt comforting and gave me a sense of belonging somewhere and to someone. But I only felt good half the time.

Half the time, Anna was moody, contradictory, unpredictable, and always probing, always ready to give her opinion about what life should be like, how I should dress, look, and think. She told me she feared mediocrity more than anything. I began to realize I was mistaking strength and poise for nervous energy.

I reread Herman Hesse's *Steppenwolf* to stay sane.

On December 3, the Beatles' *Rubber Soul* album was released. It included "Michelle" and "Norwegian Wood," which featured George Harrison playing the sitar—the first time the instrument had appeared on a rock recording. It also marked the first time in pop music where making a great album had been the focus instead of the album merely featuring one or two hit singles with a lot of filler. The Beatles had moved ahead of everyone once again.

Musicians were freak royalty. Rebels with causes and attitude. The music was about love, and losing love, and finding it again, and anything but war. No one was singing about marching off to war.

Without any insulation in the walls, my garage apartment got even colder at night and in the mornings and during the rainy season than my apartment on Ellendale or the fraternity house. I bought an electric space heater to get through the coldest nights. I pretended it was a fireplace. I replaced two of the white bulbs in the ancient, hanging, three-bulb light fixture with a red bulb and a blue bulb so I had a red, white, and blue glow in the apartment. I fiddled with different lights by unscrewing one or two of the bulbs at a time to give me different color perspectives on the canvases I was painting.

The Vietnam War continued to escalate through the last months of 1965 and beginning of 1966. Heavy fighting in the Ia Drang Valley took place with heavy casualties on both sides. The US 1st Air Cavalry Division used improved aerial reconnaissance techniques to drive back the regular North Vietnamese army, but the local Viet Cong guerillas continued to vanish into the countryside and down into deep tunnels when they were pursued, only to pop out again unexpectedly with deadly force.

No matter how hard the US hit the North Vietnamese army and the Viet Cong, they quickly regrouped and went on the offensive. For the Americans, it was like fighting ghosts.

Anti-war demonstrations drew more than a hundred thousand protesters in each of eighty American cities. Returning Vietnam veterans began joining the anti-war movement in ever greater numbers and soon were taking leadership roles.

Two Americans, a Quaker, who immolated himself outside the Pentagon offices of Secretary of Defense Robert McNamara, and a Catholic worker, who set himself on fire in front of the UN in New York, were part of the growing anti-war protests throughout the fall of 1965.

At the end of November, President Johnson announced a troop increase from 120,000 to 400,000 for Southeast Asia. American troop levels in Vietnam reached 200,000 by the end of 1965. The plan was to add another 200,000 in the coming months.

Nearly two thousand American soldiers and tens of thousands of Vietnamese soldiers and civilians had been killed in the war in Vietnam during 1965. Many tens of thousands more had been injured and maimed for life.

Teach-ins, some broadcast across the country, became a regular fixture at many esteemed US universities, but not USC. Much like the rest of the country outside of the more liberal institutions, USC had pockets of people talking about the absolute stupidity of the war, but most of the student body quietly ignored what was happening beyond the campus.

"It's a sucker's war, a war for fools," Theo said. Theo was one of the few other students on campus I knew who called himself a writer besides Garry. Theo and I had crossed paths in a couple of psychology and writing classes. Theo was dark-haired with a medium build and had a slight speech impediment. He was from New York and hung around different students than me. He was one of the few students I knew outside of the theater crowd who smoked pot and dropped acid.

"Nobody's quitting school and running to sign up for this war," he insisted.

It was true. I had casual friends in many different circles around the campus from jocks to fraternity and sorority members to Republicans like Buddy, who had supported Barry Goldwater in 1964. Not a single person I knew, male or female, had anything good to say about the war.

Anna decided to go home for the Christmas break. I couldn't be sure whether I wanted to see her or not when she got back.

CHAPTER 49

After Anna flew home to Mexico City for the Christmas break, Faith called out of the blue and invited me out to a midnight movie.

I had been interested in Faith from the time I first saw her.

Faith was a couple of years older than me and good looking but went out of her way to make herself look unattractive—with her curly strawberry-blond mop of hair always unruly; eyeglasses repaired with tape and sitting on the end of her nose as if ready to fall off; sandals which were never buckled so she walked like she was cross-country skiing; and old jeans or peasant skirts and men's shirts which were always several sizes too big and hid her curves. She worked in the library and had already been to university in New York where she had lived in the Village. She was a beatnik, not a freak, an older war baby who was just old enough to ride the tail end of the beatnik era.

Over time, I learned Faith's father was a well-liked screenwriter and sometimes USC professor. She took pride in being a great disappointment to him. She scared away almost everyone on campus. She seemed to enjoy the fact that people called her strange behind her back. She had read more books and seen more movies than most people would in a lifetime.

I wasn't at all afraid of her. She liked that. It turned her on, she said.

I hadn't seen her for a couple of months. She had moved to a nicer apartment in the Wilshire district, not far from Anna's friend Donald.

"Why did you move?" I asked when I picked her up, remembering the other apartment she had lived in south of Exposition Park and deeper into the ghetto.

"I was raped," she told me matter-of-factly.

A Black man—not one of her former Black lovers but a complete stranger—had broken into her apartment in the middle of the night, sexually assaulted her, and threatened to kill her.

"He only let me live," she explained, "because I didn't struggle."

When he was done, she told him to take the money in her purse. "I swore I wouldn't call the cops," she told me. "It wasn't a Black and white thing. Just a man hates woman thing."

Faith was wholly chastened by the experience. She had let her father pay for her new apartment, something she never would have done before the rape.

After the movie, I took her back to her apartment, and she invited me in.

She wanted someone to be with, she told me. "Just for a few hours. A day. Whatever you want. I just want to feel normal."

I felt comfortable being with her. She wasn't complicated.

She was open, available, no hang-ups, no demands. We were two shipwrecked people, looking for warmth and reassurance.

We stayed in bed for two days, getting up only to eat.

She made me feel good.

But not good enough.

Anna still haunted me. Faith sensed my restlessness. She asked me if I was seeing anyone. I hesitated at first but finally told her about Anna.

She said not to worry. "Everything will work out. Go back to your old life. Come back if you feel like it. You made me feel good about myself."

I continued to see Anna for a few weeks after she came back from Mexico City. She hadn't changed. Finally, I told her, "I don't want to be with someone so complicated."

"I love you," she told me. "I always love you."

I no longer felt I could always love her, not like I had at first. I didn't care if we remained friends or not.

I was drifting again, in love with neither Anna nor Faith, feeling empty, but not discouraged.

At least I knew what I wanted.

I wanted two things.

First, I wanted a woman who was mysterious, unpredictable, surprising, exciting, with a passion equal to my own desires, and who I was wildly attracted to.

Second, I wanted a woman who was down-to-earth, uncomplicated, trustworthy, wise, calm, nurturing, thoroughly in love with me, and beautiful to me but at the same time someone who wouldn't be chased down at every turn by other men.

I wondered if it would be possible to find all this in one person.

Equally important, would I ever be worthy of such a person if she existed? What did I have to offer? What right did I have to pursue anyone?

Was my Great Uncle Lew right? Was my constant pursuit of women just hormones?

Of course, but what could I do about it, and should I care?

I wanted to know everything. I wanted to see and feel everything. I hated the thought of being stuck in a halfway world between being and becoming.

I wished I could leave school, get a job doing anything, and try to make it as a writer in my free time. No one wrote meaningful novels about struggling with school. I wanted to start my life, so I'd have something to write about.

But if I dropped out, I would be drafted. I would go to war, either directly or indirectly I would be a participant of what was becoming America's biggest crime of the century. Would I be able to write a better anti-war novel from that experience? I had already read *All Quiet on the Western Front*, *Johnny Got His Gun*, *The Red Badge of Courage*, *A Farewell to Arms*, *For Whom the Bell Tolls*, *The Execution of Private Slovik*, *The Tin Drum*, and *Catch-22*. I had heard the combat and prisoner-of-war stories from my uncles. No one needed another novel to tell them how senseless and inglorious war is, I assured myself.

"Never think that war, no matter how necessary nor how justified, is not a crime. Ask the infantry and ask the dead," wrote Hemingway in *For Whom the Bell Tolls*.

I had taken enough acid and seen enough in a half dozen days of the Watts Riots to know the insanity of war. I realized that comparing Watts to Vietnam was like comparing a match to an inferno, but I didn't need to see the inferno to understand how ugly it was. I had no illusions about why some men and women in the midst of war become addicted to it.

Being so close to death and killing heightens every sensation. War and the fear of death lowered inhibitions and heightened sexual desire. Slaughter made some sick and makes others feel more alive, more powerful. Some even discovered they enjoyed killing. No one should be forced to find out if they enjoyed killing. War was a plague on humanity's sanity.

CHAPTER 50

Back East, my parents were being visited by their own plagues.

First, the truck driver, who delivered the home heating oil for their furnace, screwed up. Normally, the oil was piped in through an outside oil fill opening at the front of the house. It flowed directly into the storage tank in the basement. This time, the driver fell asleep in his truck. He missed the signal to shut off the flow and several hundred gallons of toxic heating oil flooded the finished and unfinished halves of the basement. The driver failed to report the accident. My mother only discovered the oil when she returned home and smelled it. It took more than a week to get the oil out. My parents had to throw away everything soaked in the brown slime—some of it was artwork my mother had saved from her days as a Seventh Avenue sketcher and dress designer. The insurance covered most of the physical damage and none of the emotional harm. The smell lingered for months.

A few days after the cleanup, a pipe burst in the outside utility cellar and the basement was flooded again, this time with several inches of water.

Adding to their troubles, the weather turned unseasonably warm and the hoped-for recovery in the glove business never materialized. Even if it had, they would have been hard pressed to get the factory up and running. Their chief cutter, Red, an overweight, chain-smoking fur worker and most recent foreman of the shop—one of two people my parents had kept on salary during the hiatus—dropped dead of a heart attack. There was no money to replace him even if my parents could find someone with his skills.

My parents had even more debt at the end of the year than they had at the start.

The Plainfield Glove Company, which had been shuttered since July, was officially closed at the end of December 1965. My parents started the New Year broke and in debt to loan sharks for a total of forty thousand dollars, about six times the median annual family income in the US. The only thing to do was to sell the fifteen-acre property, take out what equity they still had in the house, try to sell the business and the equipment, and hope for the best.

Even the little bit of money my mother had been sending me had to stop. I was earning more than enough part-time at the library to support myself, so I had simply been saving what she sent. Again, I offered the money I'd accumulated to my mom, but she insisted I save it for a rainy day.

I kept drifting, hunting for love, thinking about dozens of different career paths, and always returning to writer or painter or both as my personal answer to everything.

More of my contemporaries were being drafted, snatched away as if by ghouls in the night.

I discovered a drafting pen with a needle-like point that was even better than the felt-tip pens I had been using. The new double-zero point made it easier for me to create the cartoon-like drawings I had been experimenting with.

I got caught drawing in my playwriting class by my teacher, veteran Hollywood writer and producer, Morgan B. Cox. [45]

I thought I was going to get reprimanded when he took my notebook and began leafing through the pages. "These are really good. Each one's a story," he said to the class. He held up the drawings and showed them to the small seminar group before handing the book back to me with a smile. Cox gave me an A for the semester. He said I should think about writing for the movies as well as theater. I had been thinking about the movies for more than a year. I took the playwriting class because Garry had signed up for it.

I painted more, too. Friends brought their friends over to my little shack to see my latest paintings and drawings.

I found my sixty-two-year-old fencing teacher, Francis Zold, captain of the Hungarian Olympics fencing team in 1948, intriguing. He was a refugee of the 1956 Hungarian Revolt. [46]

He had escaped to another country and reinvented himself in America as I might have to do if I went to Canada. I mentioned this one day to Theo in the student union, Like me, Theo was also concerned about his draft status. Theo pointed to an elderly, gray-haired woman who was cleaning tables in the corner of the room and asked me, "Did you know that she came at the same time as Zold? She was a medical doctor in Hungary, but she doesn't speak English well enough to retake her exams. So, she's picking up garbage in the Student Union. Some people just can't reinvent themselves."

The truth was I didn't have the guts to go to Canada. I wasn't that brave. I was just shooting off my mouth.

Mike Vosse was investing more of his time working with Jan Ward, his young folk-rock, singer-songwriter.

When Jan got behind in his rent, his roommate Rick Smith, dumped their apartment and moved across town, leaving Jan on his own. Mike moved Jan and Jan's girlfriend, Betsy Ross, into a spare bedroom in the 32nd Street house.

Over the course of the fall and early winter, Jan had evolved from a solo act into a new duo after pairing with an extraordinary singer with a rich, haunting voice named Pam Polland. Pam was a veteran of the folk scene. She had been playing in local clubs, including the Ash Grove on Melrose, for a couple of years with a young unknown guitarist named Ry Cooder before they parted ways. Mike was already working on a record deal with Columbia for Jan and Pam.

I loved hearing them rehearse in the living room at the 32nd Street house, especially hearing the soaring voice of Pam.

Mike was high all the time whether or not he was taking drugs. This was his ticket into the music industry as a producer. By mid-winter, the

Columbia deal for Pam and Jan was close to happening. Everyone was excited, even the hangers-on like me.

Then, everyone started getting busted.

CHAPTER 51

Within a three-week period, six of my friends were busted for pot in three separate incidents.

The first was Rick Kaplan in Venice Beach. Police raided his apartment, confiscated his Chinese waterpipe collection along with a small amount of grass, and hauled him off to jail. The second bust was Theo, my writer friend. He had moved out of his fraternity by then and was living in a rundown apartment on Ellendale Place.

The third and scariest bust was at the house on 32nd Street.

Jan was feeling especially invincible with his new record deal in the works. So, he bought a kilo of grass from someone in San Francisco.

The weed arrived from San Francisco by plane one Saturday night while many of the usual crew at the 32nd Street house came and went. Jan got someone to drive him to the airport to pick up the grass. I was at the 32nd Street house most of that evening, listening to music, and sitting in a corner, sketching away in my notebook. I finally got tired and decided to go home.

Jan arrived about ten minutes after I left.

Shortly after that, the LAPD drug squad swarmed the house, coming in through the front and back doors with guns drawn. Garry, Mike, Jan, Betsy, and one or two others were hauled away in handcuffs to jail downtown.

Also confiscated besides the key of grass Jan had brought from the airport were a couple of water pipes and some prescription pain pills for Garry's back.

Garry's mother, Suzanne, called me the next morning to let me know what happened and find out if I was okay.

I was terrified. I flushed a half lid of grass down the toilet, threw away my pack of rolling papers, and waited for the knock on my door.

The police never visited me.

Rick Kaplan's father bailed him out, and somehow the case got brushed away.

Theo got out on a technicality. He told me the only bad thing about the case getting dropped was that he remained eligible for the draft.

Mike got a lawyer to spring him within a day or two. Garry's very pissed-off Uncle Sam Arkoff sprung him within twenty-four hours. Except for Jan, the others were all released a day or so later. The case against the 32nd Street gang was dropped because of a procedural error. The police apparently should have obtained a warrant before crashing the party.

The only one who did any significant time was Jan. He wasn't held on drug charges. He was underage with no one to vouch for him in Los Angeles.

He spent six weeks in juvenile detention before Mike Vosse was able to find him a sponsor acceptable to the court. By the time Jan was released, the pending record contract for Jan and Pam Polland had been dropped. Once Jan turned eighteen, he headed to the Strip again to make it on his own.

Garry moved home to Studio City. Mike moved to an attic apartment in West Los Angeles. I spent a lot of time wondering what would have happened to me if I had been busted.

CHAPTER 52

I was happy to see that Anna had moved on. She found a new boyfriend who was madly in love with her. She told her parents he was Jewish, which he wasn't.

On March 4, 1966, John Lennon declared the Beatles were more popular than Jesus.

The comment caused a firestorm of bad press, protests, and bans on Beatle records at several radio stations across the country, particularly in the more religious Deep South. Though the protests were minor in comparison to overall sales, the incident was enough to make Lennon retract his statement later in the year though he did add a few words about his right to freedom of expression.

A Green Beret camp was captured in the Ashau Valley by the North Vietnam Army, and the US Supreme Court overturned the Massachusetts obscenity ruling against *Fanny Hill*.

A second Watts Riot took place in mid-March and lasted nearly two days. This almost-forgotten riot killed two people, including the white driver of a beer truck. A number of businesses were burned. [47]

The police soon had the second riot under control without the help of the National Guard.

I had sold my gun to a friend. So, I wasn't armed for the second Watts insurrection. I didn't think I needed to be. I was pretty blasé. If the rioting spread, I planned to throw a few things in my car and drive to someone's house in the hills. I had no interest in fighting anyone.

My brother finally saved enough to marry Linda, his college sweetheart. I couldn't afford to go to the wedding in New Jersey, so I sent them a US Savings Bond.

One night I had a very vivid dream of someone choking me. I couldn't see who it was. I tried to struggle against the hands around my neck, but I couldn't move my arms, I was paralyzed all over. I tried to yell but my voice was gone. In the dream, I was slowly sinking deeper and deeper into unconsciousness, which is weird since I was already asleep. But instead of accepting it, I continued to will my arms and hands to move. Finally, I ripped the hands off my throat and yelled loud enough that I woke myself up. If I hadn't, I would have died for sure.

The choking came from the thick smoke that filled my apartment. I quickly assessed the situation. I had kicked my blanket into my space heater beside the bed. A low flame and clouds of thick smoke were pouring from the blanket on the floor.

I absorbed the details as I coughed my lungs out and shook the fog from my brain.

Somehow, I had the good sense to turn off the heater, throw open the door, breathe some fresh air, then come back, grab the smoldering blanket, and toss it off the balcony into the driveway a few feet from my car.

I slipped into my pants, T-shirt, and boots, went downstairs, and stamped out the blanket and stood in the driveway for a few seconds breathing in fresh, smoggy air. The houses all around me were dark. No one would have noticed the fire until it was too late.

I hurried upstairs and double checked under the rug to make sure the wooden floor was untouched. I opened all the windows and ate a peanut butter sandwich while contemplating how lucky I was. The only thing that had kept the floor from catching fire was the old stained, now burn-scarred wool carpet. With all the oil paints, turpentine and a couple of canvases still drying against the wall a few feet from the heater, it was a miracle everything hadn't gone up in flames.

Lucky, lucky, lucky, I told myself, over and over.

I was alive.

It felt good to be alive.

My mother's letters and occasional phone calls kept little from me.

In a three-way race, my mother lost her bid for a second term on the regional high school board of education. She came in a weak second. She had been too busy closing the factory and looking after my dad to campaign and rally her troops.

My father's health continued to deteriorate even after the shop closed and the pressure of running it disappeared. He was so frail and shaking so hard, he was having trouble feeding himself.

One of his old business associates, who owned a clothing factory in Nashville, Tennessee, offered him a job. My father flew to Tennessee and worked there for a few months. His friend Herb had a son about my age. Herb thought my father could mentor his son, but the kid didn't want some sick, old man looking over his shoulder. My dad soon got his walking papers and returned to New Jersey feeling completely defeated and useless at fifty-five.

In March 1966, a US Senate bill to repeal the Gulf of Tonkin Resolution was defeated.

My safe status as a student became increasingly shaky as the rules for getting a 2-S student deferment kept changing and getting tougher.

On March 24, 1966, during the second half of my junior year, the Selective Service announced it would begin using school performance—grade averages—as a criterion for student deferments. My cumulative average was high, well over 3.5. So, I was safe for the moment, but the competition for good grades heated up. So did cheating.

Theo, my writer friend, got caught cheating on his term paper in psychology when he copied an article from a psychology journal and handed it in as his own work. The professor, Dr. Dan Davis, a young brainiac who had previously worked at Bell Labs, told me Theo would never have been caught if another student in our class hadn't by chance copied the exact same article from the same journal and turned it in as her term paper. Theo got an F in the class and vanished from sight. I presumed he had been drafted.

Garth showed up at my place one afternoon with a paper bag of avocados that came from his father's estate high in the hills in Orange County. I met him at a crowded beer party at the apartment that Jack Row and a couple of other theater students were sharing. It was the famous party where one student fell backwards off the ledge of the second story balcony but was so drunk he didn't hurt himself. I was standing about ten feet away when the guy fell. Carol and Garry introduced me to Garth shortly afterward.

Garth had dropped out of university before finishing his degree and was working on Wilshire at one of his father's corporations. He showed up at my place at odd hours with one or two girls on his arm, coaxing me to go with them to all-night eateries like the seedy Barney's Beanery on Santa Monica Boulevard and Canter's Deli on North Fairfax Avenue. Canter's was a favorite hangout for actors, television personalities from the nearby CBS TV studios, and bigwigs and wannabees in the music business.

The avocados Garth dropped off were hard as a rock. He assumed I knew about ripening them. I didn't. I had eaten guacamole on many occasions, but I didn't know much about how it was made. Not knowing what to do with the avocados, I cut into one and tried to eat a piece of the flesh. It was so bitter, I spit it out and let the other avocados sit around until they got moldy, and then threw them out.

The next time I saw Garth, I told him what I had done. I didn't want him bringing me more avocados. Garth laughed and told me how to ripen them and how to tell when they were perfect for eating. Once I had that figured out, I started buying avocados all the time at the grocery store.

The next time I saw Garth, he told me he'd been ordered to report for his physical, and a few weeks after that he got his induction notice.

Before he left for the Army, his parents took a dozen of his friends including Garry, Carol and me to a very expensive restaurant in Beverly Hills.

And then, just like that, he was gone, maybe to Vietnam, maybe forever.

More friends got drafted.

My options after graduating in a little over a year were graduate school, the Peace Corps, Canada, or Vietnam—none of which appealed to me.

Despite my recent visit to Montreal, I still saw Canada as the least likely option.

Nevertheless, wishing to keep all my options open, I drove to the Canadian Consulate in Los Angeles and obtained an application for immigrating. I kept the application handy but continued to see Canada as more fantasy than reality.

I applied to the Peace Corps. That seemed viable. The Corps wasn't an alternate service. But it would provide a draft-age person like me with a two-year deferment. The Corps also had a program that allowed those accepted to take basic training over the summer between their junior and senior years. After they finished training, they returned to school for their senior year, and then went right into the program after graduation and were sent wherever the Corps assigned them. One of Garry's old girlfriends had done that the year before, so I was hopeful I'd get in.

Grad school in psychology looked like another possible hedge since I was pretty sure I could get a fellowship. I had a 4.0 in psychology and had been elected to Psi Chi, the international honorary society in psychology. If I played it right, I believed I could stretch my studies out for at least a couple of years for a master's degree, and possibly a few more years for a doctorate.

The competition for grad school had heated up dramatically over the past year since I wasn't the only one thinking this way. More male draft-eligible undergrads were now applying.

I started to think about an edge to get me into one of the better grad schools.

Over the next few months, my mother managed to sell the fifteen-acre property for twenty-five thousand dollars to the egg farmer whose property bordered on part of her land. She worked out deals with loan sharks in New York, fought off lawsuits from suppliers who hadn't been paid, sold the factory machinery and leather, and somehow managed to save the house from the shylocks by remortgaging it and giving them the cash. She also began working through the various federal and state government agencies to get disability for my father. She took two part-time jobs as a salesperson, one at FabricLand, a sewing and fabric supply store on the highway, and one at Pratt's, a high-end local furniture store one town over where she sold furniture and did rough drawings of floor plans to help her clients visualize the pieces of furniture in their homes.

Somehow, she continued to sound positive in her letters and rare phone calls. Thankfully, I was earning enough from my part-time job at the library to keep my head above water since I was on my own and going to school full time.

My job at the library continued to expand. I worked part time in the mailroom to pick up extra hours.

Dr. Stieg also assigned me a new special project—to go through the old clippings files and microfiche of the *Los Angeles Times*, the *Los Angeles Herald Examiner*, and other local California papers and find any and all articles on smog going back as far as I could.

The project was to be the first step in building what I was told would be the first research center about smog and air quality issues.

In the four years since Rachel Carson had written *The Silent Spring*, about how humans were poisoning the earth, more people were beginning to talk openly about the environment and the harm we were doing to it if we kept throwing chemicals and waste everywhere.

In April, *Time* magazine's cover asked, "Is God Dead?"

Of course, I thought, and he or she has been replaced by the Beatles.

I went to the Rusoff-Arkoff Seder for the second time. As much as I loved being a loner, I also loved having a touch of home to experience. This time their family Seder was at Uncle Sam and Aunt Hilda's place. No one mentioned Garry's most recent bust. Uncle Sam and Aunt Hilda—they asked me to call them that—were warm and delightful hosts, making me feel like I was part of their extended family.

The newspapers and magazines published stories about freaks in 1966, but they began using a new word—*hippie*, a variation on hipster.

The hippie was the latest term for the non-conformist, outsider, bohemian, beatnik, avant-garde, folk revivalist, and freak—people who felt like they didn't want to or couldn't fit into the mainstream and were looking for or living unconventional lives.

In China, Chairman Mao urged the youth of his country to rise up and revolt against their current leaders and culture. This was the start of the ten-year-long, bloody, and highly destructive Cultural Revolution that killed more than a million Chinese and sent many more millions of the country's educated class to prison or into menial jobs in the country-side—all because the vain, cranky old Mao felt his influence on China was fading.

Some of the people on the periphery of my circles started calling themselves Maoists. I was as suspicious of them as I was of the self-styled Marxists. I knew a lot of people over thirty I didn't trust, but I knew as many under thirty I was equally wary of. I was the perpetual outsider even among my outsider friends. I continued to try to resolve my feelings about war and *the* war on my own or with one or another of my friends who were thinking about it.

CHAPTER 53

I started looking more seriously for an edge to get into a good master's or doctorate program in psychology. I needed extracurricular activities that would look good on my applications. I also craved something that would possibly give me material for a novel.

As much as I loved the library, I had to think ahead.

I told Dr. Stieg my plans. He assured me he would find me a place on his staff anytime I wanted a job. With his blessings, I soon started looking for part-time work in something more closely related to social services.

Within a few weeks, I found a new job as a recreation counselor at the Variety Boys Club of America across town at 2530 Cincinnati Street in Boyle Heights. The club was sponsored by Tent 25, the Southern California branch of the Variety International service organization, which raised money for needy boys. The organization had not yet begun admitting girls. Active members of Tent 25 included such luminaries as Cary Grant, Danny Kaye, and Sam Arkoff, who were all heavily involved in fundraising for the club.

The all-male recreation club for needy boys was seven miles from my place, or about a fifteen-minute drive by freeway. It was in the heart of what was considered one of the toughest Hispanic neighborhoods in the city.

The double front doors of the building opened into a two-story room the size of a basketball court. A half dozen pool tables and an equal number of ping pong tables were scattered around the room. A full-sized gymnasium, locker room, a large outdoor swimming pool, a library, and offices branched off the main room. The shop and arts and crafts area were on the second floor.

The first objective of the organization was to get the local street kids through the doors of the facility to the pool tables. Over time, the aim was to wean as many kids as possible away from the pool tables to the ping pong tables, library, gym, pool, shop, and arts and crafts department—all considered more socially acceptable activities than the pool tables. During the school year, I worked the three-to-five-thirty shift after school three to five days a week, ate dinner in one of the neighborhood Mexican restaurants and sometimes the original Canter's delicatessen on Brooklyn Avenue, and then worked the evening shift from seven to nine thirty.

The area was a study in how fast Los Angeles changed.

Only a generation before, the neighborhood around the Boys Club had been a mixed middle, lower-middle, and poor immigrant community made up largely of immigrant and first generation Jews, Mexicans, and Japanese with smaller populations of Russians and Yugoslavians mixed in. After World War II, the Jews migrated west to the Fairfax District and the Russians and Yugoslavs also moved out. Most of the Japanese had been uprooted at the start of World War II and interned in concentration camps. Few ever returned to the area.

The Boys Club was now at the center of a predominantly large population of Americans of Mexican descent and new Mexican immigrants and a small number of other American-born and immigrant Latinos, Blacks, and Romani (known derisively as gypsies at the time).

I was told when I interviewed for the job with the director of the club that 25 percent of the members were on probation or had been to jail or some type of juvenile facility. The kids who had been locked up were mainly the older kids, the oldest of whom were in their mid-to-late teens, or just three or four years younger than me. Some had been in and out of juvenile facilities and jails several times.

The local gangs in the area were among the oldest continuous gangs in the US, some dating from the 1920s. A few of the older boys were in gangs their grandfathers had been in. Some gangs had once been a mix of Jews, Blacks, and Chicanos, but by the 1960s, the Chicano gangs ruled Boyle Heights.

At any time, we had seventy to a hundred-and-fifty kids in the building, with each section supervised by one or two people. I worked the front room with the ping pong and pool tables. I was usually paired with an old social worker near retirement, named Romy (short for Roman). Romy had been a social worker in the Boyle Heights area for forty years and was very knowledgeable about the families in the community and the gangs. I tried to imitate his quiet, attentive style. He had a sixth sense about when to intervene and when to let the kids let off steam.

The toughest kids were always the ones hanging around the pool tables, which were segregated by age. The ten-year-old kids were the most boisterous. They were also the most malleable. The toughest were the seventeen- and eighteen-year-olds. None of them, from the youngest to oldest, needed any instruction in pool.

Occasionally I'd play ping pong with one of the kids, and once in a while I'd teach guitar or sing a few songs for a handful of kids in the library, the least popular station in the building. The few kids who regularly visited the library had crushes on the young, attractive librarian.

The Boys Club was also the only place by 1966 where I saw anyone eager to join the military. One of the club members turned eighteen and joined the Navy while I was there. We had a little party when he came back from basic training, beaming with pride in his new uniform. While the younger kids wanted to test his strength with arm wrestling and pushing, the librarian told me worriedly, "I just hope he comes back in one piece." Like me, she was anti-war, not anti-military.

I was still in a state of limbo, hoping the Peace Corps would provide me with sanctuary.

In May, a battle between Buddhist monks and the South Vietnamese army resulted in scores of deaths.

I got almost straight A's in both of my junior semesters, making the Dean's list both times, and bringing my overall average above 3.7, well above the 3.0 I needed to keep my scholarship for my final year. The psychedelics had not done me in, partly I suppose because I hadn't let them take over. School and work always came first.

I did not go back to New Jersey for the summer. After school ended and summer began, I worked the fulltime schedule at the Boys Club—from one to five thirty during the week and ten to one on Saturdays.

I continued to wait to hear from the Peace Corps. The deadline for early training for the summer of 1966 had already passed, but I still hoped I would be accepted for the following year.

Since I started my shift at one o'clock and worked the afternoon and evening shifts over the summer at the club, I often went to Venice Beach in the mornings to sit in the sun and read or go swimming. The drive from the beach to the club was a breeze. The traffic on the Santa Monica freeway was always light. I could easily be on the beach in under half an hour. With all the driving I was doing, my battery remained well charged, so I always had the radio on.

My favorite song of the day on August 1 was "(Hot Town,) Summer in the City," a gritty but happy-go-lucky song by The Lovin' Spoonful. It was a week away from making it to number one on the Billboard's Hot 100. It was so popular I could usually find a station playing it on the drive to work.

The song matched the heat and grit of the inner city where I worked. I often found myself singing along, tapping out the rhythm on my steering wheel as I cruised from one freeway to another, circling the downtown and landing in Boyle Heights.

On August 1, I had gone to the beach in the morning, driven across town, and just exited the freeway for the last short leg of my drive when "Summer in the City" ended, and the news came on. I heard the first reports about the mass shootings at the University of Texas at Austin as I neared the Boys Club.

Over the next few days, the story was told and retold about how the highly disturbed Charles Whitman, a twenty-five-year-old student, Eagle Scout, and former Marine, had stabbed his mother and wife to death, and then went to the university tower and began shooting everyone he could see on the campus below. Before he was finally killed, he had murdered fourteen people and wounded thirty-two, a record for university killings in America that stood for forty-one years until the Virginia Tech massacre in 2007.

I was shocked to learn that one of those killed was Tom Ashton, a kid who had been in one of my classes. He had just graduated from USC in the spring and was taking his Peace Corps orientation at the University of Texas that summer. I couldn't help wondering if I had been accepted into the Peace Corps for that summer, whether I also might have been sent to Texas to train.

The Beatles' album *Revolver*, one of the very first truly psychedelic albums, came out five days after the Charles Whitman rampage at the University of Texas and two days after Lenny Bruce's death from an overdose of morphine across town in Hollywood.

The new sounds and lyrics on *Revolver* seemed to burst out of some deep sub-consciousness in songs like "Eleanor Rigby," "Yellow Submarine," "I'm Only Sleeping," "Love You To," and "She Said, She Said." The cover featured the "acid" art of Klaus Voorman.

Days later, my reply from the Peace Corps finally arrived. I had been rejected for that summer. I was advised to reapply the following year.

I never reapplied. During the year, the draft rules changed once again. Peace Corps volunteers were no longer deferred from the draft.

My options continued to shrink. All that remained were grad school, Canada, and the military, none of which I wanted any part of.

More than anything I wanted to be master of my own destiny and not some pawn in a war that no one had convinced me was worth fighting in or dying for.

CHAPTER 54

What did I really know about leaving the country?

Nothing.

I had been to Canada twice. I had been to Juarez once and Tijuana twice.

Except for Anna, I hadn't met anyone my age who had burned their draft card or refused their draft call.

My father and mother had both supported World War II. Both had been born in America and never once thought of living anywhere else. My father was thirty, married, and had a son (my brother) when the US entered World War II. He had a war job as night manager of a munitions plant while running his glove business during the day. He had passed his physical and was on standby for the Navy, but he was never called up. He said he would have gone if he had been given notice. Two of my uncles, one great uncle, and several of my parents' male cousins had served during the war. Several had served in World War I. One had been gassed. Another cousin, a career Marine, had earned a Silver Star for his role in the famous Battle of Belleau Wood as one of the notorious Devil Dogs.

But what of the generations that came before them, the ones who had turned their backs on Imperial Russia and immigrated to the US?

My great grandfather, Joseph Kipnees (aka Josef Kipnis)—the "Joseph" I had been named after—had been a draft resister. Who could blame him? He fled Russia at the beginning of the Russo-Japanese War in 1905 after several years of pogroms had undermined the well-being of Russia's Jewish population. His own family had gone from upper middle class with servants and the children in private Russian schools to having their house burned down and being forced to live in a neighbor's basement with burlap hanging from the ceiling to make room dividers. He was thirty-seven years old when he left Russia ahead of his wife and five children.

He brought his family to America a year later where they had struggled among the poor of the Lower Eastside and Brooklyn.

My grandfather Isaac William Glazner left Russia even earlier. He had been drafted.

Grandpa Ike had died when I was four. I had only the vaguest snapshot memories of him. He was my godfather. He was already eighty-one years old when I was born.

A working-class boy from a family of metal workers, he had been trained in a Ukrainian-Russian high school as a tool-and-die maker. He had apprenticed for five years, and just as he was ready to start his career, he was drafted during a period of stepped-up repression against Jews in the late 1880s. Grandpa Ike was sent to the cavalry, reputed to be the most anti-Semitic branch of the Russian military. He was assigned to the stables to work at the lowest jobs. The older Jewish soldiers there told him he could expect to spend the next five years shoveling manure and doing other menial jobs the cavalry officers used Jews to do. The Jews were the Blacks of Russia in those days.

The story I heard was that twenty-three-year-old Grandpa Ike stole a horse and rode off the military base in the middle of the night. Using identity papers of a relative, he took a train across the border and lived for a short time in Germany before heading to America a year or so after the Statue of Liberty was unveiled. He had lived under an assumed name for the next seventeen years.

Was I, at twenty-one and a half, about to follow in his footsteps?

Karl Marx noted in *The Eighteenth Brumaire of Louis Bonaparte*, "Hegel remarks somewhere that all great, world-historical facts and personages occur, as it were, twice. He has forgotten to add: the first time as tragedy, the second as farce."

Did I have the nerve to leave, or would I end up like my other friends and simply try to make the most of whatever was thrown at me? Garth had refused Officer Candidate School. He was a private doing deskwork at a base in Europe.

CHAPTER 55

I met my sister-in-law Linda for the first time late in the summer when my brother and his new bride drove to Las Vegas on their delayed honeymoon. As the airlines switched from prop planes to jets, prices for air travel dropped quickly. So, I took my first commercial flight and flew to Las Vegas. My brother and I had been to Las Vegas in 1962 on our way back from California to New Mexico, but I had only been seventeen, so I couldn't get into the casinos. This time I was twenty-one, so I was able to gamble and see several shows.

My sister-in-law said she had no idea how to play roulette and then jumped up and down like a cheerleader when she won a big jackpot. I liked her. She was short, blond, and heavyset like my brother. She had a cheery smile and an infectious laugh. She was a graduate of Columbia University and had started teaching nursing at the hospital in Plainfield where I had been born. Most important of all, I could see she was crazy about my brother. I was happy to see him so content and so proud of her. He had had little luck dating in high school. Now, he had found true love when I wasn't even sure what love was anymore even though I was supposed to be one of the ambassadors of the love generation.

I flew back to Los Angeles thinking about how easy it was to change channels in real life by hopping on a jet. In hours, instead of days, I could be in New York, Montreal, London, or Saigon.

With one exception, I never saw any of the parents at the Boys Club. Romy told me it was part of the culture of machismo and a code of silence that the Latino families maintained outside the home. The one exception was Larry, the only Romani boy that I knew of at the club at that time.

Dark-haired, dark-eyed Larry was there most days with about a dozen hardcore ten-year-olds who hung around the pool table and vied for top dog each day. Larry was good enough to win once in a while, which made him as bold and self-confident as any of this crowd—until his mother showed up.

One day the old social worker Romy and I were getting ready to take a half dozen younger kids by van to the Shrine Auditorium to see the circus. The kids were already in the van. Romy had gone inside the club for a second. I was standing beside the vehicle waiting for Romy to return when a woman in her forties and a man in his twenties appeared on the sidewalk heading toward me. Both had stern looks on their faces. I had never seen the woman before, and I had never seen anyone on the streets in the neighborhood looking like her. She was wearing a fluffy white blouse; long, dark, wavy hair tied in a red kerchief; silver and gold chains around her neck; and wrists heavy with silver bangles. The young man was about my age and height but with another twenty pounds of muscle on his frame. I recognized him. His face showed no emotion as he stared at me through narrow dark eyes. I had seen him in the neighborhood before. He was Larry's brother. Romy told me he sometimes carried a gun. The family lived a few blocks away from the club and had been in occasional conflict with the police and their Latino neighbors.

I saw no sign of a gun but the frowns on the faces of the two made me a little nervous.

The woman stopped in front of me. Larry's brother stopped a few paces back.

"Where is Larry?" the woman demanded in a sharp, no-nonsense voice. "I'm his mother. I want to see him now."

"He's in the van," I said. Larry was squeezed into the back of the van with several other boys.

I opened the door of the van. Larry's mother stuck her head in, spotted him, and ordered, "Larry. Get out here. Now."

The grim-faced mother and older brother were not only giving me the jitters, but the kid was visibly trembling and embarrassed by his mother's presence. The other kids were dead silent, riveted by the drama.

Romy came out of the club but stayed by the door. I gave him a questioning look. He returned it with a shake of his head—enough to tell me to stay out of it.

As the kid stood on the sidewalk grim-faced, his dark-eyed mother bent over him and demanded, "Where do you think you're going?"

"To...to the circus, mama," he stammered. "I already told you."

She squinted at him for a few seconds longer as if thinking about it, and smiled.

"The circus?"

Larry nodded.

She gave him the are-you-sure-look for a couple of seconds.

Larry nodded.

She opened the small purse she was carrying and took out a quarter.

"Okay, then buy me an elephant," she laughed, handing the quarter to her son.

We all burst out laughing.

She kissed Larry on the forehead, tussled his hair, turned him around, and pushed him back in the van, and then turned and marched off with her grown son behind her without a look back.

Larry, gripping the quarter in his hand, took his place in the back of the van, grinning.

On another day, out of the blue, Larry walked up to me and a couple of the staff members and asked us, "You know why everything is all mixed up in the world?"

"No," we all said.

"It's easy. When you're inside your mother before you're born, you're upside down. Then, you get born and they put you on your feet. They tell you that's right side up. But it isn't. That's why everything is mixed up. Right?"

We laughed, and he returned to the pool table with a grin to wait for his next shot.

CHAPTER 56

Early one Sunday morning at the end of the summer, I was driving back from grocery shopping, grinning from ear to ear when I spotted Kim Charney. He was driving toward me in his XKE coupe along University Avenue. He recognized me and pulled to a stop beside me in front of my place.

"You got a minute?" I asked.

"Sure. What's up? You look like you just won the World Series."

"I got something that'll blow your mind. You're not going to believe what I found."

He parked on the street.

I drove down my driveway. By the time he reached me, I had pulled my bag of groceries from my car. I told him I had to run the food upstairs. If he wanted to help, he could grab the album I just bought off the back seat and wait for me to return.

I put the food away and came right down to find Kim holding the album and twisting and turning it so the daylight hit the surface from different angles.

Kim was my last close friend from my freshman year who was still hoping to get into medical school. At the moment, he was facing the possibility of losing everything he had been working toward for years. I was hoping that what I just found might take his mind off his troubles.

Kim and I had met in our freshman year during rush week—the week at the start of the school year when fraternities and sororities throw parties and invite potential new members into their houses.

Kim and I had crossed paths at several parties and joked about the weirdness of being cattle for sale. We joined different fraternities but remained friends and had a few classes together. I had lasted only a year in the fraternity. Kim had stayed through our junior year until his fraternity got kicked off campus. He and a half dozen others in his frat house were expelled from USC on hazing charges at the end of the school year.[48]

Kim hadn't been involved in the hazing, but he had been charged by the school and expelled, because he was an officer of the fraternity, and USC had one of the strictest anti-hazing laws in the country. If Kim couldn't return to school, he feared he might be blackballed from medical school—the only thing he wanted to do since he was a child. He was fighting the expulsion in court and suing the school. The case was taking forever.

On top of that, his long-time girlfriend had just dumped him.

"Is this what I think it is?" he asked as I joined him beside my car.

"Yes."

"Where did you get it?" His eyes were popping out of his head.

"At the Ralph's near the Forum ten minutes ago."

"Wow."

He was holding my new copy of the Beatles' *Yesterday and Today* album, which had been released weeks before. Kim was a big Beatles fan, but it wasn't the record that got his attention. I had found the holy grail—a first edition of the album cover with the new cover pasted over it.

The original cover for the album for *Yesterday and Today* showed the Beatles dressed as butchers surrounded with dismembered, bloody doll parts. The album with the notorious Butcher cover was pulled from record store shelves almost immediately after its release after a flood of complaints. It was banned in some cities. Shipments were halted and most copies were destroyed, but some in cities around the US survived. The music company, eager to continue to distribute the album, quickly produced a new cover with a new photo of the four Beatles standing or sitting around a large steamer trunk in casual clothes. The new album with the steamer trunk cover was quickly sent out to replace the recalled albums. Somewhere along the way, some music company executive tried to save money by having employees paste the new Steamer Trunk cover over the old Butcher cover. A small number of these were distributed for a few days before they, too, were discontinued and recalled because the original Butcher covers could be seen through the photo of the Steamer Trunk cover.

In the end, the original Butcher cover and the paste-over had become the stuff of legends in a few short weeks. And I had just found one of these rarities in the discount bin at the big Ralph's 24-hour supermarket.

"This is amazing," Kim said still gripping the album in both hands. Then, suddenly, he looked up and added excitedly, "If there's one, maybe there's two."

A brilliant idea. I hadn't thought of that.

We hopped in his car and flew over the empty streets to the store. We spent the next couple of hours going through thousands of discounted record albums, each for eighty-eight cents, sitting in no particular order in rows of bins in the supermarket.

By the time we had finished checking out every album in the store, we each found one more.

We both walked out of the store grinning.

"Maybe your luck is changing," I said as we headed back to my place.

"I hope so. I don't know what I'm going to do if I lose in court."

"What about medical school?"

He had done something unusual. He had applied to medical school toward the end of his junior year.

"None of the places I applied to accepted me. It's too late in the summer to try to apply anywhere else."

If he lost the fight and remained expelled, he was also immediately eligible for the draft unless he could transfer to some other undergraduate school, and he hadn't gotten around to applying.

"Could you go back to acting?" I asked. Kim had worked as a child movie and TV star and a pop singer from the age of six to eighteen when he quit the business to study pre-med at USC. He had been in over fifty movies and TV shows, playing opposite Frank Sinatra, Debbie Reynolds, and many others.

"I don't want to," he said. "Even if I wanted to act, it wouldn't be the same. I was a child actor. I'd be going back as an adult. It's a completely different business. I'd be starting over. Besides, I only acted to earn money to pay for medical school. I missed a lot of normal things. I didn't have a bar mitzvah. I never wanted to be anything else but a doctor."

"Whatever you do, stay out of the draft," I told him when he dropped me off in front of my place.

"I'll do my best."

What a waste it would be to draft this guy, I thought as he drove away.

A week later, he came by my place still grinning. He was carrying a life-sized top half of a store mannikin and a large, brightly painted plaster bust of the Egyptian Queen Nefertiti.

"What's this?" I asked.

"Presents if you want them. Part of my pop art collection."

"Don't you want them?"

"No, I'm moving home. I got accepted into med school. UC Irvine is starting a new medical program. They had an opening. I'll be starting in a few weeks. I don't have to worry about being expelled because I'm done with USC."

"What about your court case?"

"I won. I was readmitted and the expulsion was erased from the records."

"You're going to be a great doctor," I told him.

"And I'm going to be reading your books one day."

After he left, I set the statues on the deck outside my door so people passing by on the sidewalk could enjoy them, too.

Maybe, Jeff's dad was right. Some people have all the luck. I was hoping I would have a little.

Donovan's psychedelic love song "Sunshine Superman" topped the charts during September 1966.

The hardest class I had in the first semester of my senior year in the fall of 1966 was Statistics II, a graduate level class in psychology taught by my old friend Dr. Dan Davis, the psychologist who had caught Theo cheating and flunked him.

The math in Statistics II was incomprehensible even after I read the books and reviewed my notes repeatedly. I just didn't get it. I knew I wouldn't. I didn't have that kind of mind. I knew I was doomed. Even so, I gave it my all. I had enough money saved from the summer to leave the Boys Club, so, I could spend more time studying. I picked up a bit of extra money for a couple of months, doing some research for Dr. Davis in the psychology department.

One day, I got a phone call at my place from a sociology student in another class who was writing a paper on hippies. She wanted to interview me. Dr. Ted Hadwen, my sociology professor, had recommended she call me. He had given her my number.

Hadwen's focus was on opening up students to the cultures and worlds beyond their own. Hadwen was one of the first to study Watts before the riots and afterward. [49]

I had two classes with him in past semesters. In one class for our final, he assigned everyone a country and told us to bring food from that country to a lunch on the last day of class. We had to hunt down specialty shops all over the city to buy fruits, vegetables, and other foods native to that country or part of the world. We shared the food with each other at a picnic in the backyard of some wealthy friends of Hadwen's where we all drank wine and ate dishes from two dozen different countries most of us had never been to or heard of. In another class, I wrote a long paper for him on the gangs of East Los Angeles with the help of Romy and a few articles I found in the library. The paper received high praise from Hadwen. We talked about hippies in class, and I had offered my opinion on what I thought freaks and hippies were trying to do. Hadwen often asked me to comment when anyone asked a question about hippies.

Still, I was a little surprised and flattered that he remembered me from his old classes and thought I was knowledgeable enough on the subject to be interviewed by another student.

I invited the woman who phoned me to come to my place.

A tall, well-dressed young woman with straight short blond hair showed up a few days later at the appointed time with another buttoned-down, studious woman with glasses and long, straight brown hair. The interviewer, Barb, introduced her friend as Karen. They both lived in the dorm and were juniors.

Barb asked all the questions and took notes. Karen listened without expression when I talked. Occasionally, I saw her looking at my paintings with the same unreadable eyes. I got the feeling Karen was there to make it two against one if I turned out to be too freaky.

We covered a lot of ground in the next thirty minutes. Barb wanted to know what hippies believed in.

I told her I thought being a hippie was a state of mind. If everyone's mind was different, then every hippie was different. If unifying principles existed, they boiled down to peace, love, and hope, back to nature for some, creative jobs and businesses in the city for others, being anti-war, anti-military-industrial complex, anti-mindless consumerism, anti-pollution, and anti-rat race.

"How do you stay out of the rat race? By not working?" Barb asked.

"By working smart," I said. I told her about a favorite passage I'd read in Thoreau's *Walden* as a freshman in high school. It seemed even more relevant in 1966.

"In *Walden*'s first chapter, Thoreau says something that was true in his time and yet makes no sense today on the face of it," I explained. "Thoreau mused that he could walk faster than a train. He could walk fast enough, he said, that he could walk from his hometown of Concord to Fitchburg thirty miles away and beat the train by two hours."

I explained that he said this in 1846 during the early years of railroads when trains averaged fifteen miles an hour while the average person walked about three miles an hour. I explained how Thoreau had made a valuable economic argument, important because hippies were trying to live in an alternate economy.

"The cost of the train ride between Concord and Fitchburg," I explained, "was ninety cents, about what the average worker earned in a ten-hour workday."

Barb's eyes narrowed. I could see she was finding faults.

I plowed on, "Thoreau's argument rested on logic—he could set out in the morning, go to work in a factory like his father's pencil factory near the train station for ten hours, then hop on the train to Fitchburg, and be there two hours later, for a total of twelve hours in all. Or he could start out first thing in the morning walking to Fitchburg, skip the day in the factory, and reach his destiny in a total of ten hours, two hours less than if he had worked for ten hours and then bought a ticket. And he could get exercise and see interesting sites along the way."

Barb shook her head at the obvious flaw in the argument. "But that makes no sense today."

"Of course. No one can walk faster than a train or a car or plane today or even a bicycle. I can earn enough to take a bus from Los Angeles to New York in a forty-hour week and be there in seventy-two hours. It would take me a hundred days at three miles an hour for ten hours a day to walk there. Thoreau's illustration is irrelevant today, but not the economic lesson."

I told them what Hadwen had discussed with the class when I had him the year before.

"Thoreau was the original hippie. He was trying to see what life was all about by thinking about what was important to him. The hippies I know are asking themselves what they really need and what they can do without. For me, Thoreau was saying, don't waste time working for what you don't need."

I told them about how Thoreau had been an anti-war protester against the Mexican-American War because he, like Abe Lincoln and other intellectuals of his day, viewed the war as a plot by the Southern states to expand slavery. His protest was passive. He refused to pay his taxes and was jailed briefly. Later, he wrote his famous essay on civil disobedience and became the father of modern civil disobedience—the disobedience of Gandhi and Martin Luther King, Jr."

I told her that a small segment of society—from the transcendentalists and utopians of Thoreau's time to the socialist movements, artist colonies, avant-garde, and beatniks of the first half of the century to the folkies during the late Eisenhower years and Kennedy years to the freaks and hippies today—is always looking for a better way to live and be.

"What may be different this time is there are so many of us, and the society we live in is so rich. It can support more idealists than ever. The idealists are following the music—young people like us that are singing the truth. For the first time in history, an army of young people are taking their marching orders—their directions—from singers and songwriters. The Beatles, Bob Dylan, and hundreds of other musicians are more popular and influential than all the politicians, professors, and business and religious leaders combined."

I told them about Adlai Stevenson's idea of earth as a spaceship. The spaceship model was different than the older models of human existence. Survival of the fittest, the laws of the jungle, winner takes all, and might equals right don't make sense on a spaceship. "I believe we're just in the beginning of changing the way humans think. If there's a new way of doing things out there, then, I want to be part of it."

When she asked about drugs, I reminded myself of the recent busts and deflected the question. "Look at what the mind drugs were supposed to be doing. Expanding our minds. That wouldn't be a bad thing if some answers to how we're supposed to live over the next hundred or thousand years came from expanded minds. If a drug makes you more lethargic, more violent, more confused, addicted, or anything else that you consider beyond your control, then you shouldn't do it." I told them to read Aldous Huxley, Timothy Leary, and Richard Alpert.

"I can't change the world, but I can change myself and that's a start. We should all be aiming for that."

Barb seemed pleased with the interview. Karen gave me the tiniest smile, and then they were gone, leaving me wondering if they thought I was nuts.

I ran into Barb, the interviewer, a few weeks later. She told me she received an A on her paper. She thanked me profusely. It would be six months before I crossed paths with Karen again.

I voted for the first time in November, casting my ballot for Governor Pat Brown, the Democrat. I was certain he would win. He was running against the actor Ronald Reagan, a one-time Democrat who had become a Republican. I couldn't imagine why anyone would want him as governor.

I felt bewildered when Reagan beat Pat Brown. It was like California had gone from Kennedy to Nixon.

My high school friend Fred married Cecile. My high school friend George was expecting to get married the following spring. Most of my old college classmates were in serious relationships or married. I was still wandering in the desert of no love.

Mike Vosse and David Anderle, who had discovered Frank Zappa and played violin on the *Freak Out!* album, were now completely immersed on the other side of town with Brian Wilson, the most famous Beach Boy. I got regular updates from Mike and Garry who frequently visited Wilson's home. Anderle and Vosse were central to the team working with Brian on the legendary *Smile* album. Vosse was hired by Wilson and given a vague assignment to work on possible film projects for the Beach Boys. Anderle was hired to run their new production company and work on new business ventures for Brian and the Beach Boys.

Brian Wilson was having trouble pushing through his ideas for his *Smile* album with the other Beach Boys and family members, most of whom didn't like the direction Brian was taking the band. They also didn't like or understand some of the music, and didn't like the outsiders, particularly musician Van Dyke Parks, David Anderle, Mike Vosse, and others who showed up at Brian's house and the recording studio every day. The gang hanging around Wilson was sometimes fondly, sometimes derisively, referred to as Vosse's Posse. [50]

Tiny, frail, and always high, Mike provided lots of laughs. He was also fearless. He was often the one designated to go somewhere to pick up more pot or LSD for anyone who wanted it, because he was the least paranoid of any of them. From what he told me, he was there to remind them that whatever they were doing, life was supposed to be fun.

Garry was an occasional visitor to Brian's house, content to observe and tell me tales of listening to private renditions of Brian playing the guitar and singing the latest cuts from the *Smile* album. [51]

I got a vicarious high just being close to people who were working with people who were blowing our collective minds.

Kim Charney told me medical school was brutal, like learning a new language and how to walk and talk all over again, but he was doing well and loving it. He spent all his time studying or in classes at the Los Angeles County Hospital where UC Irvine was holding its first medical school classes.

He was back with his old girlfriend, but he had only seen her once in the past month.

CHAPTER 57

Out of nowhere in mid-December, I suddenly felt dizzy and nauseous in the middle of my graduate statistics class. The class was held on the second floor of the new Von KleinSmid Center.

Feeling a sense of panic, I simply got up and left the class.

Halfway down the empty staircase to the first floor, I passed out.

I was only out a second or two, but when I came to, I found myself sitting on the floor at the bottom of the stairs with my books scattered around me. Luckily, I hadn't hurt myself in the fall. I was woozy, but I managed to walk to the school's infirmary two blocks away before I passed out again in the waiting room.

The infirmary staff checked me into one of the beds with a high fever, sore throat, swollen glands, and fatigue.

Even before the blood work came back, the nurse predicted correctly that I had mononucleosis.

The mono knocked me for a loop for the first day or two, but I started rallying once I discovered Jan, one of Jeff's old girlfriends, who was in bed in the next room also with mono. Pretty soon we were spending all our time together. The Christmas break was just starting. Everyone else in the infirmary began heading home. Jan and I were two of only a half dozen patients left behind. Jan, who was much sicker than me, was also more bored. The doctor insisted we both had to stay for several more days at least, but Jan decided we had to break out.

We waited until visiting hours were over to make our escape. We must have looked like two drunks as we wandered down the hall and out the side door to the street, holding each other up. We stopped every few yards to rest. It took us a half hour to reach my place a half dozen blocks away.

I managed to drive her home to Long Beach and return to my place where I curled up in bed, trying to stay warm, using the brief periods between high fevers to drive to the 32nd Street Market two blocks away to replenish my stock of food.

Most of the people I knew or heard about who had mono had been forced to drop out of school. If I had to drop out in order to get better, there was a good chance I'd get drafted before I could get back in school.

More than 6,000 US military personnel had died in Vietnam in 1966 and tens of thousands sustained physical and psychological wounds. Tens and maybe hundreds of thousands of North and South Vietnamese soldiers and civilians, including children, were also killed. Many hundreds of thousands, maybe millions were seriously injured and maimed.

CHAPTER 58

By sheer luck, I was able to nurse myself through the Christmas break and emerge as if from a cocoon in the first days of the New Year 1967 in reasonably good health. I was still weak as a kitten but determined to complete the semester, even if I had to crawl between classes, which I felt at times I was doing.

The first single from a new group, The Doors, came out on New Year's Day. "Break on Through to the Other Side" was electrifying. Overnight, the song catapulted local Los Angeles singer Jim Morrison and his band to the same heights as Dylan, the Beatles, the Byrds, and other poet-prophets and spiritual muses leading us to a new world and a new way of thinking.

I wanted to write like Jim Morrison.

Nine days later, another local, almost unknown group, the Buffalo Springfield, with Stephen Stills, Neil Young, Bruce Palmer, Richie Furie, and Dewey Martin blew my mind again with "For What It's Worth." [52]

It was also the day I ran headlong into a new cataclysm by the name of Kaye, a wild child a year younger than me.

By chance, I met Kaye on the same day I received a telegram from the president of the university, telling me I had been elected to America's national honorary society Phi Beta Kappa. The invitation to the Phi Beta Kappa ceremony had specified immediate family and special friends as guests. [53]

I was exiting the library when I saw Don, a friend of mine, taking photos of a slim attractive woman with long, light-brown hair down to her shoulders, a round, cheerful, innocent face, dazzling blue eyes, and an impish, I'll-try-anything smile.

The woman was posing by the fountain in front of Doheny Library. Don was a budding photographer who had taken a series of photos of me a few months before. His model beside the fountain was dressed in jeans and a white sweatshirt. She was jumping in the air with her arms and legs outstretched like she was flying. Don stopped shooting as soon as he saw me. The young woman stopped jumping and joined us. Don introduced Kaye and me. I was immediately attracted to her. She had a sunny, animated, and carefree way that made me feel as if I already knew her.

Don and Kaye were taking a break from studying. We were all heading into finals in a few weeks.

Kaye said she was studying English, but she intended to leave USC after finals. She had applied to Berkeley for the spring session. UC Berkeley had switched from the semester system to a quarter system, so their next session wouldn't start for a couple of months.

"I probably won't get in," she said. "If I don't, I'm not sure what I'll do."

Don was thinking about heading back East to New York, his hometown. He was looking for a new school to apply to. "I'd quit and just go to New York," he told me, "but I'd be drafted in a second."

When Don asked me, what was new in my life, I said, "I've just been elected to Phi Beta Kappa."

Don and Kaye congratulated me, and on a whim, I explained the invitation said family and special friends were welcome. I invited them to the ceremony and tea as my special friends. I gave them the time, day, and location.

Don said he couldn't go. He had a class. I thought that would be the end of it, but Kaye asked, "Am I still invited?"

"Sure, if you can make it." I repeated the time, date, and location.

"I'll see you there."

I was happy with her response, but I didn't expect her to come. I ran into Don a day later, and he told me Kaye was dating a graduate student in the film school, so I was even more certain she wouldn't show.

On the day of the ceremony, I arrived in front of Bovard Hall and found her waiting for me at the entrance.

The ceremony was short and sweet with tea and cookies served afterward. Kaye was at ease with the crowd. We wandered around the room and made small talk with a half dozen others before we headed for the door.

On the way outside, Kaye told me she wanted to see my place.

"When?"

"Right now, if you're not busy."

She slipped her arm through mine as we walked. "You're an artist and writer," she said.

I looked at her quizzically.

"Don pointed out your place when he walked me home the other day. It's the garage apartment with the two statues on the front deck. Everyone knows about you. Don said you're writing a novel."

"I'm trying. I'm just not getting anywhere. I have to learn to let go."

"Let go with me," she said. "I'll be your muse."

I asked her about her boyfriend.

"That's over." She pulled me closer.

Kaye was just what I thought I needed at that moment. I had been telling myself that I needed to let go and somehow jump into the middle of my life. I needed to be in the moment and not be thinking about a future I couldn't control.

Kaye was my perfect muse. I could imagine taking off with her to parts unknown. She was intent on shaking free from her past. She was a local girl from San Marino, a wealthy small town next to Pasadena. She was living in one of the most exclusive sororities on campus but was questioning everything and finding real passion in sex, drugs, and folk dancing.

Kaye told her sorority-house mother that she was heading home to study for finals so she could spend nights with me.

I couldn't be happier. She loved making love and wanted to spend all her time in bed as much as me. Living in the moment was an aphrodisiac for both of us.

When not in bed, we studied furiously for our exams. I had a lot riding on my statistics exam. I studied until my eyes hurt. Sadly, I had to be honest with myself. I did not understand the higher math.

Kaye had recently discovered dancing and thought she might like to study dance instead of English if she got into Berkeley. We drove to a dance hall in Pasadena that held folk dances on weekends. She spent the night whirling around the floor to Russian, Ukrainian, and Scottish tunes, while I awkwardly tried to keep up. The place was filled with young freaks getting off on dancing and trying to get back in touch with their roots. I loved the physicalness of dance and the ecstasy on Kaye's face as she lost herself in the music and movement.

We played house at my place, buying groceries, cooking together, and eating in bed. I drew pencil portraits of her face, trying to capture the sparkle in her eyes. I sketched her in the nude in pastels while she lay on my bed reading, sometimes to herself, sometimes aloud to me. She hated the war. "I hate it more now," she said, "because you could go there and die."

We talked about going to Canada together and living in the woods. I imagined spending my days writing, painting, and playing my guitar. She imagined herself cooking, gardening, making our clothes, and dancing. We needed nothing else to live but each other.

If there was no war, I told her I wanted to live high up on the side of a mountain in Big Sur overlooking the ocean. She said she had dreamed of doing the same thing. She traveled there as a teen with some friends and tried to find Henry Miller's place. She liked him for the same reason I did. His honesty as a writer. He wrote what was inside his head.

We were in love and got along well. She was pretty sure she wouldn't get into UC Berkeley, and she couldn't stand the idea of continuing to live at the sorority or going home to San Marino.

Kaye and I talked about living together. We felt married and toyed with the idea of running off and making it official.

We went to her house in San Marino one afternoon to pick up a few things of hers and bring them back to my place. While there, her mother came home, and Kaye was forced to introduce me. They retreated to another part of the house, and her mother and Kaye had a fight about Kaye bringing a Jewish hippie to the house.

Kaye told me what had transpired shortly afterward when we left her house without any of the clothes Kaye had originally come to collect.

"That's what I want to get away from," she told me on the way back to my place. "My father's even worse. You're the first person I've really felt comfortable with since I started USC."

I felt the same.

Except for the time we spent in our respective classes, we were inseparable. We talked about taking a trip to San Francisco to look around over the hiatus between the end of our finals and the start of the spring semester.

Unexpectedly Kaye went home to San Marino after her last final to get the clothes she had originally set out to get on our last trip. While home, she found her acceptance letter to UC Berkeley for the start of the spring session a couple of months away. She called to tell me.

The letter changed everything for her. She was a different person. She was warm and passionate on the phone, telling me how much she missed me, but she wanted to leave right away for Berkeley to check it out. She had a number of old friends living in the Bay area, some of whom she had introduced me to when they had been visiting Los Angeles in the past few weeks.

I was still a couple of days away from finishing my exams. I expected her to be back at my place in a few hours, but she called me later to tell me she loved me and had decided to stay overnight in San Marino and leave from there late in the morning. "I'll call you before I leave," she said.

When she didn't phone in the morning, I called her house. Since I knew I wasn't a favorite of her mother, I told her I was an old friend from high school and wanted to get in touch. Her mother said Kaye and her had gotten in a fight, and Kaye had left very early that morning without telling her where she was staying. "That's all I know. She never tells me anything." She offered to take a message but I said no.

The sudden loss of intimacy, sex, and our carefully laid plans for a future together were shocking, but I had no time to think about it. I put her almost completely out of my mind to take the last of my exams—almost, because I kept hoping she would phone. If she did, it was when I was out at an exam or shopping for food.

The only good thing about my statistics exam was that it was the last of my exams for the semester.

My Volvo had been running rough for the past few weeks, so I decided to hitch to San Francisco and back in the ten days I had before the start of the spring semester—a trip Kaye and I had talked about before she got her acceptance letter. I was pretty sure that I had flunked my stats exam. If I did, I could lose my deferment and would soon get drafted. This could be my last shot at freedom. If I got drafted, I still didn't know what I would do. Statistics had so bummed me out that I hadn't applied for graduate school in psychology.

I had a friend from my stats class drop me off in Malibu with some cash in my pocket, my gym bag, and two phone numbers of people I knew near San Francisco, one of them a friend of Kaye's from high school.

My friend tried to talk me out of going, telling me I could get killed hitchhiking. I laughed it off.

I'm probably fucked, I thought as I walked backward along the edge of the highway, thumb out, trying to coax someone to stop. I smiled at every car that went by.

I tried to feel happy. Ahead of me lay ten days to take a look at San Francisco. Kaye and I had both heard stories about a growing community of freaks converging on San Francisco over the past two years. There were urban communes in an old part of town.

I was eager to see what was happening outside the university and my circles of friends.

I wanted to see Kaye one last time and see if anything that we had was going to continue. Going to San Francisco seemed like a much better use of ten days than sitting in my place trying to think up a story to write when I could be out living one.

I was hurting, too. I was miserable. I didn't want to believe that something so good could end so quickly with no words.

Life begins when you let go, I told myself as a wet mist rolled in off the ocean. I had been walking and unsuccessfully hitchhiking for nearly an hour. I was more than two miles from the Malibu commercial strip I started at. About a half mile back was a fish place. I calculated how long it would take to get back there on a run if it started to rain.

The traffic was heavier and there was plenty of time to see me and stop where I was, so I decided to stay.

I thought as much about Kaye as I did about the rest of my own life. I wasn't saving the world. I was no leader. I didn't enjoy being with groups enough to be a follower.

After nearly four years of university, I still wasn't sure what was set in stone and what I could change.

Would I end up in the military?

I didn't have any serious medical problems that would keep me out of the service like Mike. I didn't have an arrest record like Garry.

Could I continue forever in school?

I was tired of school.

Canada was an illusion.

The mist turned to a light drizzle.. My Army surplus jacket was water resistant, not waterproof. It would soon be soaked through.

I saw a string of three vehicles coming toward me and decided to wait before heading back toward the fish shack. The two cars whizzed by but the third one, a non-descript light-colored van, slowed down and pulled to the side of the road beside me. A clean-shaven man with deep-set eyes and angular features and short, light brown hair leaned out the passenger side window and asked, "How far are you going?" I guessed he was in his mid-to-late twenties. He looked like he worked in a bank or an office. Definitely not a freak, I thought. He had an easy-going manner and a friendly smile.

"San Francisco," I said.

"We're going part way. To Aptos. If you don't mind sitting on the floor in back, we can give you a ride."

The thought of getting out of the rain and getting a ride was so exciting I said yes without knowing or caring where Aptos was. The worst-case scenario would be they could drop me in some town where I could get a bus.

The man in the passenger seat opened the door and pulled his seat forward to let me in. The rear was crowded with camping and fishing gear.

"Thanks," I said, as I climbed aboard. The driver turned around and greeted me with a pleasant grin and a friendly hello. He was about the same age as the other guy, also clean cut, straight looking, short, dark brown hair, and a fleshy face.

"Just move what you want around. Make yourself comfortable," the passenger told me as the driver put the car back on the road heading north. "I'm Jack," We shook hands between the seats.

"I'm Henry," the driver said without taking his eyes off the road. We were about a mile up the road when the rain began falling harder.

"I'm Joseph." Kaye liked calling me Joseph. She thought it sounded more like a serious writer's name.

Lucky me, I thought as I shifted the sleeping bags and packs into a nice nest. I had gotten a ride before getting soaked. The floor where I was sitting seemed a bit higher than I would have expected, which made it easy for me to see the road between the two men.

"So, where's Aptos?" I asked, having no clue where we were heading.

"Near Santa Cruz," Jack told me.

"Where's that?"

They both seemed to think that was funny and laughed good-naturedly at my ignorance.

"Aptos is about eighty miles south of San Francisco. On the Coast," Jack said. He explained that it was five or six hours by the freeway, but they were in no hurry. "We're taking the coast highway most of the way. We should be there in eight or nine hours."

Calculating ahead, I started to think about where I might land that night. The only two phone numbers I had were for Steve, one of Kaye's friends from San Marino who was attending Berkeley and who I knew slightly, and Jeff, my old roommate. Jeff had graduated from USC the previous June and started grad school at San Jose State in September. He was wrestling with a few problems of his own at the moment, but I expected he would be happy to see me.

Staying with Kaye was out of the question. I had no idea where she was. My only hope of finding her was through Steve, who, for all I knew, might not know where she was.

It was already getting late. We wouldn't make Aptos until nine or ten—several hours after it got dark. I was starting to wonder where I'd sleep.

"How far is San Jose from Aptos?" I asked.

"Forty-five minutes. Why?" Jack asked.

I explained my situation.

Jack kept asking me questions, and soon I was telling them about Kaye, school, the purpose of my trip north, living in sunny California and growing up in rural New Jersey, my thoughts about my immediate future, my ever-present wrestling match with the war, and the latest novel I had started writing—a contemporary version of Nelson Algren's *A Walk on the Wild Side*, told in the first person and set in the tenements of Brooklyn, Greenwich Village, and Coney Island. I hadn't gotten very far with it.

Jack and Henry seemed to find me extremely amusing. They laughed a lot, sometimes when I wasn't even trying to be funny.

"You have a writer's heart," Jack told me, laughing in a way that said he was laughing with me, not at me. I found comfort in being around people I felt safe with. These guys were fun. Easy going. Like a couple of young professors.

Whenever I paused, they kept me going with more questions. I felt like a real comedian, like I was the funniest guy on the planet. I told them more about Kaye and me, a story that bordered on the ridiculous even to me. What was I really doing? I was chasing after a woman who had probably taken off to San Francisco without leaving me her address because she didn't want me to find her.

"Sounds like you're in love, man. Go for it. Go find her. See what she's like in a different place. Who knows?" Jack insisted.

Who knows? I thought. That was the secret of every great adventure.

I tried a dozen times to find out more about Jack and Henry, but they always deflected my questions back at me.

"Don't worry about a place to stay," Jack told me. "Once we're in Aptos, Henry and I have to make a few stops, then he's heading home, and I'm heading to my girlfriend's place. So, you're welcome to stay at my place as long as you aren't afraid of dogs."

"What kind of dogs?"

"A very friendly dog."

"I like friendly dogs."

"Then, we're good." He turned to me, flashed a peace sign, and grinned. I took it as a sign that he was trying to be hip. I grinned and returned his peace sign.

"What do you guys do in Aptos?" I asked again.

"We make surfboards," Jack said, grinning at me, "and other things."

"Cool," I said.

"Cool."

"What kind of other things?" I asked.

"We know you're cool, man," Henry said.

"Thanks," I said.

Jack turned around in his seat again and held out his hand palm up. He had three small white tablets in it.

"We're going to drop some more acid. You're welcome to trip with us if you feel like it."

I must have looked surprised because they both couldn't stop laughing.

"You should see the look on your face," Jack said.

"You guys look so straight," I told them. They definitely didn't look like freaks.

Their look was part of their modus operandi. The camping gear in back was their cover. Under the floorboards, Jack explained, where I was sitting (and the reason it had felt higher than normal) was a customized airtight compartment made of the same polyurethane, fiberglass cloth, and resins from which they made their surfboards. Inside the compartment were hundreds of pounds of marijuana, carefully pressed into kilo bricks wrapped in cardboard, aluminum foil, and plastic so carefully and tightly that the border patrol dogs couldn't smell anything.

"We've been making regular runs to Mexico for nearly two years. This is our last run with the van," Jack explained. They had accumulated enough cash to buy a small plane and planned to bring their grass in that way from then on.

Halfway to Aptos, we stopped at a diner and laughed our way through hamburgers, French fries, and milkshakes. By the time we got out, the rain had stopped.

We drove for a couple of more hours along the coast highway through Big Sur, Carmel, and Monterey. Three quarters of an hour later, we finally stopped at a cabin in the middle of a pine forest somewhere in Aptos. It was overcast and dark, so I couldn't see much of my surroundings. I helped them unload the keys of grass into the garage of their friend.

Jack told me the keys of grass would be divided over the next few days among contacts in hippie communities along the coast and in the coastal mountains as well as in San Francisco and Berkeley.

Jack and Henry had more business to take care of after we finished unloading the grass. So, they dropped me at Jack's house, and left me there for the night with a large shorthaired dog that looked like a small pony. Pluto, the dog, would have scared the shit out of me if he hadn't been so friendly and I hadn't been so stoned.

I spent the night drinking tea with honey, writing epic poems, drawing crazy pictures, listening to the rain beating down on the roof, staring at the fire in the fireplace, and laughing with joy at simply being alive.

When I got hungry, I raided Jack's kitchen. It had all I needed. I made a peanut butter and avocado sandwich and some more tea.

I catnapped.

I fed the dog as the sun came up. The rain had stopped.

I took a walk outside and felt as if I had been transported to another world. Through the trees and foggy patches, I could see down the mountainside across fields, past the highway to the ocean. I could see around me dozens of small cabins half hidden behind trees. Heads poked out the doors of a few cabins as I walked by on the country road. Every person I saw was a long-haired freak, earth mother, or kid dressed in country clothes. Everyone who noticed me gave me a friendly smile and a peace sign.

Where the heck am I? I wondered. Was this the past or the future?

Henry and Jack's van was parked in front of the cabin when I returned.

Jack was in the kitchen squeezing fresh orange juice and making toast from fresh baked bread he brought from his girlfriend's place.

The fog was already burning off. The sky was a warm blue.

Over breakfast, Jack asked me what I wanted to do.

I told him I was planning on hitching the rest of the way to San Francisco. He said he would be happy to drive me to the entrance of the freeway if I didn't mind a quick detour to the surfboard factory for a few minutes while he checked on his crew.

I was happy for the ride.

The surfboard factory was housed in an old building with lots of open windows a couple of blocks from the freeway entrance. The big main room had a half dozen long-haired freaks working there, making very trippy looking surfboards, some decked out with psychedelic designs. Everyone looked happy or stoned or both. Jack hinted that at least one of his crew was on the run from the draft.

"You're welcome to stay and join us if you want," he offered.

And just like that, I had another option to add to grad school, Vietnam, or Canada. Just drop out and disappear. The idea was appealing. [54]

"Not now," I told him. I still wanted to find Kaye.

"You can always come back," he said as he drove me to the freeway entrance. "We can always use good heads here. The war's no good, man. Don't go fight if you don't have to. It's not making the world a better place. Okay?"

I nodded. This strange and comforting corner of Aptos reminded me once again that I had to be crazy to let myself get dragged off to this war.

I stood in front of the entrance to the freeway after Jack dropped me off. I was a little sad to be on my way. Aptos was my first glimpse into rural communal living. I had heard about groups springing up around the country, but they were still rare, and this was the first one I'd seen firsthand. I liked what I saw. Part of me wanted to turn around and head back to the surfboard factory. No one knew where I was. I could disappear and erase all thoughts of the draft, the war, and school.

A car pulled alongside me a few minutes later.

As I opened the door, I reminded myself that Jack said I could always come back.

My ride sped up the ramp to the freeway seconds later. I wrapped my mind around finding Kaye.

CHAPTER 59

I was a little more relieved than I wanted to admit as I left Aptos.

Could a person just disappear inside America? Would the government eventually find me? Would all the freaks be rounded up and put into concentration camps?

Could the freaks and hippies really change anything? Or were our growing numbers of pot and acid heads and the anti-war protestors just making the government that hated us stronger. Were we just giving our enemies a larger target to shoot at?

The driver who picked me up in Aptos was a middle-aged salesman heading into San Jose where Jeff lived. The driver dropped me off downtown at the bus station. I phoned Jeff. He was thrilled to hear from me. He insisted I stay in town. He had just moved to a new apartment on Lancaster Drive and had plenty of room. Since I still didn't know if I'd even find Kaye or a place to crash once I reached San Francisco, I welcomed a temporary safe house.

Jeff was in the middle of planning his wedding. He had met Cindy, a tall, willowy, blond freshman, during the first weeks of his first semester in grad school. He brought her home from San Jose to meet his parents in Tarzana over the Thanksgiving holiday. I drove to Tarzana to see him. She was very sweet, and it was clear she and Jeff were deeply in love. A couple of weeks later, she found out she was pregnant. Jeff's parents were against the marriage. Dorothy, Jeff's mother, tried to enlist me into talking Jeff out of getting married. She was sure, and Sid agreed, that Jeff was about to ruin the rest of his life. I told his parents I would speak to Jeff. What I didn't tell them was that I was happy for Jeff. I envied him in some ways. I also thought it just might be the best thing that could happen to him.

The wedding was going to be in three weeks in San Jose.

Jeff had changed profoundly in the last month. He had always been more carefree than me. Now, he was much more serious. He worried about how his impending marriage and future child would affect his financial ties to his parents. He wasn't just becoming self-supporting like I had been for the last couple of years. He was taking on the responsibility of supporting himself and his new family. He was both scared and exhilarated, not only about starting a family but about finally breaking away from his parents.

The bonus in the combination of wife, baby, and graduate school was a deferment from the draft, probably for the rest of his life. Jeff, I suspected, was going to make a good father. His parents were still worried, but they were coming to the wedding.

"I want this, and I'm going to make it work," Jeff assured me.

He's lucky, I thought. Cindy is intelligent, calm, had a great sense of humor, and was very in love with Jeff. She was going to be a wonderful mother.

The three of us went to see *Georgy Girl.* I wished Kaye was there beside me.

I wondered what kind of father I would make or even if I wanted to be a father. My head was exploding with unknowns. Kaye, I hoped, would provide some of the answers.

The next day after lunch, Jeff dropped me off at the San Jose bus terminal for the short ride into San Francisco.

It was cold and overcast when I reached San Francisco, but my luck continued to hold. I phoned Steve, Kaye's old classmate from high school. He was happy to hear from me, and yes, I could crash at his place. He also had a phone number and address for Kaye's friends in San Francisco, but, he said, "She's been sitting in on classes at Berkeley. She may or may not be at her friends' place."

I found a tourist map and navigated my way through the city via bus and foot. I arrived at the friends' place in the middle of the afternoon. Kaye's friends lived in an old row house on Oak Street opposite the

Panhandle—a narrow strip of parkland on the east side of Golden Gate Park. I rang the bell.

No one was home.

The house was only three blocks from the intersection of Haight and Ashbury Streets, the crossroads of the low-rent district also known as Haight-Ashbury, the Haight, or Hash-bury.

I had never been to the Haight, but it was already legendary. It had recently become a subject of study for the American mainstream media. Newspapers, magazines, and TV were full of stories describing it as a mecca for local and newly arriving hippies in their teens and twenties. Young people were arriving daily on rumors of free and cheap acid, easy-to-get marijuana, the promise of free love, and a vibrant music scene that was just starting to become a leader in the psychedelic sound.

This is a different kind of dropping out, I thought as I wandered into the center of the Haight.

The creative energy was visible everywhere. The psychedelic art appeared on posters plastered on the sides of buildings and lampposts, album covers in storefront windows, the covers of underground newspapers and magazines, the storefronts of headshops, bookshops, and clothing shops, and on the sides of cars and vans. A woman went by with one side of her face painted red.

The art had a lot in common with the earthy, back-to-nature designs of the art nouveau era but with psychedelic colors. Some of the art carried political or social messages; some just illustrated a dream or an imaginary state of mind of peace, tranquility, or ecstasy. Some of the art tried to capture the fragmented and distorted drug-induced hallucinatory experience.

The streets weren't very crowded. I walked slowly to try to take it all in. The people loitering about were a mix of old people, who I suspected had lived in the rundown neighborhood for years, and young people in their teens and twenties, who looked like the regulars who had descended on Sunset Strip in the past two years. The outfits of the young ranged from white, baggy cotton outfits like Hindu gurus to the back-to-nature look—jeans, boots, and lots of leather. The back-to-nature look was part of the dream of getting back to agricultural self-sufficiency and the simplicity of old-time transcendental philosophers, like Henry David Thoreau and Ralph Waldo Emerson, and of utopian communities and art colonies of long ago. Others were dressed like the freaks on the Strip in Los Angeles in brightly colored clothes and colorful beads. Others wore top hats, bowlers, and other pieces of secondhand outfits from the Victorian, Edwardian, and Flapper eras, and war surplus.

The cheaper the better.

Saving on clothes, saving on rent by living together in urban communes, saving on cosmetics for the women, and haircuts for both sexes drove down the cost of living to practically nothing.

But even in the Haight, the disconnect between the idealism and reality was obvious. Money did matter. Not just saving it but making it. The evidence was all around me as I walked down the gently sloping Haight Street toward the center of town. I lost count of the times someone tried to sell me grass, speed, or acid, or asked for spare change. A young girl with a face full of acne sat on the steps leading to apartments over one store asking everyone who passed by if they knew of a place where she could crash that night.

A straight-looking, clean-shaven guy with a crew cut and dressed in black slacks and a white shirt, stood in front of a free medical clinic handing out illustrated pamphlets outlining the symptoms of several different venereal diseases.

I walked back the way I came, and it seemed like one pass along Haight had already made me a regular. Street people nodded at me, grinned, and flashed the peace sign.

I returned to Kaye's place but again found no one home, so, I wandered around San Francisco for a few hours before finally taking a bus across the Oakland-Bay Bridge to Steve's place in Berkeley.

Steve had a small apartment on the second floor of an old wood-frame house on Telegraph Avenue just a few blocks from the University of California Berkeley campus.

I thought about calling Kaye but instead decided to eat dinner with Steve and go with him to a lecture by Richard Alpert, the acid guru and former colleague of Timothy Leary. The event was pay-what-you-can in an off-campus hall, which attracted only two dozen people. The audience appeared to be equally divided between serious, earnest followers, who had come to listen to the LSD philosopher and life-style counselor, and another group of young people who had come stoned and were there to trip on the message or pick up or be picked up by other like-minded freaks.

Everyone was looking for something. Everyone was preaching some sort of way to reach nirvana. All I wanted to do was see Kaye one last time, if for no other reason than to say goodbye in person.

"Why don t you call Kaye," Steve said on the way back.

"It's late. Besides, I want to see her." I feared more than anything that she'd tell me she didn't want to see me. I didn't want my illusions to end on the phone.

CHAPTER 60

The next morning was gray and misty. I headed out early along with Steve. He showed me the building and classroom where Kaye was supposed to be auditing the dance class later that morning.

After Steve went to his class, I had several hours to kill. I walked to the little village of stores closest to the campus.

To my surprise, I ran into someone I knew, the poet Paul X, who I had last seen before the bust at Garry and Mike's place two years before. Paul X had a place on Oregon Street. He took me to a coffee shop nearby. There he repeated the story he had told me at the 32nd Street house. The federal government, he insisted, had a list of all the freaks and protesters in America and had plans to send us to concentration camps.

"You and I are on the list for certain," he said.

By then, I had heard the same story from several other people, including Mike Vosse who said everyone around Brian Wilson and the Beach Boys knew and believed the story. By then, I thought the rumors were possible.

Paul X showed me a few of his latest poems. He was hoping to get them published as a book. He asked me about my novel. I told him I was disappointed in myself. I still hadn't figured out how to write one.

"Just keep writing," he said. "That's what we do." He gave me his address and took off to attend to some other business.

I continued my walk around the campus. UC Berkeley was beautiful, a mix of old and new buildings set in the hills overlooking the Bay. The weather was different than the desert climate of Los Angeles. Berkeley was part of the coastal rain forest, home to redwoods that could grow to the sky. The climate remained wet and lush with no noticeable smog.

I could live here. Or in San Francisco. Or in Aptos. Or in Montreal.

I returned to the building where Kaye's class was being held. I watched the students filing in. I waited until the class started. Kaye never showed.

I returned to San Francisco by bus. I went to the house where Kaye was staying.

Her friend Grace was there. "Kaye's visiting other friends of ours from high school a few blocks away. She'll be back late afternoon."

"You mind if I come back then?"

"No. She talks about you all the time. She's been thinking about heading back to Los Angeles to see you. Come by later. I won't tell her you're here. You can surprise her. You know she likes surprises."

I was even more anxious to see her after talking with Grace. And yes, I knew Kaye loved surprises. She had brought me little gifts on several occasions when we had been in Los Angeles.

It started to rain.

To kill time, I took a bus across town and hopped on a streetcar to Fisherman's Wharf.

It was practically empty in the middle of a cold, rainy day in January.

I ducked under the overhang of a building and spent ten minutes talking to a Salvation Army soldier sheltering from the rain and waiting for someone to drop a coin in his pot. The Sally Ann collector told me about a big new store around the corner that sold all kinds of gifts.

I dashed through the rain and found this crazy store called Pier 1 Imports. It had unusual and cheap items from all over the world.

It was easy to kill a few hours in a store like this.

I bought a teleidoscope, a couple of giant beeswax candles, and a kite for Kaye, and extra candles for Steve and Kaye's friends. Kaye had bought me a teleidoscope when we were together in Los Angeles. I was very excited to find one among the sea of gifts and trinkets. [55]

The rain had stopped by the time I paid for my gifts and left the store. The sky was aluminum gray with streaks of clouds that looked like giant white birds with their wings stretched.

I took the bus toward Kaye's and got off several blocks from where she was staying so I could walk part way through the park. The rain brought out the scent of grass and earth along the Panhandle. I felt nervous as hell as I approached Kaye's door for the fourth time.

Grace answered and smiled. "She's back. I didn't tell her you were here."

"Thank you," I said, handing Grace one of the giant candles from Pier 1. "This is for you."

I walked into the living room not knowing what to expect. I saw Kaye sitting on the couch reading a book. She looked up as I crossed the room. My heart raced as I watched her recognize me. Her whole face lit up into the sweet smile I had fallen in love with when I first met her. She jumped from the couch and threw herself into my arms.

"I can't believe you're here," she said over and over, kissing my lips and cheeks.

Grace's roommate, Denise, emerged from the bedroom and was introduced to me. She had been studying but said she could study on the kitchen table, letting Kaye and me retreat to the bedroom by ourselves.

I recounted my journey to Kaye. "I wish I had been with you," she said, "but then none of what happened would have happened."

She told me she had been stoned since she left San Marino. She was so happy to be away from her family and southern California. She was even happier to have me with her, she said. She told me she had tried calling me in Los Angeles over the last couple of days and had begun to worry when I hadn't answered. By then, I was already on the road. We spent the rest of the afternoon listening to music, looking through the teleidoscope, making love, and getting to know each other again.

She told me about the fight with her mother, and how she had left on an earlier flight than she had originally been booked on. "I was afraid if I called you before I left, I would talk myself out of going. I needed to go. You understand, don't you?"

I said I did, but I wasn't completely sure.

She swore she still loved me, but she couldn't decide between being with me and being alone to find herself.

Grace and Denise's apartment was too small for me to stay with Kaye. So, I continued to sleep at Steve's place in Berkeley. I saw Kaye intermittently—at Berkeley after the classes she was monitoring, at her friends' place, and in the city.

When I wasn't with her, I explored Berkeley and San Francisco on my own. Both places felt good and exciting to me. I enjoyed the sense of the sprawling student village around Berkeley. I liked walking around San

Francisco. If I had to get somewhere fast across town, the streetcars and busses worked just fine, not like Los Angeles where you had to have a car.

One morning, while crossing the Berkeley campus, I ran into another old friend from Los Angeles—Theo, my former classmate from USC, who had been busted for pot and caught cheating on his psych paper. He appeared on the sidewalk heading right toward me.

I wasn't surprised when he told me he had dropped out of school, but I was even more curious about why he hadn't been drafted.

"They'll never find me," he said. He hadn't let his draft board know where he was and had no intention of telling them.

Theo led me to a quiet corner of the campus, pulled a small briar pipe packed with grass from his pocket, and lit up. He offered the pipe to me. Students were walking along the walkways only a few yards away. They could smell the smoke. A few glanced our way but kept walking. I hesitated.

"Nobody cares about smoking grass here," he told me. "I wish I had left USC a year ago. This is the place where the future is happening right now. You can do what you want here."

We finished the pipe and walked toward the student union.

Suddenly, he put his hand out to stop me. "Look."

Coming out the door of a building, not twenty feet away, surrounded by a dozen students was Allen Ginsberg, dressed in white baggy cotton pants and shirt, munching on an apple. He passed right by us with his entourage.

"See? It's like this all the time," Theo laughed. "This is where the world is being remade. This is the center of the universe."

We drank coffee in the student union, and he told me about the first Human Be-in the week before. It was this amazing event, he said, where freaks for miles around filled Golden Gate Park.

"Everyone's going to be smoking grass and dropping acid in a year from now," Theo predicted.

Or locked up in one of Paul X's concentration camps, I thought.

Even in Berkeley, the majority of the students I saw on the campus and surrounding streets had relatively short hair, wore conventional clothes, and were mainly clean shaven and earnest.

Theo said he earned what money he needed by going into San Francisco and panhandling or selling nickel and dime bags of pot and hits of acid to students at Berkeley.

We said goodbye, and he gave me an address he was staying at but told me it would probably only be good for another week or two. He was planning on moving but didn't know where.

I couldn't see myself dropping out and living like Theo. I needed more time to figure things out. The first day of my last semester as an undergraduate at USC was about to start. My best chance of staying out of the draft was to go back to Los Angeles and finish my senior year.

On the way to see Kaye, I decided to leave on the overnight train to Los Angeles.

Kaye's friends were out, so we spent the afternoon together in bed. She still had a couple of months free before starting her first term at Berkeley. She wanted to come with me, she said, but I could sense she was torn between leaving with me or staying in San Francisco. I could see what she was seeing in me. I wasn't settled. I had nothing to offer anyone but uncertainty.

I made it as easy as I could for Kaye. I told her I had to go back to Steve's to pick up my stuff. I said she could meet me at the train station if she wanted to.

Right before I left for Steve's, Kaye told me that running away from me in Los Angeles had been a colossal mistake. "I'll meet you at the train station by ten. I promise. We can take a sleeping car back to Los Angeles. I love you."

I was elated.

Of course, she never showed up.

CHAPTER 61

I spent the night in San Francisco's Union Station, writing stream-of-consciousness free verse about losing my mind while stuffing myself with candy bars from the newsstand, hoping against hope that Kaye would eventually appear. I saw no point in phoning her once the last night train left. I knew it would be stupid to go to her friend's place. She wasn't coming even to see me off.

That was okay. She was doing me a favor. I had to do what she was doing—get myself into the moment and do what was best for me.

Of course, it wasn't okay. I was miserable, but I had to move on.

In the morning, I hopped on the first train to Los Angeles. It was a milk run that took twelve hours.

The trip was astonishingly beautiful. The tracks ran along the coastal cliffs and beaches in places far away from the Pacific Coast Highway. I saw large parts of the coast I had never seen before—sheer rock faces where only birds lived, pristine beaches without people or footprints, tiny coves where pirates may have left buried treasure, and occasionally, a cabin on the mountainside overlooking the ocean where I could imagine living, loving, and writing.

I felt miserable without Kaye, without someone to love and someone who loved me. I wanted to be sitting next to someone I felt close to looking out the window together, seeing the amazingly beautiful scenery for the first time.

I envied how easily she had let go of me and simply gone off to join a different world.

I wasn't ready to be free. Maybe I never would be. The hard truth was I wasn't going to find that part of myself that I needed to find by looking for it in someone else.

I welcomed the idea of reentering the cocoon of my little house and rejoining the friends who still remained. The postcards with my grades—one from each of my professors—were in my mailbox when I arrived home. Dr. Davis had come through, giving me a C in Statistics II. A C in graduate school was as good as an F, but all it meant for me as an undergraduate was a passing grade.

My A in Social Psychology, B in Industrial Psychology, and pass in my pass-or-fail physics class balanced off the C in statistics, giving me a 3.0 for the semester, the lowest since my first semester as a freshman. My cumulative grade average was still well above 3.5, enough to make high honors at graduation if I didn't totally screw up my final semester. I was a fraud, of course. I wasn't a genius in anything. I was just smart enough to figure out the system and game it. For the most part I had taken easy classes. I had also saved the easiest for my last semester.

My lineup of new classes was almost all electives. I had a writing workshop with Glenn Meeter, a painting class, a freehand drawing class, a psych seminar in mental hygiene, and a senior colloquium in philosophy and science which was supposed to be a no-brainer, pass-or-fail requirement course for idiots.

I had already missed the deadline for applying to the top grad schools in psychology. To hedge my bets, I decided to take a shot at social work, which I thought would be easy enough that I'd have time to write on the side.

I applied to UCLA and UC Berkeley. Both were publicly funded state schools. Since I had changed my residency to California when I turned twenty-one, I could attend them at a fraction of the tuition cost at USC.

I began working again at the Boys Club a few days a week.

I also landed my first paid writing job.

Dr. Floyd Ruch, my industrial psychology professor in my fall semester, had been impressed with a paper I wrote on advertising. Ruch was one of the pioneers in the field of industrial psychology and was also the author of the most widely read psychology textbook in America—*Psychology and Life*. It had been in use in colleges and universities across the country as the basic Psychology 101 text for decades. Ruch had just published the seventh edition and was already getting ready to publish the eighth edition. He phoned me and asked if I'd like a writing job. I said yes before I knew what the job was.

When I found out, I was relieved. It was something I was sure I could do. My new job consisted of reading his latest text and writing a series of multiple-choice questions for each chapter for a workbook for use by professors and instructors who taught Psychology 101.

It paid well, and I could work at my studio and turn out the material at my own pace. I was thrilled.

Maybe I wasn't a complete fraud. I had gotten a liberal education, and I kept writing. I had perfected a skill that I could use to earn money. All I had to do was keep writing.

I rarely attended classes with two exceptions—my painting class and my life drawing class. The subjects in both classes were female models, mainly in the nude but sometimes wearing ethnic or historical costumes. Each model worked for several sessions and then was replaced by another. We worked with a half dozen models during the next four months.

By then, I had been painting with oils for five years, so, I was surprised when my painting professor told us we were going to work in acrylics, a relatively new medium.

Painting with acrylics was perfect for me. The paint barely smelled and required only water to clean up instead of turpentine. The new kind of paint also dried quickly. It was an excellent medium for working fast or painting quickly over mistakes. Because the material was porous, even large globs of paint dried all the way through within hours instead of forming a skin like oil paint and taking weeks, even months to fully dry.

"Draw less and think less about telling a story. Think more about color and about what you see in front of you," my painting instructor, Keith Crown told me. He was a respected abstract painter. I experimented with different colors as background against the image of the model posing for us for each class.

I often sketched the same models in my evening drawing class with Morton Dimondstein that I had painted in the morning in Crown's class. Dimondstein, another well-regarded professional painter and sculptor, was fun to be with. While Crown was grumpy and didn't seem to like teaching, Dimondstein loved having people around him. He wanted us to draw what we saw. Shapes were important to him. My drawing became more relaxed, more fluid. For the first time, I was beginning to get control over what I drew. I loved the way confidence gave me more control, and control gave me more confidence. Practice was the key to doing anything well.

An older woman, Matilda Moore, in her fifties, who had been a mentor to Kaye and her friends in high school in San Marino, heard about me from one of Kaye's friends and asked if I would paint a mural in her home.

I went to her place in the Fairfax District and showed her my sketch pad of psychedelic and conventional drawings. She lived in a complex of two-story attached townhouses facing a small, nicely landscaped, common courtyard. She wanted me to paint the floor-to-ceiling front windows looking onto the courtyard. She asked me to do something psychedelic. The painting, she hoped, would work like stained glass, letting in light but blocking the view from the sidewalk when the curtains were open.

I painted the window from the inside, making the giant blocks of color swirl around like interlocking petals of flowers, like nude bodies mixed with leaves and branches. The painting had a matted look, like a giant pastel drawing from inside the house. It looked crisper, almost like stained glass from the outside. In addition to paying me fifty dollars, Matilda gave me the most amazing art book. It was the English translation of a coffee table book called *Pablo Picasso, Les Déjeuners*, with text by Douglas Cooper, and printed by Thames and Hudson in 1963.

The book changed my understanding of art. Picasso's *Les Déjeuners* (Lunches) was a homage to Edouard Manet's painting, the *Le Déjeuner sur l'herbe*, which translates as *Lunch (singular) on the Grass*. Matilde told me the painting had been ridiculed at the time by critics for its depiction of two men, fully clothed, eating lunch on the bank of a river beside one completely nude woman and another scantily clad woman.

The impact for me was seeing such a large collection of work by one artist—Picasso—centered on a single subject. Previously, I thought of art as a linear progression from rough sketching to a finished work. I saw art in terms of control and a goal. The control was the process of getting better—drawing more precise images—each time you attempted a visual work. The goal was a perfection of the vision. The finished painting was supposed to be better than the sketches. Not so for Picasso. The book reproduced all his "Lunch" sketches and paintings between the summer of 1959 and the summer of 1961, just short of the hundredth anniversary of Manet's "Lunch." [56]

It showed Picasso repeating his many different styles from his past—from the lyrical drawings of his early Blue and Rose Periods to classicism, surrealism, and cubism—all of which he was still toying with. His work showed no linear progress in a conventional sense. It was picaresque. Each drawing was a unique play on the Manet theme. *Play* was the important word. I couldn't help seeing the fun that Picasso had creating each drawing and painting. There was no linear progression. There was no goal. Each work looked like he had started fresh.

I wanted to paint and think like Picasso.

By the beginning of March, I had received a letter from my draft board in New Jersey reclassifying me as a student for the current semester.

My deferment would only last until I graduated in three months.

One morning after my painting class, I was walking with a couple of friends across the campus when we saw a movie being shot on the front lawn of Doheny Library. The last time I'd seen a film production on campus had been the previous year when Alfred Hitchcock had shot parts of *Torn Curtain* on the other side of the street between Bovard Hall and Founders' Hall. He had used the buildings as stand-ins for a dreary East German setting from which Paul Newman and Julie Andrews were escaping during the Cold War. I watched Hitchcock strut up and down University Avenue in a dark suit and tie, talking to the lovely Julie Andrews while

Paul Newman chucked a football around with several crew members, waiting for the next take.

This time, my two friends and I couldn't see anyone we recognized in the shoot in front of the library. A crew member between the Von KleinSmid Center and the library pointed out the director, Mike Nichols. Mike Nichols had directed *Who's Afraid of Virginia Wolfe* the year before. He was already an important director but he was hardly a recognizable face.

The film they were shooting now, we were told, was about a recent college graduate. The guy playing the recently graduated college student was short with a big head, a biggish nose, and way too old to be mistaken for anyone my age. His name was Dustin Hoffman. None of us had ever heard of him. It took the film crew an hour to set up everything for a shot of a crowd of extras pretending to be students, strolling out of Doheny and down the front steps.

My two friends snuck behind the extras while the cameras were still rolling. They were excited they might get into the film. The movie was supposed to come out later in the year, but it didn't look like anything I'd want to see. Nevertheless, I made a small mental note in the back of my mind to remember the title, *The Graduate*. I thought I might watch it one day to see if I could spot my friends. I had no idea at the time that the buildings were being used as stand-ins for the UC Berkeley campus, or that the plot of the film was laughably close to my own recent trip to San Francisco to find Kaye. Only, my story had a much different ending.

I began to hang out with a new friend John Beck. I met him one evening when I dropped by the rooming house where Kaye's old boyfriend lived. John was renting a room from him for eighteen dollars a month.

John was an actor. He had grown up on the rural edge of Joliet, Illinois on four-and-a-half acres of woods and vegetable gardens—similar to the environment I had grown up in. Having a common background made it easy for us to relate. We were both rural kids trying to make it in the big city. John was a few steps ahead of me, but we were both poor. John was getting some work by playing the occasional small parts in episodes of *I Dream of Jeannie*, a short-lived series called *Hank*, the soap opera *Days of Our Lives*, bit parts in a couple of low-budget movies, and a handful of commercials, but he was barely making enough to pay his rent, food, and gas for his 350 Honda Scrambler motorcycle.

Like me, he thought the war was a stupid waste. John was two years older than me and very eligible for the draft since he hadn't yet finished his undergraduate degree. He was going to auditions all the time and taking classes at a junior college in the San Fernando Valley to try to maintain his student deferment. Tall, athletic, and handsome with a strong jaw and dirty blond hair, John had at one time been a light-heavy-weight Golden Gloves boxing contender. He had knocked out other boxers in the ring. He was also one of the best-read people I knew, and he had been classically trained for the stage in a highly regarded local theater company in Joliet. He was usually cast in Hollywood as a handsome jock, lawman, military officer, cowboy, and sometimes a tough guy or bad guy.

We hung out quite a bit, eating cheap meals and drinking at dives around town and on the Strip, going to movies, and endlessly talking about films, books, music, and ways to beat the draft. John was also the first person I knew who took the Canadian option seriously. Both of his grandparents on his mother's side had been born in Canada on family farms on the north shore of Lake Erie. He still had great aunts and uncles and second cousins in Canada. He didn't know any of them, but it made Canada seem less remote to him.

John had been a Boy Scout and 4-H'er growing up in Joliet. He had raised a few farm animals, so the idea of homesteading and getting back to nature seemed more genuine than when I heard others talking about it. John had raised a calf to adulthood and helped butcher it when he was a teenager.

"If we don't want to be farmers," he said, "We could get jobs in the forestry industry or in the fisheries."

Going to Canada with a buddy sounded like more fun than ending up in the jungles of Vietnam with strangers. Canada sounded almost possible.

Someone stole the mannikin and the bust of Nefertiti that Kim Charney had given me. They took it right off my front landing in broad daylight. The statues were there when I went to class in the morning and gone when I came home at noon for lunch.

CHAPTER 62

The world's first event called a "Love-In" took place in Elysian Park in Los Angeles on Easter Sunday, March 26, 1967.

I was hanging out with another new friend, Bruce Beery, a senior who was drifting like me toward graduation, trying to decide what direction to take. We had been introduced by Clementine "Pinkie" Van Deusen, a tall, slim junior with strawberry blond curls, Kewpie-doll blue eyes, a pink-white complexion, and splashy clothes that were always ahead of the latest fashion. Pinkie made it her business to discover raw talent on campus and bring people together from different disciplines who might never otherwise meet.

Bruce had just dropped out of USC's School of Architecture after a fight with one of his professors. His new major was sculpture. He was taking a painting class in the studio next to my painting class. He was working on a giant canvas, trying to capture in acrylics the grooves in a record blown up so many times that you could see the words and music in the composition of the grooves.

Bruce looked like a cross between a surfer and a freak with long, blond hair, a handlebar moustache, surplus Army jacket, and jeans. We'd both been to the same school for nearly four years but had never met until Pinkie introduced us. When Bruce mentioned he'd been hashing—waiting tables, washing dishes, and cleaning up—the semester before at the same sorority Kaye had belonged to, I asked if he knew her. Bruce turned out to be the boyfriend before the boyfriend of Kaye's who had preceded me. Small world.

Like John Beck, Bruce was another comrade trying to stay out of the war and live a life where he could create.

We talked endlessly about ways to beat the draft. We told stories of dozens of people we knew who had suddenly come up with medical conditions. We hashed over the idea of signing up for Officer Candidate School. We'd be second lieutenants if we were accepted and passed the training.

The worse thing about signing up was the length of time volunteers needed to serve. Two years if you were drafted; three or four years if you enlisted.

The worst part of going to war in Vietnam or supporting the war machine was the glaring truth that America's involvement in Vietnam was a war crime.

We joked about shooting ourselves or each other in the foot or getting married and having a child—still a deferment. We talked seriously about going to Canada or some other country, going underground in the States, or a combination of these. Neither of us knew anyone who had gone to Canada or to another country.

Of the two of us, Bruce was the most likely to get married first. He was in the beginning of a new relationship with a woman named Karen, who he had just met. He sounded about as crazy for her as I had been about Kaye.

It took a week before I finally met Bruce's new girlfriend, and when I did, Karen and I took one look at each other and started laughing. "So, this is your new friend, the guy you wanted me to meet?" Karen asked Bruce.

"Yeah," he said, not quite knowing where this was going.

"I already met him." She turned to me. "You're the freak my friend Barb interviewed for her sociology paper last semester. "

Karen was the quiet one.

Bruce just stood there with a dumb look on his face until Karen and I brought him up to speed.

Karen was studying fine arts and design. Bruce and Karen were crazy about each other. Bruce had just met her parents. Her mother had grudgingly accepted Bruce, but Karen's father, a World War II Air Force officer and now a high-tech executive, had not been favorably impressed with Bruce's hair, moustache, ideas on the war, or choice of professions, which, of course, made Karen even more in love with him. She had already told Bruce she'd go wherever he had to go. She had nothing but disdain for the war.

Karen had gone to her parents' house in Arcadia for the Easter weekend. Bruce wasn't invited.

On Easter Sunday, Bruce picked me up early in his ancient VW Beetle, and he drove us to Elysian Park around nine to go to the world's first Love-In. The gathering filled a giant grassy, saucer-like part of the park. The park was in the same neighborhood as Dodger Stadium and the Los Angeles Police Academy. The Love-In was meant to be a Los Angeles follow-up of the San Francisco Be-In in January.

The world's first Love-In had been billed over the radio for the past few days as a giant Los Angeles gathering of the tribes of creative people, freaks, love children, flower children, and the curious.

The place was already filling with smiling, happy, colorfully dressed people, many with small children.

Some came with faces painted with sunbursts and flowers. Local Los Angeles bands played on a stage in the corner of the park. One guy brought his parrot, another, his iguana. A sky diver jumped out of an airplane and parachuted into the middle of the park close to where we were standing. Acid and weed were passed around discreetly. So was bananadine, a new substance made from the inside scrapings of banana skins and baked until dry and black.

Smoking bananadine was supposed to produce a psychedelic high. The rumor gained momentum in late November 1966 when one of Donovan's biggest hits, "Mellow Yellow," was released in the US as a single. Looking for legal alternatives to marijuana and LSD, the bananadine craze increased in popularity all winter in Los Angeles. With a shortage of weed throughout the city around the time of the Love-In, due mainly from the surge of young people starting to trip, ovens around the city began to work overtime in the apartments and houses of freaks, trying to dry enough banana skins to make a substance that could be smoked.

Unfortunately, no amount of baking could do much to make banana skins burn like tobacco or weed. And the only high anyone got from bananadine was purely a product of the fertile imaginations of the idiots who tried smoking it, including Bruce and me. Nevertheless, it gave everyone who tried it the feeling of omnipotence, not from any psychedelic effects but from being able to smoke bananadine joints in the open.

Openness was the unwritten theme of the Love-In as the Spring of Love got underway.

Everyone at the Love-In was peaceful, smiling, and flashing peace signs to everyone. Some passed out food, flowers, and the occasional joints with real grass as a few cops stood around the edge of the gathering—apparently with orders to do nothing but report back if any real trouble broke out.

No one was there looking for trouble, and soon, the cops were smiling and chatting with the gentle freaks. Counterculture families held picnics on large blankets, looking like they had just stepped out of a painting by Georges Seurat, Maxfield Parrish, or Edouard Manet.

Refreshingly, no one was selling anything. There were no food or drink stands, no trinkets or T-shirts for sale, no walk-about peddlers. Spontaneous musical events sprung up around the great bowl as individuals or small groups played impromptu gigs with drums, flutes, guitars, cymbals, and bells, while others swirled around dancing and laughing.

The gathering had achieved what it had set out to do—bring together thousands of people with no other purpose than to have a peaceful afternoon in the park together.

We ran into dozens of people who we knew—Pinkie and her sister, the folk singer Pam Polland and her friend Betsy, who used to hang out at the house on 32nd Street before the bust; John Beck; Don the photographer who had introduced me to Kaye; and others we knew from different circles. It was easy to meet anyone who passed by. Everyone was smiling and friendly. One of the most interesting people Bruce and I met was a photographer named Jay Thompson. We watched him photograph the sky diver who floated into the center of the park. We came upon him a second time while he was snapping photos of people walking by. It was obvious from the equipment he was carrying that he was a professional.

Bruce and I stopped to talk.

Jay was short, about five feet six or seven, with medium-length, dark brown hair, clean shaven with a round face and a dozen years older than us. He was with a stunning woman named Indus, a young model who I later learned was supposed to be having an affair with one of the Everly Brothers.

Jay and Indus seemed to know a lot of people. Someone was always stopping to talk with them. Bruce and I wandered off but kept running into Jay. He gave us business cards and told us to keep in touch. He was there taking photos for a book he was planning on freaks and hippies.

If there was a turning point when the underground came out and moved above ground, this was it for me. Thousands of freaks had come to the park. The idea of creative people being part of an eclectic tribe that might be able to help save the planet from humankind's greed and stupidity appealed to me. I felt a sense of power from all the beautiful, interesting people wandering around that day. Maybe good change was possible.

The trouble with the Love-In was it ended. It had to. We had to go back to our everyday lives. But it left me with a sense of hope. I wanted to believe that the simple message of peace and love could overturn the war machine.

In those early months of 1967, it seemed possible that we could simply change the world by thinking differently as we innocently hurtled toward what would soon become known as the Summer of Love.

CHAPTER 63

Just weeks after the Love-In, I fell in love with Gabrielle, a brilliant, beautiful woman with dark, cat-like eyes and long, straight, raven-colored hair. She appeared in my art class one day as our newest model.

Gabrielle was aloof when she posed, seemingly lost in her own world, oblivious to the eyes riveted on her.

Male and female art students alike were mesmerized by her. All the other models were old. One model, Cleo, was so old that one of the art students said Cleo had been the model for her mother's art class back in the 1940s, and she was old then. Gabrielle was our age, young, vibrant, and mysterious.

In my drawing class late in the afternoon, we drew portraits of Gabrielle in black ink with Chinese paint brushes. Dimondstein complimented me on my drawing to the class. For a second, I felt Gabrielle's gaze on me as Dimondstein talked about my work. Her look was instantly exciting, like a jolt of electricity.

Our paths crossed outside the art department the next time she came to pose. She was there early, standing beside the door to the building smoking a cigarette. I stopped to talk with her. She was warm and funny. The distant look she wore when she posed vanished. She told me I was the first person at USC who had ever bothered to talk to her.

She ended up at my place that evening.

I told her how all the guys were crazy about her but were afraid to approach her.

She had been modeling nude at USC, UCLA, and art departments elsewhere in the city for a couple of years. She was two years older than me. Her father had been a radio writer in New York when she was growing up. The family moved to Hollywood in the 1950s when her father began writing for television in the early years of the new medium. Gabrielle had been a beatnik since leaving high school six years before and had lived for long periods in Greenwich Village, sometimes hitchhiking back and forth between New York and Los Angeles, and posing for art classes at universities whenever she ran short of money. Posing nude was always in demand. It was a portable job she could take anywhere.

Her passion was art and design, but she had no formal training. She was living with her divorced father for the time being in Studio City a couple of blocks away from Garry's house.

I was mesmerized by her free spirit. She didn't care what anyone thought. She made love when she felt like it, smoked pot, and was toying with opening an antique shop. She wanted to specialize in the arts and crafts and the art nouveau movements, eras that had struck a strong chord with the new wave of psychedelic artists.

For the next few weeks, Gabrielle and I wandered the city, checking out the antique and secondhand shops, particularly a cluster of low-end shops in Venice Beach.

She had this idea for creating a wall of old photographs that we found in one of the junk stores. Cartons and cartons of old photos—smallish cartes de visite and larger cabinet cards from the mid-1800s to the 1920s—were randomly thrown together in one corner of the shop. Gabrielle bought several cartons. We spent hours looking through the images, some of children, some of weddings, some of old people who had dressed up in their finest, gone to a studio, and posed in front of fake scenery. We found group shots of early settlers to the California coast near Ventura, and workmen at the turn of the century putting in a street in downtown Los Angeles. Gabrielle showed me a photo of an attractive, stylishly dressed woman on a park bench.

"Paris in the 1890s," Gabrielle said.

"How do you know?"

"You just pick up things if you listen and keep your eyes open."

So, true. I was absorbing information from everywhere, not just school. I couldn't help wondering how many of those long-gone people in the photographs got to live the lives they dreamed of when they passed through on their way to who knows where.

We were still seeing each other when I got accepted to the graduate programs in social work at both UCLA and UC Berkeley. Both offers came within days of each other and with full-fellowships of $2,000, enough to cover living expenses for the nine months I would be in school. I picked UCLA, because I felt comfortable in Los Angeles. I knew where things were. I had friends in Los Angeles. I was hoping grad school in social work would be easy enough so I could spend a lot of time writing and painting.

Free love as Gabrielle defined it was sex and friendship with no commitments. She was not someone I imagined would run away with me. She was just with me until she felt like being with someone else or no one else. She was the one who had insisted on our relationship being open. She liked her freedom as much as she liked sex. I was swept away, fascinated, and attracted to her joy for life and her free spirit.

After a few weeks, Gabrielle left for San Francisco. She said she would phone when she returned. I never heard from her again. I was jaded enough by then not to be surprised.

Bruce and I went to Jay Thompson's house in the Hollywood Hills to see the photos Jay had taken at the Love-In. The black-and-white shots brought back the wonderful craziness of the day—the sky diver, the guy with the parrot, the guy with the iguana, a number of the spontaneous dancers and musicians, Jay's model friend Indus, Bruce, and me, and hundreds of other freaks who had passed in front of his cameras.

The most impressive photos I saw that evening weren't of freaks. They were a half dozen framed photos he had taken that hung on the walls of his living room of famous people like Cary Grant, Bette Davis, and First Lady Eleanor Roosevelt. He had captured a softness in Mrs. Roosevelt's face that brought her to life in the photo. I was impressed. Jay was a pro like the photographers and artists my Uncle Sam represented on Madison Avenue.

Jay was experimenting with new ways to make money. He and his roommate Paul Sheriff, an actor, made hash pipes. Jay and Paul sold the pipes and postcards of Jay's photographs through their own mail-order business. What interested me most was Jay's upcoming book of photographs on the new peace movement. He had been jetting between Los Angeles, New York, and San Francisco, photographing hippie celebrities.

Jay invited me to a party at his place, so I could meet his agent, the West Coast representative for Random House. The agent said he would be glad to read my book once I finished it.

I felt cool and sophisticated. I was making connections in the real world on my own.

I was invited once again to the Rusoff-Arkoff Passover Seder at Uncle Sam and Aunt Hilda's home. It wasn't the dinner or the company that dazzled me this time. Garry, in his usual kindness, realized how little contact I had with my own family. By then I hadn't been East in nearly two years. So, when I showed up early at Garry's suggestion that night, he took me into Sam and Hilda's bedroom, handed me the phone, and told me that I could call home to New Jersey and speak to my family for as long as I wanted. I was reluctant at first since I didn't want to run up the Arkoffs' phone bill, but Garry explained Uncle Sam had a special phone line. For a flat fee each month, he could make calls anywhere in the US at no extra charge. I had never heard of anything like this. It was magic to me, and since it was only five o'clock in California, I was able to reach New Jersey at eight in the evening and talk for free with everyone in my family, something that I would not have thought possible.

Aretha Franklin's hit song "Respect" was released in late April. I was convinced that all the good that would come from the sexual revolution would come from women feeling as free and worthwhile as any man ever felt. How could America be great if it failed to develop the greatest minds of the population regardless of sex, race, creed, religion, or other fake division.

Buddy and Teri, my two friends who had dropped me off in Barstow two years before at the start of my hitchhiking trek across America, were both getting married but not to each other.

Teri was marrying her long-time boyfriend from USC.

Buddy and his girlfriend Terri were also getting married. Buddy had returned to USC and was in business school studying accounting. Terri had transferred from UC Santa Barbara to UCLA. Both couples were planning to get married over the summer.

I continued to hedge my bets by taking the physical and written exam for Officer Candidate School for the Air Force, reckoning that this branch of the service would be the most selective. I still worked out almost daily. I ate carefully. If something was wrong with me physically, then the Air Force would find it, and I might just get a 4-F.

I went to an office building downtown. I checked in and was segregated from the ordinary potential draftees and sent to a separate line reserved for the OCS candidates. I told the doctor about my allergy to bees, my stomach troubles, my periodic disabling headaches, and seeing with one eye at a time. [57]

He told me not to worry. No one cared about little things like that. He assured me I'd pass the physical. He ran me through a series of tests and then sent me to another room to take the written exam.

I whizzed through most of the written exam until I came to the section on mechanics, which I had absolutely no knowledge of. I did have an advantage though. The test was multiple choice. After weeks of writing multiple choice questions for Dr. Ruch's *Psychology and Life* workbook, I imagined I could hear the answers to the questions simply by saying the questions in my head.

I checked off the answers, guessing what I would write if I were creating the test.

I got my notice from the Air Force a month later. They had not only accepted me into the program but assigned me to study aeromechanics, the one subject I had completely faked. It left me wondering if I had passed the test with flying colors by accident or if I had done so poorly that they wanted to upgrade me in this field.

I turned down the offer. Joining the Air Force meant serving for four years. I couldn't imagine joining anything for more than four minutes.

I continued to drift toward graduation, not sure what would become of me.

CHAPTER 64

Allen Ginsberg was invited to read his poetry at USC. He spent several days on and around the campus. He was only regarded as a minor celebrity at my school, known certainly as a famous poet but not idolized like he was in the more intellectual environment of Berkeley.

I had previously mentioned to Jay Thompson that Ginsberg was coming to the campus. Jay said he had just returned from San Francisco where he'd taken photos of Ginsberg for his upcoming book. Jay gave me a message for Ginsberg if I ran into him.

So, when Ginsberg appeared one afternoon at the fountain in front of the library, I decided to approach him.

Ginsberg, a consummate showman, had managed to gather only a few students around him. He was entertaining them by answering questions, signing copies of his poetry collections, and occasionally breaking into a chant or a little dance.

I stood at the edge of the group until I saw my chance to speak with him. I told Ginsberg, "Jay Thompson sends his greetings. He said to tell you the photos he took of you have been developed, and he'll be making prints and sending them to you next week." I was expecting Ginsberg's face to light up.

Instead, Ginsberg frowned. "What photos?" He looked suspiciously at me.

"The ones for his book. You're in it."

"I don't know anything about any book. I don't know anyone named Jay Thompson."

I was startled and embarrassed. I hadn't seen the photos, but I trusted what Jay said.

"The photographer Jay Thompson," I said, but Ginsberg had turned away. A couple of other kids quickly grabbed his attention.

Bummer, I thought, I must have misunderstood the message.

I headed back to my place, thinking that was the end of my Ginsberg adventure.

I was wrong.

My phone began ringing as I started up my stairs. I raced to the door, unlocked it, and grabbed the phone halfway through a ring.

It was Carl Emerich. Carl was a big man in student government, so we normally traveled in very different circles.

"What are you doing later?" he asked. Carl and I had had a sociology course with Dr. Hadwen the year before. Carl was working for the school administration as a liaison between students, faculty, and the administration. He was also part of a campus organization dedicated to bringing important people from different walks of life to the campus. This group was responsible for bringing Senator Robert Kennedy to Bovard Hall in 1965.

"I'm writing a paper for my philosophy class." It was my pass-or-fail class, and I had written nothing and needed to catch up.

"Want to go to a party?"

Carl Emerich had never invited me to a party.

I was curious. "Where? When?"

"It's a small gathering after the Allen Ginsberg reading this evening. We need someone who's a little more far out than the rest of us to make him feel at home."

"A token freak?"

He laughed. "You'd be helping me out, Joseph. We need a few people who won't bum him out."

"I haven't read much of Ginsberg's poetry," I told Emerich. In fact, I had never been a big poetry buff. What I had admired about Ginsberg was his stature in the peace, love, and psychedelics world.

"It doesn't matter. It's just a social evening. We need to show him that we have some people on campus who are thinking about taking different paths than the straight and narrow."

I was flattered. "I'd be glad to go."

Carl gave me the address for the party and told me I could meet him at the poetry reading or just show up at the party.

I decided to go to Ginsberg's lecture and party. I wanted to watch how he performed.

I studied for a couple of hours, cooked, ate dinner, washed up, and changed clothes for my night out.

The decision about what to wear wasn't difficult. I only had one sport coat, a mustard yellow corduroy jacket that I had bought at a bargain store a few months before. It had been marked down to nearly nothing because it was so ugly no one else wanted it. Of course, that was exactly what appealed to me—it was loud, unloved, and well made. I had worn it to the Love-In. [58]

I gave no thought to bringing any grass. For one thing, I was out, and we were in the middle of another pot drought. For another, I was still quite mindful of the bust at the 32nd Street house the previous year. I wasn't interested in calling too much attention to myself.

Or was I?

I had a small mix of bananadine and tobacco wrapped in tinfoil in the fridge. Gabrielle had cooked a batch of banana skins at her father's house and brought it to my place. With the tobacco mixed in, it burned like grass. We smoked it a few times on the outside chance that we might get a buzz. We didn't, but I hadn't thrown it out.

I decided to bring enough of the mix for a couple of joints—along with a pack of rolling papers and matches.

I called Jay before I headed out and explained what had happened earlier when I had spoken with Ginsberg on the lawn outside the library. Jay was as puzzled as I was.

"Ginsberg can be a little paranoid when he's stoned or in a strange place," Jay explained. "People like him are always concerned someone they don't know wants something from them. If you talk with him again, just don't say anything about me or the photos, and you should be okay."

I had underestimated Ginsberg's popularity. The auditorium was three-quarters full. Ginsberg was a superb showman. He loved performing. The audience laughed and enjoyed the poetry and Ginsberg's message of peace and love. I sat quietly at the back of the auditorium, taking in the performance and the audience as he talked about finding one's inner self, being a creative person, and finding cosmic truth. Ginsberg was an apostle of hope and a bearded, doughy cheerleader for living a free and interesting life. He earned his money as a writer and speaker. How could I not be impressed?

I ran into Pinkie after the reading. She was there with two of her friends from the film school. We talked until the hall cleared out. I asked Pinkie if she wanted to come with me, but she and her two friends were heading for a movie and were running late. So, I headed to the party alone. Carl told me years later that he thought the house was Taylor Hackford's place, but he wasn't certain. Hackford was the student body president. He was working closely with Carl and another friend John Sullivan in student government. John Sullivan was the driving force behind bringing some of the most important cultural icons of the day to Bovard Auditorium.

The party was on the ground floor of an old house just off campus on one of the side streets behind the athletic building. [59] [60] [61]

About two dozen people were already there. I recognized about half. They were either faculty, grad students, or student government big wigs. The mix of men and women was about even.

Ginsberg was on the far side of the living room near the front windows. He was sitting cross-legged on the floor surrounded by a dozen faculty and student government people sitting on couches and chairs in a circle hovering over him.

Carl was right. The crowd looked like a convention of off-duty narcs.

Carl, Taylor Hackford, and John Sullivan were halfway across the room, talking to other students and faculty and greeting the late arrivals. I approached Carl and made small talk for a few minutes before he put his hand on my back and said, "Go talk with Ginsberg. He doesn't look like he's enjoying himself."

Ginsberg squinted through his glasses at me as I sat down in an empty chair opposite him about a dozen feet away. I wondered if he recognized me from earlier in the day when I had mentioned Jay's photos.

He spent no more than a second looking at me before politely returning to the conversation in progress. Ginsberg was having an academic discussion about modern poetry and older forms of poetry and fielding questions. Some were the same ones he had answered on the lawn outside the library earlier in the afternoon. I wondered how many times he had to answer the same questions.

He was polite but looked disinterested, like he couldn't wait for the night to end.

I glanced over at Carl. He frowned and gestured with his hands, palms up, as if to say, do something. Anything. Lighten things up.

Since I had absolutely nothing smart to say about Ginsberg's poetry, and I wasn't about to bring up Jay Thompson's photos again, I took out my stash of bananadine, rolling papers, and matches and slowly and methodically began rolling the perfect joint.

Ginsberg carried on with his conversation but never looked away from me. I was quite skillful at rolling joints by then, which must have been entertaining to this audience.

As the joint took shape in my hands, Ginsberg stopped talking and simply stared at me, eyes full of anticipation, mouth partially open. Several of the others close by purposely turned away, pretending they didn't see what I was doing. They were talking to each other in increasingly loud voices as if someone (me) was undressing in public.

I was having fun, knowing that I was in no danger of getting busted for bananadine. I was also enjoying the look of curiosity on Ginsberg's face.

When the perfect joint was finished, I lit it, took a hit, blew out the smoke, and then held the lit joint out toward Ginsberg. "Here, Allen, try this."

The conversations on the entire first floor of the house had completely stopped by this time. Ginsberg looked around for a second to see if it was okay to take the joint from me. Everyone else in the room seemed frozen in time, pretending not to see, unable to take their eyes off of us. Unable to speak.

"It's okay," I coaxed him.

Ginsberg moved close enough to reach out and take the joint from my fingers. Without hesitating, he put it to his lips and inhaled deeply.

"Have another toke," I said, when he tried handing it back. He exhaled, took a second hit, and waved the joint around offering it to anyone who wanted it. Each person he made eye contact with turned away. As quickly as it had stopped, the conversations around us started again, but no one was looking at or talking to Allen or me.

I slid to the floor to be on the same level as Ginsberg as he passed the joint back to me. I could see the expectant look on his face as he waited for the first buzz. Others sitting around us got up in ones or twos and wandered off to refresh their drinks or talk with someone else.

"What is this shit?" Ginsberg asked me in a low voice, eyes wide and puzzled.

"Bananadine and tobacco," I told him. "Sorry. It's the best I could do. Everyone I know is out of pot. I thought, if I lit up, someone else holding might light up." I looked around at the others who continued to ignore us. I laughed. "Apparently that's not going to happen."

Ginsberg lowered his voice even more and said, "I got some good stuff on me. You think they'll mind?"

A few people were watching us from a distance. I saw Carl standing on the other side of the room grinning at me.

"I don't think anyone here would know the difference."

Ginsberg smiled and pulled from his pocket a worn, brown leather billfold with lots of compartments. I watched as he sifted through the folds until he found a thin, flattened joint.

"This is good shit, man," he said. "You only need a couple of tokes." He gently rolled the flattened joint between his fingers to make it round again, then lit it, took a hit, and passed it to me.

I took a hit, waited, and blew out the smoke.

He said it was a mix of grass and hashish.

A few of the bolder students and faculty wandered over to where we were sitting and sat down again. We passed the joint back and forth between us a couple of times, blowing smoke in the air. Ginsberg offered the joint again to everyone who made eye contact with him. The others shook their heads no, but they stayed this time and watched.

Ginsberg and I laughed and tripped. The others smiled. Ginsberg started having fun, chanting away, clacking his little hand cymbals, and beaming at everyone like the Cheshire Cat.

A couple of the student government kids began chanting with Ginsberg, first as a joke, but soon I could see they were having fun, letting themselves go, getting into something that they hadn't done before and didn't quite understand. They seemed to be enjoying a contact high.

Ginsberg showed several of us how to entwine our fingers and turn them in a certain way to create a lotus flower.

The party turned into a real celebration, with people talking to each other and to Ginsberg like an ordinary person instead of a celebrity.

I stayed long enough to get him to write out all the words of his trademark "Hare Krishna" chant on a sheet of paper. He signed it at the bottom "to Sr. Joseph." He also drew a symbol which he said was a guide for me to follow. It was a triangle with an eye in the middle and the bodies of three fish, each coming off each of the sides of the triangle, so it appeared to be three fish with one head. "It's an ancient symbol of humankind, best known as the Buddha's Footprint," Ginsberg explained to me.

I was having fun, but I was getting tired and could feel one of my bad headaches coming on. I needed sleep.

The party was still underway. Ginsberg was smiling and talking with a couple of the students. I said goodbye to Carl and a couple of others in student government. Before heading for the door, I glanced one last time to flash a parting peace sign at Ginsberg as a way of saying thanks for the smoke, the talk, and the drawing.

He saw me out of the corner of his eye and interrupted his conversation to address me. "Nice meeting you, Joseph. Tell Jay I'm looking forward to seeing his photos when he sends them next week."

Hahahaha, I laughed as I wandered home. Ginsberg knew what I was talking about during our afternoon encounter. He didn't know me then. He couldn't trust me. Now, he trusts me.

Even famous people like him didn't feel safe. If a government list of dissidents existed, his name was surely on it, and maybe mine, too.

CHAPTER 65

Throughout the first half of the year, the music had been pushing the popular culture toward the idea that love could win over war. The sounds simply washed over us, cleansing the past, alluding to a better future or Armageddon if humans didn't get their shit together.

In addition to the Doors' debut album in early January 1967, the psychedelic rock of the Beatles' single B-side, "Strawberry Fields Forever" and the A-side "Penny Lane" made our heads spin and our hearts sing.

In February, the positively surreal and electric second album of the Jefferson Airplane, *Surrealistic Pillow*, with "Somebody to Love" and the utterly mind blowing "White Rabbit" echoed a feeling that great changes were coming.

Late spring brought the highly influential, haunting, slowed down, hard rock version of an older Supremes' hit, "You Keep Me Hanging On." It was the first single by the Vanilla Fudge, a Long Island band.

The Beatles upliftingly wild *Sergeant Pepper's Lonely Hearts Club Band*, released at the beginning of June, promised peace, love, and goodwill to humankind. All we had to do was believe it hard enough. At least three songs on the Sgt. Pepper album, "Lucy in the Sky with Diamonds," "A Day in the Life," and "With a Little Help from My Friends" appeared to be making overt references to the power of mind-expanding substances.

Bob Dylan had reappeared in our midst after a horrendous motorcycle accident the previous summer. I saw him a few times along Sunset Strip, twice at one of his favorite watering holes, Fred C. Dobbs, named after the Bogart character in the film *The Treasure of the Sierra Madre*. No one bothered him. But I could admire him from afar. I wanted to live like he did. Create songs that helped others see clearer. If I asked him for advice,

I was pretty sure what he'd say: Figure it out for yourself. Do a lot of writing.

The spring of 1967 seemed like one long coming-out party for the love generation, led by our beloved troubadours. The hippies were no longer living in a secretive underground of the previous year. The media couldn't get enough of the story. The freaks-hippies-heads, the music, and the anti-war sentiments were news. So were the busts.

In January, Bruce Palmer, Canadian bass guitarist and founding member of the Buffalo Springfield, was arrested for marijuana possession and deported to Canada.

On February 12, the police raided the home of Rolling Stones' guitarist, Keith Richards, and arrested and charged Richards, lead Stones' singer Mick Jagger, and his girlfriend, pop singer, Marianne Faithful, with various drug offenses.

The Lovin' Spoonful was permanently crippled when guitarist and singer Zal Yanovsky and bassist Steve Boone were busted for marijuana. Yanovsky, a Canadian about to be deported, was said to have given up his drug dealer to keep out of prison. He returned to Canada to start a new life.

The celebrity busts weren't only limited to drug infractions. During the early part of 1967, Beach Boy Carl Wilson had been drafted. He was busted for draft evasion when he refused to take the Oath of Allegiance. He was held in custody for five days in May. He was out on bail, but he faced a precarious and uncertain future. Early in the spring, another war baby, boxing's heavyweight champion of the world, Muhammad Ali, refused induction into the military on religious grounds, arguing that he had "no quarrel with those Viet Cong." In June, he was fined $10,000 and sentenced to five years in prison. He remained free on appeals. Celebrities with money, I noted, had different options than the rest of us. I had no doubt if I simply refused induction, I would spend years in the slammer.

Karen took Bruce and I to a showing of a film called *Ladies and Gentlemen...Mr. Leonard Cohen*. She told us, "If we end up in Canada, we should look this guy up." He was a poet and all-around cool guy that few people had heard of living the life of a writer in Montreal. I was taken as much by Cohen as I was with the style of the film. It had a personal intimacy that I found enticing. I wondered what it would be like to go to a place like that and make small, intimate films.

Beach Boy Brian Wilson abandoned the *Smile* album by the spring of 1967. Some said he had a near nervous breakdown. He was depressed as he continued to argue over money with his old record company and tried to work out artistic differences with his bandmates. David Anderle and Mike Vosse were no longer on the payroll, but soon, Mike was telling me about a new gig he had, working with Derek Taylor on something called The Monterey International Pop Festival.

"It's going to be the biggest gathering of freaks ever," he insisted. "You can come and work backstage. Nothing like it has ever been done before."

CHAPTER 66

Derek Taylor, the Beatle's first publicity agent and mentor to American film and music royalty since moving from London to Los Angeles in 1965, was one of the brains behind the Monterey International Pop Festival, along with promoters Al Pariser and Benny Shapiro, musicians Mama Michelle and Papa John Philips, producer Lou Adler, and a number of iconic musicians who acted as figureheads. Those supporting the project from behind the scenes included musicians Paul McCartney, Mick Jagger, Brian Wilson, Donovan, Smokey Robinson, Johnny Rivers, and Paul Simon, and producers Andrew Loog Oldham and Terry Melcher.

John Phillips of the Mamas and Papas wrote "San Francisco (Be Sure to Wear Some Flowers in Your Hair)" and gave it to Scott McKenzie, his friend and former folk-singing band mate when they were part of the Journeymen. Released on May 13, "San Francisco" was number four on the Billboard Hot 100 in the US by the first week in June. It was virtually a three-minute commercial for the Monterey International Pop Festival and San Francisco. It reenforced the idea that San Francisco was the new Mecca of sex, drugs, and rock 'n' roll despite the Haight's declining reputation among those who had been there in the past few months.

Derek Taylor was in charge of the communications for the festival. Mike Vosse was the editorial assistant on the full-color program for the event.

Jay Thompson was also planning to cover the festival for his much-talked-about book. Jay planned to drive to the festival and camp out with a few of his friends. He invited me along. He planned to stay for a few days.

Mike Vosse asked me several times if I wanted to go with him to help out as a volunteer backstage or work with David Anderle, ferrying celebrities to and from the show. I thought about it. It was tempting.

During the weeks leading up to finals, spontaneous Sunday mini-gatherings of the tribes became a regular event in Griffith Park as the hippie-freaks and motorcycle gang members peacefully swarmed the mountain park and turned it into a giant Love-In and Smoke-In for a few hours.

Everyone was friendly. There were twenty times more hippies than Hell's Angels. And no cops. The cops stayed away.

An enormous Human Be-In was also in the works for the Grand Canyon over the summer. I was thinking of going to that as well.

I didn't think the war was going to end just like that, but I did feel we could be witnessing the start of the end.

I didn't have any real finals—neither of my art classes nor my writing class had finals. Marks were based on papers for the rest of my classes.

This is the way school should be, I thought as my undergraduate years came to an end.

Physically, I felt like I was at or near the center of the universe of the people who might change the world, push back on the war, push for civil rights for everyone, and solve the growing menace of pollution.

My health was the best it had been. I regularly did laps around the track behind the athletic building and worked out with several football players at the school gym. The Air Force had found nothing wrong with me. In fact, they had listed my height as five ten, the tallest I had ever been. I weighed a hundred and thirty-five. I was ready and primed for something big. I had to get started being a writer or I might never do it.

I gave up the job at the Boys Club because I was pretty sure I could make it through the summer on the savings from my writing job with Dr. Ruch. If things got tight, I would get another job. At the moment, I wanted to just feel what it was like to live a free life as a writer and painter.

My mother wrote that one of her friends in the township owned a big advertising agency that did a lot of work for Johnson & Johnson, the makers of first aid equipment and medical bandages. He told my mother I should write to him. I wrote a brilliant letter. J&J had recently come out with flesh-colored bandages, but they were all light tan—flesh colored for white people. I thought this was crazy. They needed to have at least five different flesh toned bandages. I wrote that having different colored bandages would help remind people that humans come in different colors. I pointed out that they would sell more bandages if more people could relate to them. I sent off the letter and waited for the reply.

I also sent one of my short stories to the *Evergreen Review* hoping to earn a little extra money over the summer.

I skipped my graduation ceremony and headed to New Jersey by plane. I hadn't been to New Jersey in two years. I owed my parents a visit. I was hoping I'd have time to get back for the pop festival in Monterey.

I felt accomplished, polished, finished, and ready for life as I boarded the plane in Los Angeles and headed for Newark. I was a member of the college class of 1967, *magna cum laude*, Phi Beta, Kappa. I was settled in California. It was my home. I was ready to take on the world.

CHAPTER 67

"The love business," as my mother called it, had been irking her long before I arrived home. She wrote me in one letter, "By the time this letter reaches you, there may be another girl. Gosh, you really had your pick of faces and shapes. Wonder who will get you finally—and even at that, I'll bet it won't be final. You are much too hungry & thirsty for an answer—but that's what will always keep you young—at least in mind—if you don't wear out the body."

A couple of weeks later, she wrote, "Do be careful & don't get too drowned with that love bit. It's good but—people are people and some are sincere and some are not."

The plane ride was my first cross-country trip by air. I could travel the three thousand miles in hours instead of the three-to-five-day, bone-jarring ride by bus or car. Prices for commercial jet travel was so cheap, even I could afford to fly.

Several of the passengers were in military uniforms. None of them looked happy. I wondered if any of them knew they weren't saving the world. They were fighting a war and dying by the hundreds each week because the government was lying to America. I felt bad for them.

My old world in New Jersey had changed dramatically in my two years away from home.

My mother was stretched to the limits working two jobs and looking after my father and sister.

My father looked terrible. He weighed even less than he had two years before. His skin was gray. He was so shaky that he could barely walk. He shuffled around the house like someone crossing an icy street, afraid he might fall at any moment. Even with his food cut for him, he had to work hard to get each bite on his fork and then struggle to get the fork from his plate to his mouth. My mother said that she didn't know what would happen when he could no longer feed himself.

"Maybe the operation will help," she told me. My father had been accepted conditionally for a second time by Dr. Irving Cooper at St. Barnabas in the Bronx for the brain freezing technique. The new date hadn't been set yet.

Dad had mixed feelings about the operation. His friend, who had owned the Esso station at the top of our hill, had had the operation, and it hadn't done much for him.

At fifty-six, my father was scared, angry, and humiliated by life.

And he still had to go through a series of tests with Dr. Cooper's team before getting final clearance for his surgery.

My brother and my new sister-in-law, Linda, had moved out of the house and had their own apartment in a leafy part of Plainfield.

I naturally thought I would have my old bedroom to myself, but in the year since my brother moved out, my mother began using the room as a storage area for antiques, old family photos, fabrics, second-hand designer clothes, costume jewelry, her stamp and coin collections, extra linen and towels, blankets, and packages of socks and underwear for the family, bought at discount clothing stores in Plainfield and on the highway, which she planned to dole out in the years to come.

"That's so you won't even think about coming home," my mother told me when I questioned her about the junk piling up in the room.

The basement was even worse than my old bedroom. The finished cellar with the wet bar and my guns and swords on the walls was packed to the ceiling with leather, fur, factory equipment, and boxes of gloves they couldn't get rid of when the factory closed. My father's favorite chair and the old couch were stacked with my mother's collection of old and new *Life* magazines she saved when the basement had been flooded with heating oil and later with water. I was happy to see that some of the boxes with my mother's drawings from the 1920s and '30s had survived the floods.

I moved enough of my mom's treasures and junk to reclaim one of the twin beds in the boys' room. I stayed until my father's appointment in the city and drove him in.

He saw several doctors at St. Barnabas. At the end, Dr. Cooper told my father and me that Dad was an excellent candidate for the operation, because his mind was sharp, and he was younger and fitter than most patients they saw. Cooper said his secretary would send Dad a letter indicating the next available date for the operation.

On the way home, my father talked a bit more. He asked me if I had enough money. I told him I did. He asked me if he should go through with the operation.

I wished I was strong enough to tell him yes, but I couldn't, because I couldn't say what I would do. The only thing I was facing was whether to go to war or not. I took the coward's way out, telling him, "I don't know what you should do because I don't know what I would do."

We talked a little about my plans for the future. My mother had warned me Dad thought I had defrauded the University of Southern California by taking their scholarship money and not becoming a doctor. He wasn't mad at me, just disappointed.

I tried to reassure him that I would be all right and the school had no quarrel with me changing majors.

"You're smart. I hope you know what you're doing," he said.

I hoped so, too. "Don't worry," I told him. "I'll be okay."

We drove in silence for a few minutes before my dad added, "I wish I could help you out more. But I have nothing to offer."

"You helped by letting me be myself," I said.

My father nodded and disappeared behind his Parkinson's mask for the rest of the ride home.

"I'm glad you two didn't fight," my mother said. "I think you were a good distraction for your father."

"He asked me if he should have the operation. I told him I'm not sure."

"I think he should. If it were me, that's what I'd do, but I told him the final decision has to be his."

The two jobs my mother was working were bringing in enough to pay the mortgage and put food on the table. She told me the same thing she had told me each time I had gone home. "Don't come back. You'll never be happy here."

She was right. I wouldn't be happy in New Jersey, and I couldn't help her.

My sister Daisy said Dad hadn't lost his sense of humor. She saw him one day answer the front door to two evangelicals. He started to speak before they could, telling the holy solicitors he was a poor, sick man who needed money from them right away. He told them he knew they had been sent by God and held out his shaking hands palms up as if waiting for the coins to rain down. The proselytizers turned and left without a word.

As strong and athletic as my father had been before he got sick, he was also kind and had a soft spot for the underdog. I was lousy at just about every sport I tried with the exception of swimming when I was young, and that took me years to master. I could not catch a ball to save my life because I could only see with one eye at a time, so I had little depth perception. I had been hit in the head and knocked out by baseballs a half dozen times. In high school, I had gotten a concussion from a dodge ball that left me with blinding headaches ever since. If I did manage to catch a ball when I was younger, I almost always sprained a finger or a wrist. Yet, my father never made me feel bad about being a poor athlete. He never tried to humiliate me into trying harder.

"You should love him more," I scolded my mother as we got ready to leave the house the next day.

I knew where the thought came from. I was talking about myself.

My mother gave me a dirty look. She saw right through me.

My father was already asleep in the middle of the morning in front of the television. Since the business had closed, his life had been sitting in front of the TV and dozing. He had nowhere to go and nothing to do.

I followed my mother outside to her car. She was on her way to Fab-ricLand, so, she was able to drive me to North Plainfield to catch the next bus to New York.

"It isn't easy to be lovey-dovey all the time," she said as she drove.

"I know. I'm sorry. I wish I could do something to make Dad feel better without giving up my own dreams."

"The only thing you can do is live your own life. That's all any of us can do."

I wondered what she'd feel if she smoked a joint instead of puffing on one of her cigarettes. What would she be like if she dropped acid?

"You're not for the war, are you?" I asked.

"Of course not. Don't be silly. I don't believe in dead heroes. Just stay in graduate school, and you'll be okay."

She had told me many times how the war had changed her two brothers. Uncle Joe had become introverted. Uncle Sam had become erratic and boisterous.

I hopped out of the car just as the bus approached the stop.

"And none of that dope stuff," she called after me.

"Peace and love," I shouted, grinning, and flashing the peace sign before hopping on the bus to the city.

I wished she could leave her life of disappointment behind. I wanted desperately to believe that I wouldn't be disappointed by life. I wanted to believe I had an inalienable right to pursue happiness.

CHAPTER 68

My old high school friend, George, had an apartment on West 68th Street, close to Central Park. He said I could crash at his place for as long as I wanted.

George was the only high school classmate who had written to me after I left New Jersey. Like me, he had gone through seven or eight different lives since we had been in high school. To be closer to his high school sweetheart, he had dropped out of Ripon College in Wisconsin and moved in with his parents for a year while commuting to Upsala College in East Orange, New Jersey. George lost a year in the transfer and expected to earn his bachelor's degree in five years, a year after me. Two months before I arrived on his doorstep, his high school sweetheart broke their engagement. George quit college, got a job as a junior researcher at *Time* magazine, and found a great apartment near Central Park West.

He was learning everything he could about journalism by day. At night and on weekends, he was dating several young women he had met since moving to the city. It did not surprise me. George was movie-star handsome, bright, funny, and easy going. Half of the girls in high school had crushes on him. Now, he had his feet on the first rung of the ladder of the news business.

An old knee injury, which kept him off the football team in our senior year in high school, now guaranteed him an exemption from the military. His life was good, leisurely, smart, stylish, and everything that I had dreamed of when we had graduated from high school four years before. We sat outside at a place near Central Park drinking beer after he finished work. He was on his way up in the world of button-down shirts, ties, sport jackets, and suits.

Long-haired, bearded, and colorfully dressed hippie-freaks were barely in evidence in the high-rent districts around the park. I was dressed down, in a button-down shirt, white jeans, leather boots, and a moustache. I wasn't trying to stand out. This was not hippie land. Most people passing by were men and women wearing business clothes and carrying briefcases. The suits still ruled the Upper East and West Sides and most of the rest of America.

I wondered how many people passing by spent even a minute each day thinking about the war.

I had lunch with my Great Uncle Lew at his club. He had been writing me on average once a month for the past three years, always enclosing some sage advice and a ten-dollar check. Although everyone in the family thought he was fabulously well off, he confided to me that life as a commercial real estate broker was a mercurial business.

"I'm in a slow period right now. Few deals are closing," he told me. He'd been living off his capital for the past year. He told me the life of a writer was even worse because unless I was one in a million, "writers starve to death. You'll never have enough to take a girl out for dinner."

His advice on women continued to be to love them and leave them. He had been tough on the samples of my writing I'd sent him, calling my short stories juvenile with no reader interest. "You need to travel, live, and learn more. Like Jack London." He thought Jack London was a writer I should read and emulate.

He was even more concerned about the war and how I was dealing with it than about my writing. He had warned me from the start that, in his words, Vietnam is going to be "a long draggy messy war." He seemed to know things about it that even my most paranoid friends hadn't told me. He wrote earlier in the year that he had heard on good authority that 20-25 percent of shipments to the war zone were being stolen or sold on the black market. "You'll only have a fifty-fifty chance of living if they send you to the hell of Vietnam." He predicted that in the fall of 1967, President Johnson would call up the most draftees ever. General Westmoreland wanted another 100,000 men. Uncle Lew thought the president would probably send 60-70,000 over. "Remember I warned you," he told me. "Join the Navy. It's the safest place to be, and they have the best food and quarters."

I didn't dare tell him I was seriously thinking about going to Canada. He was having too much fun introducing me to his cronies in the real estate business as a recent graduate of USC, *magna cum laude* and a Phi Beta Kappa.

"Every decision you make now is irrevocable," he warned me. He saw life as a very fixed pattern. Choices were made, hard knocks overcome, and reality meant I needed a practical career that would one day allow me to get married, support a family, and put some savings away for my old age—if I was lucky—his words.

I wasn't so sure. Uncle Lew was fifty-one years older than me. His world was a half century behind mine. I thanked him sincerely for the lunch. I left him with his illusions of me, wondering how much of a disappointment I would turn out to be.

I understood that he didn't want me to make the same mistakes he had made.

I wouldn't. Or I would.

I wanted an excuse to just let go and find out if I could make it as a writer.

I wondered how moral a writer had to be to write something moral.

CHAPTER 69

My parents, brother, and sister would be momentarily saddened if I died in Vietnam or anywhere else, but their lives would go on. No one cared if I went off to war and was killed. I would disappear into the ether. Occasionally, someone would say, "Poor Joe," and for a moment, think about me. This wasn't unique to me. Anyone with a conscience and awareness knew at some point in their lives that they lived outside of whatever the fuck everyone else believed and thought. We were alone in the end, traveling from birth to death in our own little body-like spaceships, making contact with other body-like spaceships when we could.

The next day I had lunch with my Uncle Sam. He began to talk about the Vietnam War as soon as we sat down in the restaurant. "Get out of it anyway you can," he told me. "It's total bullshit over there. They'll use you for cannon fodder. They don't know what they're even trying to do in Vietnam. Go to Canada if you have to. Don't let them take you."

I repeatedly reminded myself he had been a combat soldier, a POW, and a Purple Heart and Bronze Star recipient during World War II. And he was wholeheartedly against the war in Vietnam. He was smart and successful and working on Madison Avenue.

"Of course, the government has concentration camps set up for kids like you. Of course, they have lists. They have to. They're clueless about what you kids are doing and thinking. Stay in school as long as you can," he said as we parted after lunch.

The next day I went to lunch with him again at another one of his favorite restaurants. It was during the early hours of the Israel-Arab War of 1967. No one could predict the outcome. The radio news was being broadcast over the restaurant's sound system. As we were eating, a story broke about a major clash. Sounds of gunfire mixed with static over the radio. Sam jumped to his feet and began yelling, "That's it, that's it. The start of World War III." He sat down again, barely noticing that the entire restaurant had gone dead silent. "We might have to go and fight there," he told me quietly, and then ate another bite of his sandwich.

It took a minute for the other patrons to stop staring and return to eating, It took a few minutes before the din in the restaurant returned to its former volume.

Uncle Sam would have recited his name, rank, and serial number if I had asked him. He had done it before. He told me it had been seared into his brain. He would never forget it. He had been interrogated several times in the month he had been a POW. He had been marched across Germany and into Austria where the Nazis were intending to use the POWs as slave laborers during their last stand in the mountains. One night on the long march, he fell into the hands of several fanatical young Nazis, who had joined the march. They wanted to execute Sam because they suspected he was a Jew. He was grabbed by them and taken behind a barn. Sam was only saved because the commander of his prison group, a German sergeant in the regular army, stepped forward to prevent it.

Everyone in the family knew Uncle Sam could act a little crazy at times.

My mother's words echoed in the back of my mind, "None of the boys who went overseas during the war came back the same."

I headed to Chinatown late in the afternoon.

George and I were meeting there for dinner at a Chinese restaurant he said he liked. He had given me the address. As I walked along a side street that the map said would take me to Mott Street, I suddenly recognized the block I was on as the same one where my mother, brother, sister, and I came across an old man lying on the sidewalk being kicked and yelled at in a foreign language by a tough looking young man.

I was ten. My brother was fourteen. My sister was five. My mother was walking ahead with us while my father parked the car. We were a couple of blocks from our favorite Chinese restaurant. We always ate at the same place on the second floor in the middle of Chinatown. My grandfather had been friends with the family that started it. He knew good food and he promoted it to his friends. The children of the original owner still recognized my mother and always gave us the best table in the place.

The tough-looking, wiry Asian teenager, probably a few years older than my brother, was kicking the old Asian man as hard as he could. The Asian man was curled up in a ball.

Without hesitating, Mom dropped Daisy's hand, walked right past my brother and me, and stopped right in front of the tough. "Leave him alone," she said in a timbre powerful enough to stop a train.

The thug turned and gave her a look like she might be next.

"Shame on you," she continued, staring right back at him. "He's no different from your grandfather or father. Go home to your family. Or go to your friends. It doesn't matter."

The thug continued to stare.

"Go, get out of here." She waved her hand at him like she was shooing flies.

The thug backed away without a word so we never knew whether what my mother said had done the trick or if it was just the sound of her voice and the look she gave him. We had no way of even knowing whether he understood English.

The old man reacted much like the thug. He said nothing and wanted nothing to do with us. He waved away any attempt by my mother to help him up. He got up slowly on his own and walked away, limping past my dad who had just caught up to us. My father thought my mother should have waited for him. "You could have gotten killed." She shrugged it off and said to everyone, "Let's go eat. I know what I'm having. Does anybody else?"

I ran into George a block from the address he gave me. I showed him the downstairs shop my brother discovered that sold firecrackers under the table to him.

It turned out George had discovered the same restaurant my family had been eating at for years. I hadn't remembered the name, but as soon as I saw the front of the building I recognized it. Small world.

I tried to think what my mother would feel deep down if I went to Vietnam and died. She would be sorry, but she would survive.

By the spring of 1967, the US and South Vietnamese had knocked out most of the airbases in North Vietnam and destroyed about half of the North Vietnamese MIG fighter jets, but the ground war seemed to be an endless grind of back-and-forth battles pitting the US and South Vietnamese troops against North Vietnamese regulars and the Viet Cong, the wily and effective underground army of resistance.

On June 12, the Supreme Court issued the landmark civil rights decision *Loving v. Virginia*, ruling that laws banning interracial marriage violated the Equal Protection and Due Process clauses of the Fourteenth Amendment to the US Constitution.

CHAPTER 70

I tried to contact everyone on the list Jay Thompson gave me to phone in New York. He called them "fellow tribesmen." I was to tell each one the same thing. "Jay said to tell you your photos are almost ready."

The first number I called was Paul Krassner, the editor, publisher, and founder of *The Realist*, the first of the modern underground tabloids of the 1960s. Krassner had been a child protégé on the violin and wrote for *Mad* magazine. He had invented for my generation the irreverent, cheeky journalism that mixed leading-edge news stories with satire and humor.

The Realist was one of the first publications to support a woman's right to an abortion, the legalization of pot, and civil rights for homosexuals (the term "gay" came much later.) He wrote about his own LSD trips, the only drug, including tobacco and alcohol, he consumed at the time.

Krassner became an early and ongoing vocal critic of the Vietnam War. He was responsible for forcing the mainstream media to pay attention to the war and America's illegal support of it shortly after President Kennedy's assassination. [62]

Krassner was particularly horrified by the widespread napalming of civilians. He blamed President Johnson and actively attacked him like a pit bull.

Jay thought Krassner would "dig" meeting me. Jay had called Krassner on other business before I left Los Angeles. Jay told me Krassner would be expecting a call from me.

Although I only read *The Realist* sporadically, the writing style and content influenced my own writing and the writing of legions of other writers. Krassner's writing was intimate, gutsy, raw, funny, and yet clear as glass and informed. His newspaper was news and his personal diary.

If only I could write like that.

Each time I called, Krassner was either out or tied up. When I did reach him, he apologized and asked me to call back. When it was clear he was too busy to see me, I stopped calling.

I didn't know at the time that he was in the middle of a firestorm surrounding the May issue. I would learn more about this later in the summer when I finally met him.

I met with one of Jay's contacts in the film industry.

Bob Margouleff, the co-producer, and a few of his friends had been shooting an underground film earlier in the year when Jay visited and photographed them. By the time I arrived, the film, *Ciao, Manhattan*, had spun completely out of control. The star of their film, Edie Sedgwick, was being uncooperative. She had just run off with a photographer, leaving the film without its star. Margouleff had to halt production because of money problems. Margouleff and everyone in his studio were depressed and in no mood to entertain some kid like me fresh out of college, even if I was Jay's friend.

I was disappointed to strike out with the second of Jay's contacts, but in a weird and unexpected alignment of the stars, I would meet Edie Sedgwick later that summer with the photographer she had run off with.

On Saturday night, my friend George and I had a few drinks before dinner. He had a date later. So, I phoned the last of Jay's friends, an artist named Paul Thek, from a pay phone in the Village. Thek said I was welcome to come by, but it had to be that evening as he was leaving for Fire Island in the morning and wouldn't be back in the city for a week.

The sun was setting as I headed from the West Village to the East Village. I saw fewer and fewer long-haired freaks as I traveled east. The streets got seedier, poorer, and tougher by the block.

I passed near the place where I had spent the night with Evelyn four years before. I wondered if she was still in Ibiza. Happy, I hoped.

An old man wobbled along the empty sidewalk on the other side of the street. He appeared to be drunk. As soon as he saw me, he started crossing the street, heading straight for me with his hand out.

I kept my eyes on the sidewalk and kept walking. The air that night was hot and sticky.

A drunk or junkie in ragged clothes lay in a fetal position in a doorway sleeping with one arm under his head as a pillow, the other stuffed between his legs.

A couple of young, punky looking men came toward me on the sidewalk and made me step out of the way. They laughed as they passed by, and for a second, I thought they were going to stop and hassle me.

I had walked in tough neighborhoods in Los Angeles and New York before. Usually, I felt safe. That night, I was getting enough bad vibes from the street that I considered turning around and heading back to the West Village. Instead, I talked myself into continuing.

It was dark, and the bad vibes continued to grow by the time I reached Thek's building. It was on East Third Street, a few blocks south of Tompkins Square between Avenues B and C. I peered through the open front door into the darkened lobby, A couple of tough-looking young men about my age were hanging out, passing a paper bag between them, sticking their faces in the bag, and inhaling.

Glue sniffers, I thought as I forced myself to keep walking like I belonged.

The stairwell was dark and smelled of urine and mold.

I kept going, stepping over the outstretched legs of a sullen teenager sitting halfway up the staircase.

A middle-aged derelict sat on the top step, leaning against the wall, nodding to some tune in his head as I passed by.

I found Thek's door and knocked.

"Who is it?" I recognized the same soft voice I had spoken with earlier on the phone.

"Jay's friend."

I heard several locks being unlatched.

I'm safe, I thought as the door opened inward.

I stepped inside so quickly I didn't really look at Thek until he was closing the door and relocking the multitude of locks.

Paul Thek was tall and thin and in his mid-thirties with long, straight blond hair held in place with an Indian headband. He had a big blond moustache, blue eyes, and was dressed in jeans and a white hippie shirt that hung loosely around his waist. His voice was warm, soft, and friendly. The overall impression I got was of a soulful Nordic freak with more than a passing resemblance to the Swedish actor, Max von Sydow, a favorite actor of film director Ingmar Bergman.

The apartment was small, hot, and rundown with only one lamp burning in a corner that shed more shadows than light on the darkened bare walls. It was also clean and safe compared to the derelict hallway. Thek introduced me to a clean-shaven, dark-haired man about my age in jeans and a T-shirt, sitting cross-legged on the floor in the corner of the room. He had the lid of a shoebox in his lap and was separating the leaves from the seeds and stems of a couple of hefty handfuls of grass. Thek's friend, looked up, gave me a grin, nodded, and continued to clean the grass.

"Come with me. I'm just finishing up," Thek said heading into a second brightly lit room.

It wasn't until I walked through the arch and crossed the threshold that I saw the dead man, half naked lying on a long table.

I had no question in my mind that the man was dead. He had that unmistakable bloodless pallor of the dead bodies I had seen at the funerals of Uncle Tony and my childhood friend, Johnny. At the start of my second year at USC when I worked with Buddy at the library, Buddy had made friends with a campus handyman who had the keys to the lab where the dental students worked on cadavers. The handyman invited Buddy to have a look. Buddy had invited me. The cadavers all looked like the dead man in Thek's apartment.

I fought against a sudden feeling of icy fear. I tried to take stock of what I was seeing. I told myself to be calm. The room appeared to be part kitchen and part laboratory with shelves lining the walls filled with jars of multi-colored liquids, paint brushes, carpentry tools, hoses, and surgical and other instruments I couldn't identify.

Thek nonchalantly fiddled with some tubes between the corpse and what appeared to be an IV drip containing a dark, bluish liquid.

"How is Jay doing?" Thek asked as he worked. "Have you seen the photos he took of me?"

Does he think I don't see what he's doing?

His nonchalance made me shiver. My legs trembled.

"I haven't seen your photos," I said, trying to keep my voice from giving me away, "but Jay said the contact sheets look good."

"How do you know him?"

I explained as briefly as I could, trying to sound like I wasn't the slightest bit nervous. The only windows in the apartment were along the wall on the other side of the table looking over the street. Jumping was out of the question.

"Sorry. This must not be very interesting for you," Thek said wiping his hands. "Let's go sit down and talk."

I edged backwards into the living room, telling myself, maybe if I just pretend like I hadn't noticed what he's doing I'd make it out of there alive.

"Sit down," he said, gesturing toward an old stuffed chair near the door. The cushions and springs were so shot that I would have sunk down into a near fetal position if I sat back too far. I perched on the edge of the seat while Thek sat opposite me. Thek's silent friend lit a joint and handed it to Thek, who took a hit and held it out to me.

"No thanks," I said, wondering if the dead guy in the kitchen had been drugged first before he'd ended up on the table.

I was more wary by then, than scared. I scared easily but I also recovered quickly.

Use your head, I told myself. Think.

Thek shrugged, handed the joint back to his friend and at the same time asked him, "Would you mind making some tea?"

Thek's friend, grinning, went to the kitchen to make tea beside the corpse. Thek continued to ask me about Jay, Jay's book, who else I had seen in New York, and how I happened to be back East.

While I was talking, I kept trying to remember something Jay had said to me back in Los Angeles about Thek.

Then, it hit me.

Jay hadn't said Thek was an artist. Jay said he was a sculptor.

Oh, my god, oh, my god, I wanted to shout and laugh at the same time. That isn't a dead hippie on the table in the kitchen. It's a life-sized *wax sculpture*.

I started to laugh right in the middle of something Thek was saying. It was a completely inappropriate place to laugh, but being high, he just laughed right along with me.

"You're a wax sculptor," I said.

"Well, yes, among other things," he agreed, laughing along with me without knowing what I was thinking.

After I stopped laughing, I had some tea, shared some of their grass, and stayed for a few hours talking art and life with the East Village artist while his friend rolled more joints, made more tea, smiled a lot, and never said a word. [63]

I left Thek's apartment feeling good. The bad vibes were gone from the street as I passed by the night crowd—the young couples out on dates, families and old people out on the stoop in the middle of the night because it was too hot to sleep inside, the toughs and the down-and-outs not paying any attention to me when I passed by. New York was still wide awake as I made my way to the subway to the calm of George's West Side apartment.

George was back from his date. We stayed up for a couple of hours drinking beer and talking about an idea that he had for a modern magazine that would concentrate on interviews with young, up-and-coming statesmen, artists, and scientists to bring the latest ideas to the thinking class.

George and I had breakfast together the next morning. I left his place feeling good, knowing that George would never be drafted. Neither of us had any idea he would be snatched by the military by the end of the summer, sent to Vietnam, and shot and seriously wounded three weeks after landing in country. [64]

CHAPTER 71

I flew back to Los Angeles and began hearing about the Monterey International Pop Festival, first from Mike Vosse, and then from Jay Thompson, who stayed longer and took a side trip to the Haight.

Mike brought back amazing tales of old and new musicians who had played there. The Beach Boys had cancelled, but no one seemed to care. The headliners and familiar names like The Byrds, the Mamas and Papas, Scott McKenzie, and Simon and Garfunkel were great, but the excitement buzzed around newcomers—Big Brother and the Holding Company with their lead singer Janis Joplin; the Grateful Dead; Otis Redding; The Who; and Jimi Hendrix, who had set his guitar on fire.

"Thousands and thousands of kids, people like us, are smoking dope, dropping acid, and waking up to the idea that we can change things if we just get together," Mike insisted.

Jay made a detour to San Francisco before returning to Los Angeles. The concert had been mind-blowing. He wasn't as happy with what he saw in the Haight.

He had seen more of what I had witnessed on my trip to San Francisco in January—a hundred times more school dropouts, desperate people, hustlers, pimps, and Hell's Angels.

The same thing was happening in Hollywood and on Sunset Strip.

Moustaches were suddenly in. The Beatles wore them on the album cover of *Sgt. Pepper's Lonely Hearts Club Band*.

Bright colors, clashing colors, amazing colors were in, often against a background of white which highlighted the splashes of color.

I went to a Beverly Hills optometrist and bought a pair of gold-filled, wire-rimmed glasses like John Lennon. They were the first glasses that suited my face. They were just like the glasses my Uncle Sam wore during the war. Now, those glasses were a symbol of the anti-war movement.

Bruce was busy making plans to head to Berkeley in August. He moved out of the room he had been renting and camped out in a sleeping bag on the floor in my walk-in closet. He was spending so much time with Karen and working at odd jobs that I hardly saw him.

John Beck had vanished. No one had seen him after he moved out of his rented room in the old house behind the USC playing field. I suspected John had been drafted and was either in the Army or on his way to Canada.

Canada.

People talked about it, but I still hadn't heard of anyone going there.

Jay was running around in a dozen different directions at once, working on his book, and making and selling pipes and postcards through his trading company. He was advertising in a dozen underground papers on both coasts. He was working on a scheme to manufacture psychedelic body decals. He was also working on a technique for developing black-and-white prints of his photos on canvas and turning the pieces into pop art. He intended to cut the negative and attach it to the back of the work to prove it could never be duplicated. He had already perfected a way to print portraits on medium-sized canvases.

He photographed me in a vacant lot in Hollywood for his book and his postcard business. The lot was overgrown with wildflowers, some almost as tall as me. He was toying with ideas for new postcards entitled "Flower Power" and "Flower Children."

"We need to band together and form some kind of tribe or urban commune for creative types," he told me.

I thought of the commune at Aptos. Jack said I could return anytime. I wondered if it would be possible to go underground in Los Angeles.

CHAPTER 72

The Beatles' single, "All You Need Is Love" was broadcast via satellite to 400 million people in twenty-six countries around the world on June 25, 1967. The broadcast was blasted over the first live global television link. The single was released in the US on July 7, 1967, another of the poem-songs released since the start of the year, promising something magical.

The following day, I went to an afternoon party that Jay had told me about. It was at the home of Dick Dunn, a TV producer of soap operas like *The Young Marrieds*, *The Secret Storm*, and *General Hospital*.

Dunn's house was on the south side of Mulholland Drive, the ribbon of two-lane blacktop that twisted and turned along the top of the Hollywood Hills. Dunn's house and pool overlooked Beverly Hills and was packed with young up-and-coming Hollywood actors, actresses, and other beautiful people. Jay was there with Indus. They introduced me to Dunn and a half dozen beautiful young people, including a beautiful model and her boyfriend. The model had drawn a giant flower on her face with green and blue eyeliner. Her eye was the center of the flower. The stem ran halfway down her cheek.

In one of the side rooms talking to two beautiful young women I spotted John Beck.

I was stunned to see him. I thought for sure he had been drafted or gone to Canada.

He saw me in the doorway and yelled, "Hey, Joe." He was excited to see me. He introduced the women to me as actresses in one of Dunn's shows. They wandered off as John started telling me about his life since he left our old neighborhood.

The draft hadn't gotten him after all. He had called my apartment in Los Angeles a number of times when I was in New York to tell me he was moving. He had no way of leaving a message. He knew I was graduating and figured I had left town.

He'd been making good money acting in commercials and small parts on TV in the last few months. One of his commercials was for Head and Shoulders shampoo. It was airing in the fall. John was getting enough work to pay for an apartment right off the Strip. He had been staying at Dick Dunn's house for a couple of weeks and was moving into his new place in the middle of the month.

His worries about the draft hadn't disappeared. He was on even shakier grounds than previously since he had dropped out of the classes he'd been taking in the winter.

"I signed up for a few more classes in the fall. I'm hoping that will cover me," he explained.

When he found out I was planning to move closer to UCLA, he suggested North Beverly Glen Boulevard. It was a lot like Laurel Canyon and much closer to UCLA.

"You can walk to UCLA, if you have to," he said.

I took note. My garage and a number of the buildings along University Avenue were slated to be torn down soon for the USC redevelopment project, so I had to move somewhere. My nine-year-old Volvo was on its last legs. I wasn't sure it would make it through the summer. I had enough money to pay my rent and eat for a few months but replacing my car was out of the question.

I had been looking for a place closer to UCLA and had visited a few rentals along Wilshire but hadn't found anything I liked that was affordable.

So, I headed to North Beverly Glen on Monday morning to take a look.

The first half mile of North Beverly Glen Boulevard was considered prime Bel Air acreage with several winding streets branching off to the east and west. Dozens of walled and gated estates of the rich and famous lined the streets.

Bel Air chicness vanished as the road began to twist like a snake up the side of the hill where the canyon grew much narrower. The next mile and a half—what most people called the Glen—was a two-lane blacktop road winding through a steep narrow canyon with modest houses, many not much more than shacks, nestled among old live oaks. The Glen was a throwback to an older, more rustic Los Angeles when residents built cottages in the leafy hills as hunting shacks and getaways from the settlements in the flatlands of the basin.

For most of the day, few cars passed through the Glen. The only real traffic came from brief swells during rush hours in the morning and evening during the week from commuters traveling back and forth between the Los Angeles basin and the Valley. The only commercial establishment for a mile in either direction was a country store halfway up the hill on the Los Angeles side. Otherwise, residents of the area had to go to Westwood or the Valley for groceries. John Beck told me, a restaurant was supposed to open somewhere along North Beverly Glen, but he wasn't sure where or when.

I drove from Sunset Boulevard to Mulholland Drive and back again, then up again and down again and onto several small side streets without seeing a single for-rent sign.

I was discouraged but not ready to quit. I gave it one last try. I stopped at the small country store halfway up the hill.

The place was called Odie's. It had the same feel and size as the country grocery store at the top of our hill in rural New Jersey.

Both the cashier and only customer in the store lived in the Glen. Both were friendly and talkative. The customer, a weathered older man in work clothes and a cowboy hat, told me about an old lady down the road who rented out places.

"Look for the sign that says piano teacher," he said.

I found the sign and the house hidden by a wild, jumbled garden that filled the front yard. The trees formed a canopy over the fieldstone path to a small, shingled, barn-like building set against the side of the canyon wall.

The old lady who answered the door was a tall, thin, ancient beauty queen with a brightly painted face, red-red lipstick, and a long blond wig sitting slightly askew on her head. She was the music teacher and owner of the property.

I told her I was hoping to find something for September or even August. I was paid up until August on my garage apartment at USC.

"I have a place but it's available now," she told me.

I asked to see it.

The rental unit was a wooden, shingled shack attached on one side to the main house. A wall of windows ran across the front, looking over the garden. The door at the side opened into a long, narrow room that ran the length of the shack. Near the door was a primitive gas stove with two burners and no oven, an ancient refrigerator, a sink, a scarred oak table, and two chairs. At the other end of the front room was a desk, chair, and a single fold-up iron cot that could serve as a couch by day and a bed at night.

I followed the landlady through an archway. A curtain of beads separated the front room from a small square room with a skylight. Beyond that was a bathroom with a shower, toilet, and sink, and a large storage space beside the bathroom.

The ancient lady told me her piano was on the other side of the wall of the square room with the skylight. "I teach piano, and I practice when I feel like it but not too late or too early. If that's going to bother you, you might not want to take it."

I assured her the piano playing wouldn't bother me. I told her I stayed up late and typed a lot at night, because I was writing a book. My typing, she said, wouldn't bother her.

The rent was eighty-five dollars a month, more than double what I had been paying, but I couldn't let it go. I needed to get out of the smoggy basin. The cabin was a firetrap, but so was my old place, and the Glen apartment was bigger than my garage apartment and was in the middle of a small Garden of Eden.

She agreed to let me start renting in the middle of the month. I gave her a check and told her I'd be back on moving day, a week away, with my possessions.

It was the perfect place to write and paint.

CHAPTER 73

I was supposed to take possession of my new place at 1224 North Beverly Glen Boulevard on July 17. That morning, I was organizing my stuff to see what I would take first when I got a frantic phone call from Bill Phelps.

"I need your help right away," he said, sounding distraught. He explained that he was supposed to drive Edie Sedgwick to Hollywood, but his VW bus had broken down in Malibu, and he couldn't find anyone to help him. He was calling me from the pay phone at a service station on the Pacific Coast Highway in front of the old Malibu Ranch. "I need you to pick me up, drive back to my place, and pick up Edie. It's really important to me. I'll explain when you get here. Hurry."

I hopped in my car and drove out.

I'd met Bill Phelps toward the end of my senior year through my friend Pinkie, the collector of interesting people. Phelps was living with Sepp Donahower and two others in an old store converted into a giant crash pad. It was across from the USC athletic field on McClintock Street, a block from where John Beck used to live. Sepp named it the Café Hideaway (aka the Hideaway Café). People were always dropping in, and Sepp, Bill and the other roommates threw a lot of parties.

Bill Phelps was in the film school and part of the tight-knit group of budding filmmakers who would make a major impact on Hollywood in a few years. They included future directors/producers George Lucas, John Milius, and Randal Kleiser; budding director and cinematographer Caleb Deschanel (one of Sepp's and Bill's roommates), and budding film editor Walter Murch. They all worked on each other's student films. Bill was one of the most promising auteurs of USC's School of Cinematic Arts. In May, right before the end of school, I had attended the special screening of his film *Gemini at Midnight* at Bovard Auditorium with Pinkie.

Bill was still mourning the loss of his film when he called me to help him. A few weeks before, he had been on his way to meet Andy Warhol in New York to show him his film, hoping Warhol might finance a feature-length movie. During the trip, the only print of his minor masterpiece had been lost with his luggage by the airline.

Tall and thin with bushy, long, blond hair, William Walter Phelps III, was a real New York and New England blueblood who wanted nothing to do with his past. [65]

As a teenager, he had been a protégé of Andy Warhol and a pal of Edie Sedgwick in New York before finally being sent to the other side of the country to USC film school by his father in hopes of separating Bill from the Warhol freaks. [66]

Bill had introduced Sepp to the Warhol crowd. Sepp was a wild-looking, long-haired, blond, surfer type, who rode a motorcycle around campus and came from a wealthy Palos Verdes, California family, He had been the star of Phelps' first film. He had ambitions of being a professional celebrity photographer.

Sepp met Edie Sedgwick in New York when she was filming *Ciao, Manhattan*. When she decided to drop out of the film, she headed to California by car with Sepp and a friend of Sepp's, and Edie moved in with Sepp at the Hideaway Café when they reached Los Angeles.

Edie had been there about a month.

I knew exactly where the gas station was. Bill had invited me out to the Malibu Ranch on several occasions. He had been staying there off and on as rehabilitation after the loss of his film. A friend of his lived there with a couple of children in one of the ranch houses. She was a member of the family that owned the vast estate, which ran all the way up the hill past the seminary on top and for miles in each direction. I had stayed there a couple of times earlier in the year, sleeping on a couch in a small house on the property. The pretty young woman with the kids told me mountain lions still roamed the hills. [67]

Bill was pacing back and forth in front of the gas station phone booth when I arrived. He jumped into my Volvo as soon as I pulled up.

"You don't know how much I appreciate this," he said.

"What's the rush?"

"Edie wants to leave Sepp, but she's afraid to tell him. She wants to move out. She asked me to help her move when Sepp's not home. I think maybe she's afraid of hurting his feelings. If I do this, I think I might have a chance with her. We have to go back to my place, pick her up, and take her to the Castle."

"The Castle?"

"A house near Griffith Park. She has friends staying there."

Bill was worried he'd already failed to rescue Edie, or she'd found someone else to help. He'd just called the Hideaway, and no one had answered.

"I don't know what's going on at this point," he admitted.

I was intrigued by the idea of driving the getaway car for a fading Andy Warhol superstar. Over the next half hour as we headed to USC to find Edie, Bill explained that a friend of Edie's, Nico—I thought he said Nicole—had moved from New York to Los Angeles and was renting a house called the Castle in the Hollywood Hills. Nico, another star in the Warhol firmament, had invited Edie to stay with her after Edie and Sepp had visited the Castle a few times.

The only obstacle Bill saw against Edie falling in love with him was Jim Morrison, the lead singer and driving force behind the Doors. Bill explained that Edie met Morrison at Nico's.

A few nights before Bill called me, he heard banging on the front door of the Hideaway. "Everyone was asleep," Bill explained. "I got up to see who was knocking. I found Morrison outside pacing back and forth. He didn't want to come in. He wanted Edie to come out. I went inside, woke her up, and she went outside and talked to Morrison for maybe twenty or thirty minutes."

"Now, she wants to move out, and you think you have a chance with her?" I asked Bill.

He shrugged and gave me a shy grin. "I just hope Sepp's not at home when we get there."

Sepp's motorcycle was parked out front. I pulled my Volvo to the curb right behind it.

"Just don't say anything," Bill said, hopping out before I turned off the engine. I headed inside a short distance behind him.

The Hideaway was a pigsty. Clothes were strewn about on the furniture and the floor. Dirty dishes, pots, and pans rose above the top of the sink and covered the countertop. A couple of half-eaten meals on plates sat on the kitchen table mixed in with books and Sepp's camera equipment.

Sepp and Edie were both there. Sepp was in a shirt and chinos, his long, dirty blond hair flew off his head in every direction. He was rushing around, getting ready to leave to meet someone.

Edie was dressed in panties and a near see-through, dingy, white T-shirt with nothing underneath, walking around with a coffee cup in one hand and a cigarette in the other. She was definitely not ready to go anywhere.

It was easy to see why Bill was knocked out by her. Her smile and big bright eyes made her face light up like sunshine. She was delicate and thin and moved with the smoothness of a dancer or a cat in heat. Even saying hello to me, shaking my hand with a soft handshake, checking me out with her big curious eyes felt like she was almost rubbing herself against me, sizing me up.

Sepp barely gave me a glance. He was busy looking over some 8x10 inch black-and-white photos spread out on a table. While Bill and Edie wandered off to a far corner of the room to talk, I moved closer to Sepp to get a better look at the photos. I recognized the face in one of the photos immediately. It was the model I had met at Dick Dunn's party the week before who had painted the flower on her face.

"That's Anitra Ford," I told Sepp, certain it was the same woman.

"You know her?" Sepp sounded surprised and excited, noticing me for the first time.

I explained how I met her. [68]

"I didn't have any idea who she was. I just spotted her at a park and took her photo. Here," Sepp said handing me the print. "Give this to her."

He immediately snatched the print back and wrote his name and phone number on the back along with a short note. "Tell her I'd like to meet her," he said.

I nodded. I didn't tell him that I really didn't know Anitra. Nevertheless, I would try to get the photo to her through Jay or Dick Dunn.

Sepp showed me a few more prints, including a few of Bill Phelps when he had been directing his lost opus, *Gemini at Midnight*, and one with headshots of Warhol and Nico, the blond singer who had rented the Castle. Sepp took the photos when he was in New York. He handed me six more photos with no specific instructions after signing several.

Just as he finished handing me the photos, Bill and Edie joined us beside the table.

Bill gave me a slight nod of his head to indicate that the great escape was still on, and Edie gave me a big, sweet smile like I was suddenly the nicest guy in the world.

Sepp took off soon afterward, and almost immediately, Edie pulled on a pair of slacks and threw some clothes and toiletries in a suitcase.

I carried the suitcase to the car and put it in the trunk. By the time I got back, expecting to take more suitcases to the car, she and Bill had decided to leave the rest of her things behind, worried that Sepp might return early and catch Edie packing.

We hopped in my car and were soon on our way out of South Central, heading toward the hills with me driving, and Edie and Bill in the back seat—she, looking a little spacy; he, with his arm around her, grinning like he had just won an Academy Award.

As I drove the getaway car into the hills, she thanked me enough times to make me feel like I had just helped her escape Alcatraz.

We were relying on Edie's directions. She had been to the Castle with Sepp, but he had always driven her on his motorcycle or in a car borrowed from one of his roommates.

We got lost for about a half hour but eventually found the Castle. It was high in the hills on a steep, winding street near Griffith Park at 2630 Glendower Avenue, north of Los Feliz Boulevard. [69] [70]

The Castle was a two-story house built in the 1920s. I parked on the street in front of the entrance. The outside of the house was shabby, with weeds in the yard in front. The walls needed patching and a paint job. Rundown as it was, it was a vast improvement over Sepp's place.

After retrieving Edie's suitcase from the trunk, I followed Bill and Edie inside into a large, light-filled living room with only a few pieces of old Tudor-style oak furniture scattered about. The ceiling was quite high. The bedrooms were upstairs.

I arrived just in time to see Edie disappearing upstairs with some guy who looked a lot like Jim Morrison. Bill was talking to Nico, a tall blond with a pale complexion.

Bill introduced Nico to me as she breezed past on her way through a door on the ground floor to what I imagined might be the kitchen. I still hadn't gotten her name right and told her, "Nice to meet you, Nicole," noting she didn't seem very friendly.

"That was Morrison," Bill whispered to me, nodding toward the stairs where Edie and the fellow had disappeared.

"You want to take the suitcase upstairs?" I asked, holding it out to him.

"No. Just leave it. She'll be right down."

I put it beside the stairs, and Bill and I sat in the living room and waited.

And waited. And waited.

A record player in the corner of the room was playing a Dylan album. The view through the windows at the far end of the living room provided a nice panorama of the smog-covered Los Angeles basin.

Bill kept glancing at the stairs, waiting for Edie to return.

After a half hour, Edie came downstairs alone. Bill jumped up, and they had a short conversation out of my hearing range before she disappeared upstairs again with her suitcase.

"She says she's going to take a nap," Bill told me. "We can hang out if we want."

Since the person who Bill said was Morrison still hadn't reappeared, I wondered if he was included in the nap. I was for leaving, but Bill wanted to stay. I agreed.

We sat like two dunces and waited, much like two characters in one of Warhol's films.

After another half hour, Nico returned carrying a notebook. She glanced at us as if wondering why we were still there. She sat at the other end of the living room at a table without saying anything to either of us as she wrote in her notebook.

At one point, I asked her what she was writing.

"Lyrics," she said in a way that told me she didn't want to talk. She wanted nothing to do with a couple of college kids, especially someone like me who kept calling her Nicole. [71] [72]

Edie never returned to the living room while we were waiting. Finally, Bill asked me if we should go, and I said, "No sense hanging around. I have to get back to pack anyway."

Nico barely glanced at us when we said goodbye.

By the time Bill and I left, Bill had good-naturedly shrugged off his chances with Edie, but he remained upbeat. He told me Andy Warhol was supposed to be coming to town the following week. "There'll be a big party. You can meet him," he insisted.

CHAPTER 74

The Plainfield riots, the second worse riots in New Jersey, started on July 14, two days after the larger Newark riots began.

The Plainfield riots started after a fight broke out involving some Black teenagers and young adults at the White Star Diner on Front Street, the same diner that I had eaten in after Sunday school in the early 1950s when my father's factory had been located on West Front Street and Grant Avenue behind the diner.

The violence started when a white cop, moonlighting as a private security guard, refused to assist an injured Black teenager. Soon, a hundred and fifty or more Black youths assembled in a nearby housing project parking lot, met with a Black council member, and then took to the streets for several hours throwing rocks at store windows and police cars.

The riots continued off and on over the next two days with looting and Molotov cocktails being thrown at fire trucks responding to incidents.

Police from nearby towns were called in. Riots and looting on a much smaller scale broke out in Scotch Plains, Somerville, and New Brunswick.

On Sunday night, a white policeman chasing looters into one of the projects, shot and seriously wounded a twenty-three-year-old Black man, who would eventually recover. The policeman was not as lucky. He was knocked down, stomped, shot with his own revolver, and died within the hour. A man and a woman would later be convicted of murder and sentenced to life in prison.

A nearby arms factory, The Plainfield Machine Company in Middlesex, which made military style rifles for civilian use, was raided. Forty-six M-1 style carbines were stolen and distributed among the Black community.

A fire station came under siege for five hours and was finally relieved by National Guardsmen in armored personnel carriers. Three hundred heavily armed Guardsmen and State Police searched sixty-six homes without warrants. Only three of the guns were recovered at that time.

A hundred Blacks were arrested during the riots.

My mother, always hopeful, thought there had to be a lesson somewhere from the riots. She wrote to me, "Good will must prevail, if the human race is intended to exist."

At the end of July, my father heard his operation had been scheduled for the end of August. Dr. Cooper intended to drill a hole in his skull, insert a needle, and freeze part of his brain.

General William Westmoreland also announced he was winning the Vietnam War but needed more troops. A few days later, President Johnson gave the go-ahead to send another 45,000 troops to Vietnam, close to the number my Great Uncle Lew had predicted.

I never did meet Warhol. Nor did I see Edie, Nico, or Jim Morrison again. I was too busy moving to the Glen and setting up my new home.

I felt even more like Thoreau at Walden Pond in the Glen than I had at my old place. Flowers, bushes, and trees of many different kinds and colors hid the street from the front room of my cabin. The air was fresh and alive with the aroma of blossoms and earth. I could hear the sound of bugs during the day. At night, the buzz of the insects was like a full-blown orchestra, reminding me of the symphony of sounds that came off the wetlands beside our house in New Jersey in the summer. My bank of windows opened to the garden. The hanging eave of the roof covered the windows enough so when it occasionally rained, I could still leave them open. It felt like my front room was part of the garden. My ancient landlady with the slapped-on wig and heavily painted face occasionally wandered through the garden, pruning and watering. The young fellow who rented the standalone cabin beside me was in medical school at UCLA and busy with summer classes or studying. I saw him coming and going once or twice a day. Otherwise, I had the place to myself.

The two-burner gas stove added to the feeling that I was camping out. The walk to Odie's, the country market, took five minutes. I was able to buy most of what I wanted there. They even had a butcher in the back just like the store at the top of the hill when I was a kid. If I wanted a larger selection of groceries, I drove down the hill and shopped in the supermarket in Westwood a little over a mile away.

I quickly learned I couldn't leave food out or it would be covered with ants the next morning. Green lizards sometimes hopped along the outside windowsill or clung to the screens. I often found one watching me at my desk while I typed away on my new novel. Besides lizards, the garden had a small population of little scorpions about two or three inches long. Though their sting could be painful, they appeared to have no interest in me or my food. The occasional few that wandered into my new house were easy to catch and return to the garden.

When I wasn't writing, I stretched large canvases and painted. The light was incredible. It bounced off the sides of the tree-lined canyon and danced off the flowers in my yard. My paintings were turning out better than ever. I was able to draw what I could see in my mind's eye. I began making ambitious drawings for new paintings. I painted a radiant earth mother standing in a garden, smiling. The smile was too insincere. I worked on it now and again. I drew a mermaid and mer-man holding hands, floating in the sky. I painted haunting faces that came alive on the canvas and were reminiscent of faces I had admired in Picasso's Blue Period. I drew cutaways of mysterious houses with rooms in different colors stacked on top of each other like a haphazard pile of children's blocks.

Let yourself go, just let yourself go, I told myself. I wrote every day, sometimes from dawn until halfway through the night.

The Glen was filled with interesting people. It was like a small village. I quickly made friends with the couple in the house to the north of me. Bucky was a dark-haired, strapping, clean shaven artist and writer. Sandy, his slim, brown-haired girlfriend, worked in an office and was gone during the day. So, Bucky and I dropped in on each other occasionally during the day to see how each other's writing and painting were going.

One morning when he was outside washing his car, he invited me over for lunch. Later, when I arrived I found him cooking something that smelled pretty good. "What's that?" I asked, glancing into the frying pan at what looked like little meatballs.

"Jew balls." He grinned.

I didn't quite know how to respond. His girlfriend, Sandy, was Jewish, and he knew I was Jewish.

"Does Sandy know you call them that?"

"Oh, sure. She thinks it's funny." He continued to grin while he pushed the little meatballs around in the iron frying pan with a spatula.

"How come you call them that?"

"I don't call them that." He laughed again. Then, he stopped and realized I was uncomfortable. "What I mean is that's what they call them in prison. The prisoners call them that. It's mystery meat all ground up with anything they can mix in with it to save the government money when feeding the inmates. They'd fed us these once a week. They were one of the few things I liked. Of course, I only use beef. I mix in onions and celery and a little bit of bread. They're good. You'll like them."

"Okay."

He set two plates on the kitchen table, tossed a couple of slices of bread on each one, and divided the Jew balls between his plate and mine.

"What do you think?" he asked after I'd tried one.

"They taste like meatballs," I said. "What were you doing in prison?"

"Six months." He grinned. "I got caught with a key of grass. I was lucky to get off with so little time. My lawyer got it pleaded down to possession instead of dealing."

"Lucky."

"I didn't think so at the time. But, yeah, I guess. I'm never going to get drafted."

The thought of going to prison petrified me, and yet, it had liberated Bucky.

I ran into Robin at Odie's one morning. We had run into each other a half dozen times at the store and had exchanged a few words each time. This time, she asked me if I'd like to come by her house at noon for lunch.

Robin was in her mid-forties, with a medium-build and dark, wavy hair and narrow hazel eyes. She took care of an ancient couple in the Glen. The man and woman were both in their late eighties or early nineties. They lived in a spacious old house decorated with mission-style furniture the couple had bought when they first married back in the teens or twenties. The old man and woman had both been chiropractors. The woman also had been a skillful potter. The old man had cancer and was lucid but an invalid, frail, and in constant pain. Robin and others in the Glen told me he didn't have long to live. His wife was physically healthy and sweet but in the middle stage of dementia where she needed direction and supervision full time. She could barely talk. Robin had been with the old couple for several months, living in their house and running their lives.

Robin had an assistant named Troy, a stocky, powerfully built Black man about my age who helped her move the old man from his bed to his wheelchair to the bathroom to the wheelchair and to the car when necessary. Troy was schizophrenic. Robin had rescued him from one of the local mental hospitals and kept him well medicated. He lived in the old woman's pottery studio behind the house and slept on a mattress on the floor, smoked pot, and made necklaces of colored beads, which he sometimes gave away to their friends.

Robin was a nomad, she told me. She had no home. She hired herself out with Troy to people who could no longer care for themselves but wanted to live out their last days at home. She had been living like this since her daughter, my age, had left home.

I didn't know what to think about the stories I heard about Robin. Some said she was a godsend to the old couple. Others said she preyed on old people who were dying with no heirs and got them to turn over their homes to her. Someone at Odie's said she had done it to another couple in Laurel Canyon. The few times I had lunch with her at the house, I saw her patiently feed and spend quality time with both the old man and old lady. She read to the old man and listened to his stories. She sat with the old lady, combing her long white hair, which seemed to greatly please and calm her.

I got another insight into Robin one afternoon when Troy called me and said that Robin had taken the old lady to the hospital to visit the old man. I already knew the husband had been admitted a few days before and wasn't expected to survive much longer. Troy said that I had told Robin I would drive him to the laundromat in Westwood, which I hadn't, but I was due for a laundry day, so I thought, what the heck? What could it hurt?

Troy had always appeared sullen but quiet, but when I picked him up, he seemed angry, throwing a duffle bag in the back seat of my Volvo and hunkering down in the passenger seat with a scowl on his face.

I made a few attempts at polite conversation, but if he answered at all, it was an annoyed "yeah" or "no."

The whites of his eyes were redder than normal. He sat low in his seat, glancing around in jerky motions as if he were trying to catch someone spying on him.

Not having any idea of how to get out of what was turning into an awkward situation, I fell silent and just kept my eyes on the road.

About halfway down the hill, he started talking. "I gotta get away from her, man. You gotta help me."

Oh, no, I thought. Where is this going? I decided to pretend I hadn't heard him.

"You listening to me, man? Robin's made me into her slave. I gotta get away. You gonna help me or not?"

"I thought she paid you."

"She don't pay me, man. She makes me fuck her all the time. If I stop fucking her, she's gonna make me go back to the hospital. She'll have me locked up again. I gotta get away. You gotta help me," he repeated.

"I don't know, Troy. I'm not sure I can do anything."

"You can give me twenty dollars. Drive me to the bus station."

"What about your laundry?" I asked, obviously not thinking as clearly as I ought to.

He went silent. He stared through the windshield with his eyes half closed, like he was in a trance.

As soon as I parked in front of the laundromat, he turned to me and asked, "You ever get these ideas in your head that you gotta kill someone."

"No."

"I gotta get away from her, man. She's gonna fuck me to death if I don't. Somebody's gonna get killed."

I really didn't know how to handle this guy, so I decided to pretend that everything was normal, and I hadn't really heard any of it. "Why don't we go do our laundry first?"

"I'm just going to sit here. And have a smoke." He took a pack of cigarettes out of his shirt pocket and lit up. I grabbed my laundry bag from the back of the car and went inside. I started my laundry and opened a book to kill time like I normally did.

About fifteen minutes into the wash cycle, I went back to the car to check on Troy.

He was gone. So was his duffle bag.

Not sure what to do, I tried calling Robin at the house, but no one answered. I had no idea which hospital she might be at.

I thought about calling the police, but I really wasn't sure what I could tell them.

In the end, I finished my laundry and drove back to the Glen and went straight to Robin's.

She had just returned home.

"Have you seen Troy?" she asked.

I told her what happened minus the part about him being her sex slave.

"He gets a little crazy when he doesn't take his medications," she said. "He can be hard to handle."

"He said he's been having thoughts about killing someone."

"That's why they locked him up. He's really not violent when he takes his pills." She smiled reassuringly. "Don't worry. He's done this before. He'll come back."

I really didn't want to know more, and so I left, but true to her prediction, the next time I saw Robin coming out of the country store, Troy was trailing behind her carrying a shopping bag in each arm and wearing the old zombie look on his face. When I said hello, he mumbled something back that was unintelligible. I wasn't even sure he recognized me. Robin gave me a reassuring smile as if to say: See, everything worked out. By then, I had heard the old lady had been sent to the hospital as well, and Robin and Troy were living in the house of the ancient childless couple by themselves.

The Glen buzzed with rumors that Robin had struck again.

In an unprecedented burst of energy, I poured heart and soul into my novel. The ideas danced through my mind like the lizards dancing and sliding across my window screens.

I honestly had no clue what I was doing except letting go. It felt good.

CHAPTER 75

Melanie, a stunning young woman with long blond hair picked me up when I was hitchhiking home from Westwood after my car conked out yet again. She was from Beverly Hills, starting her sophomore year at Berkeley in the fall, and on her way to visit a girlfriend in the Valley. Instead, she stayed at my place for a couple of days.

A tall blond woman from Pasadena, who had gotten married at the beginning of our senior year and left her husband by the beginning of summer, showed up in the middle of a sunny afternoon to stay with me while she got her head straight. We made love in the square room beneath the skylight.

Several old girlfriends came to see my new place and stayed in paradise for an afternoon or an evening or two or three. Half the world seemed to be trying to figure out love, sex, and relationships.

My life was simple. Nothing was permanent.

I had food, shelter, friends, grass, and an abundance of crazy ideas. I wrote like a madman.

I thought about the primitiveness of our basic sex drive. The secrets were all there. Everything that had gone wrong since the beginning of civilization was a reaction to our confusion over who we were and what our true motives were. America was a paradox, hiding sex behind puritanical walls and at the same time flashing sex everywhere—in advertising, movies, magazines, television, and billboards.

While walking back from Odie's one day, I spotted my old girlfriend Leslie driving through the Glen in her 1954 MG convertible. I flagged her down.

She was thrilled to see me and delighted I had moved to the Glen.

She had been engaged earlier in the year with a rock musician she introduced me to. I was wary of him. He had a pending record deal but was a hustler who had been supporting himself selling grass and acid on the Strip. I had suggested she get to know him a little better before marrying him. "You were right. I got to know him better, I broke off the engagement," she told me with a wry smile.

"Are you seeing anyone now?" I asked.

"I'm sort of in a new relationship. It's hard to explain."

It turned out her new boyfriend and I were neighbors, and Leslie was at his house most of the time. Leslie was on her way that day to see the Byrds' singer, songwriter, and rhythm guitarist David Crosby, who lived just up the street from me in the Glen at 10422 Lisbon Lane, the very narrow dead-end little road that ran up the hill beside Odie's. Leslie, it turned out, knew Crosby from Santa Barbara and had recently reconnected romantically with him. [73]

Over time, I learned that the Byrds had been feuding for months. No one knew it, but they were less than two months away from breaking up. David was demanding more control and recognition than the others could stomach. He was always arguing with them. One of the arguments was over a song David wrote called "Triad," which the other bandmates hated. It was about two different women David was sleeping with at the same time. As the song said, Leslie was in love with David; he was in love with all the women he ever met. She promised to introduce him to me. [74]

I was living the life I dreamed of living. I was hanging out with working Hollywood actors like Martin West and his wife Carol, who lived near Odie's, and Jeff Cooper, a friend of Jay's. Martin and Carol were renting the studio behind their house to Bruce Lee, recently out of work since *Batman* had been cancelled earlier in the year. Lee was using the studio as an office to try to develop new projects. Martin and Carol took me to the Four Oaks the first time. The restaurant was the one John Beck had mentioned. It had just opened in a house up the hill that had once been one of the Glen's notorious speakeasies. The Four Oaks was started by two actors, Jared "Jack" Allen, and Hal Buckley. The place was usually empty at lunch and dinner, so I could just drop in when I wanted. It was the only place to eat between Westwood and the Valley. The restaurant was pioneering a brand-new style of cooking that had no name but became known as

California cuisine, a fusion of French and California cooking that emphasized fresh ingredients and often raw vegetables years before anyone else was cooking that way in the US. The first time I went there I was shocked to find raw mushrooms and sprouts in my salad. The mushrooms were particularly unsettling because I had never imagined that they could be eaten raw.

I tagged along with Jeff Cooper to see the latest movie he was in. It was playing at one of the large old theaters in Hollywood to a nearly empty house. He had dragged everyone to it so many times that no one else wanted to go. He had a nice speaking part as Gangrene in *Born Losers*, the first of the Billy Jack movies that would be one of the inspirations for Peter Fonda and Dennis Hopper to make *Easy Rider* two years later. I swapped writing ideas with Terry Guerin, a writer, model, actor, and another friend of Jay's, who was spelling his name as Garren at the time because he got tired of explaining how to pronounce his last name.

I never wanted the summer to end. Instant friendships sprang up easily among people making their living in show business.

I had read the *Magus* by John Fowles earlier in the summer. It was heavily influencing me as I wrote my own tale. The *Magus* was a psychological and mystical look into the life of a young poet. It was filled with mind games that force the poet to confront deep, dark secrets related to his own thoughts.

What I admired most about the book was how Fowles had to let go of his fears to write like that.

My book developed into an allegorical tale about a young loner of independent means—something I dreamed of—who finds himself drifting through life, trying to find meaning and wrestling with the powerful and overwhelming forces of his sex drive and absence of meaningful love. The hunt to find the perfect soul mate dominates his thinking. He meets a mysterious and alluring young woman and follows her into a sex-and-drug-charged cult where he becomes the victim of a kidnapping and extortion scheme. Imprisoned and chained in a dungeon, he is kept in a drug-induced trance which he begins to believe is real. He is forced to face thoughts and fears buried deep inside as he discovers he is not alone in the prison. His fellow prisoners are hideously deformed freaks he normally would have shunned in his former life but is now forced to befriend to survive.

At the heart of the story was the question of whether anyone could ever capture what sex was supposed to be telling us. Was the electric shock of the orgasm a glimpse through a door to something magical? All the good and bad in a person could be found at the center of their sexual drives. Was this drive always going to be there, messing with everything I wanted to be and believe in? Would it go away? And then what?

Cornered by a seemingly insatiable hunger for sex and love, and trapped by a sickening war, I let my thoughts run wild, trying to find answers that would give me a direction. I found myself with a rush of thoughts and ideas like I never had before, whether or not I smoked grass.

I thought about war constantly. My earliest memories of the real horrors of war were the injuries I saw on the old soldiers who lived in the giant veterans hospital in the mountains a short drive from our house. My mother volunteered there. I went with her a few times when she was delivering secondhand magazines to the men so they'd have something to read. The missing limbs and horrible faces stuck in my mind. I taught myself how to light a safety match with my left hand when I was six or seven, so if I lost my right hand in a war, I would still be able to smoke cigarettes.

War, fucking war. If God created everything, then what was God thinking when creating war?

I tried to make sense of God and no god, trying to find a formula that encompassed everything. I asked myself: If a theist is someone who believes in God, and an atheist is someone who doesn't believe in God, and an agnostic is someone who is unsure, what would a person be called who believes the idea of God and no God can co-exist side-by-side and believes that both are true at the same time?

A *Taoist*, Bucky told me.

I laughed myself silly. I had invented an old religion.

We had to find a way to live together. We had to find a way to love each other and exist together on Adlai Stevenson's spaceship earth or perish.

I could believe in God and no God at the same time as easily as I could envision the world running like a spaceship where the best talent from everywhere worked together for personal fulfillment and common good.

CHAPTER 76

John Beck moved into his new place the same week I moved into the Glen. His apartment was a giant step up from the ratty room he had been renting beside USC. His new home was the main part of the ground floor of an old mansion at 1131 Alta Loma Road, rumored to be an illegal gambling casino in the 1940s and then a girl's school. The mansion was a short walk down the hill from Sunset Strip in West Hollywood, a then-unincorporated section of Los Angeles County between Hollywood and Beverly Hills. The mansion had been divided into three apartments: a huge apartment on the second floor, a smaller apartment on one side of the main floor, and John's apartment which contained the original grand living room and kitchen of the old mansion. It was set off from the old staircase by wooden panels. The old living room had high ceilings which made it seem even bigger than it was. John furnished it with some old chairs, a sofa, and a giant bed he'd fashioned by tying two king-sized mattresses together on the floor with no frame or box spring.

Professional acting was a lot of waiting-for-the-phone-to-ring. So, John had a lot of free time when he wasn't going to an audition or filming a commercial or guest spot on a TV show. He was one of my only friends I still had in town from my USC days who wasn't married or about to be, so, I frequently drove over to the Strip to see him, or he drove his motorcycle up to the Glen. He was putting his spare cash into camera equipment, and we'd occasionally hike up the hill to the Strip where he could snap photos of the crowds.

We slipped in and out of clubs, diners, and record shops along with the crowds. The number of long-haired young people flashing peace signs continued to grow by the day. Sunset Strip was like Haight Ashbury, crowded at night with the young hip from Hollywood and the music industry. The posers looked desperate to be seen by someone who could open a door. The seekers looked for enlightenment, fame, drugs, sex, and whatever the Strip could offer. The gawkers came to look at the colorfully dressed freaks and hippies. The frat house boys looked to pick a fight with a hippie or roll a homosexual. Motorcycle gangsters looked for fresh-off-the-bus young girls to prostitute. The county sheriffs, who policed the unincorporated patch of the city, looked mostly for car thieves, muggers, and troublemakers. They were cautious about provoking more trouble. Hippies and freaks were supposed to be peaceful.

John and I talked a lot about the war and what we would do if we did get drafted.

One day he called me and asked me to come down to his place to meet a friend of his who was coming over that afternoon. John said his friend had an idea for getting out of the draft that was foolproof. John wanted me to hear the idea to see what I thought since his friend, Bailey, wanted John's help.

"It's pretty crazy, but you have to hear it for yourself," John told me.

The problem with John, me, and the others I knew who were still eligible for the draft was the ambivalence we all felt. None of us wanted to go to war, and yet, most of the ways we had of dodging the draft—like going to Canada, going underground, or going to prison—would completely and irrevocably change our lives forever.

We talked of Canada. We reinforced the idea in each other's minds that we could actually go there, but could we? Could anyone we knew? I had watched friends work themselves into a seething hate over America's involvement in Vietnam, and yet I had not seen anyone take off for Canada. America, and all we had been taught to believe, was wired into our very identities.

John's friend, Bailey, arrived by motorcycle, already wasted. We sat around talking and passing a joint for a while before Bailey got around to explaining his foolproof idea.

He intended to take an overdose of sleeping pills while a friend stood by. He was trying to convince John to be that friend. As soon as Bailey started to go under, the friend would phone for an ambulance. Bailey would be taken to the hospital, have his stomach pumped, be charged with attempting to kill himself, and be put under psychiatric care.

Bailey showed us the bottle of sleeping pills he had bought from a drug dealer.

"Attempted suicide is an automatic 4-F," Bailey counselled us.

I told John, "This is getting crazy. We'll end up killing ourselves trying to stay out of Vietnam."

"That's what I thought," John laughed. "I just wanted you to hear it for yourself to make sure I wasn't missing something."

It was funny in a gallows humor sort of way. Fake your suicide to try to get out of Vietnam.

Bailey was a little hurt that we weren't as excited as he was about his foolproof scheme.

Bailey got busted for possession of a couple of ounces of grass a few weeks later—an instant deferment. As far as we knew, he was no longer worried about the draft. He was out on bail waiting for his court appearance.

But the thought of the draft continued to haunt me.

Going to Canada was such a black-and-white decision. My life as an American would be over. That was an incomprehensible thought. Lots of people talked about Canada, but no one was going. It was just too far out. And we knew it.

CHAPTER 77

I typed away furiously on my Smith-Corona like a concert pianist playing Mozart in double time, cramming everything I could into my book.

The process of writing had a strange, hypnotic effect not unlike some of the psychedelics I had experimented with.

After several weeks of frantic writing with the sun beating down on my shack, and me inhaling the scent of the jungle and breathing the hot, sweet canyon air, I completed what I thought was a reasonable facsimile of a novel. It was only about ninety pages, which I thought must be a little short. So, I continued to write for a few more days, turning out another twenty pages of stream of consciousness as an afterthought.

I had no real idea how a typed page translated into a printed book page. The manuscript had far more pages than any story I had ever written before, and therefore, I reasoned, it must be the right size for a book.

Never mind that much of it was pseudo literary-philosophical gibberish. Never mind that the last part of the story, added to increase the length, hung off the main story like a refrigerator off the back of a motorcycle.

None of that bothered me. I had written a book. I had fulfilled a promise to myself. I was convinced the world would soon discover me, and like a rock star, I would be internationally recognized, and every problem that I ever had, real or imagined, would soon disappear. I could smoke all the grass I wanted and hire slick lawyers to bail me out of prison if I got busted. I could send money home to my mother and father. Fame, recognition, and wealth brought happiness. At the very least, it brought advantages and a modicum of protection from the law. More importantly, if I could write one book, I could write another.

I imagined I would make enough money to leave the country and live in Switzerland, which I thought would be better than Canada, though I knew even less about Switzerland than Canada.

I had been toying with a new pen name, Anon Amos, a takeoff on Anonymous, for a few months.

Using my new name, I met with Jay's friend, Charles B. Bloch, the West Coast representative of Random House, for the second time and gave him a copy of my book, which he agreed to read.

CHAPTER 78

Part of my growing confidence came from my friends who read the manuscript. Bruce read it before he took off for Berkeley. He thought it was hilarious, a spoof on *The Magus* and *Steppenwolf*. I was delighted he got it. Garry thought it was a psychotic masterpiece. Pinkie thought it was the most far out thing she had ever read. She assured me I was about to be famous. John Beck thought I should try turning it into a movie script, so he could play a part in it. Jay thought it was plain nuts, like me, but he said it with a smile. "It's well written and compelling," he said. "You're a real writer."

Bucky, my artist, writer, ex-con neighbor, said I had metaphorically tapped into the hardest thing about prison—the sexual tension of a population of men all vying to gain power over someone else or falling victim to the more powerful.

Life, I assured myself, was about to get a whole lot better. Charles Bloch would finish reading my book and get me a huge advance—I thought twenty-five thousand would do it—about twelve to fifteen times what I had been living on annually for the past four years. That amount would be enough to leave the country, start over somewhere else, and write more books.

CHAPTER 79

I finally met Paul Krassner at the end of the Summer of Love.

Through Jay Thompson, I found out why he had been unable to meet me in June when I was in New York. Krassner had been up to his eyeballs dealing with the publication of what was probably the most controversial issue of his magazine ever.

The May 1967 issue of *The Realist* became an instant classic because of not one but two of the paper's most outrageous pieces of all time. The first was the Disney Memorial Orgy, a two-page cartoon that showed all of Disney's favorite characters having sex in a giant orgy celebrating their liberation after the death of Walt Disney, who had died several months before.

The other controversial piece was the cover story, "The Parts That Were Left Out of the Kennedy Book." These parts were purported to be the missing excerpts of the bestseller *The Death of a President* by William Raymond Manchester. The controversy over the missing material had been ignited when the president's widow Jacqueline Kennedy, who had originally supported Manchester, sued his publisher to stop publication. The suit was allegedly settled after Manchester agreed to drop certain parts of the book related to the president's family life.

Krassner penned an extra twenty paragraphs in a passable Manchesterian style. The content was vile, aimed at belittling President Johnson, showing him having sex with JFK's corpse on the plane ride from Dallas to Washington, DC hours after the assassination. [75]

Krassner, like many progressives of the day, felt Johnson was chiefly responsible for escalating the war. Krassner also took shots at the

Kennedys and their deification. Krassner regarded himself as the slayer of all sacred cows. [76]

The issue sold about three times as many copies as usual, about a hundred thousand in all, and was read perhaps by a million people in total. The climate of paranoia and suspicion in America had escalated since President Kennedy's assassination to the point where many who read the story took Krassner's piece as fact, not satire.

To me the book excerpts were liberating in a very personal way. I was blown away as much by the political intent—to vilify Johnson's war—as by the idea that it was possible to say anything and get away with it. To me, Krassner had let himself go, reached down into the depths of his absurdist mind, and surfaced with one of the most depraved "what if's" in modern times.

He did it with great vulgarity like his late close friend Lenny Bruce.

Krassner's rawness poked fun at the very foundation of American puritanism that still had a strong hold on the country.

I admired the process more than the content. Krassner was a real writer for our times.

To my delight, Krassner was visiting Los Angeles, and Jay was having a dinner party in his honor. He wanted me to come. "You'll enjoy Krassner. Krassner will like you," Jay told me.

Besides Krassner, Jay invited Scott McKenzie, whose international hit song earlier in the summer, "San Francisco (Be Sure to Wear Flowers in Your Hair)" was still getting plenty of airtime.

In addition to Krassner, McKenzie, and me, Jay invited Indus, the model, who had been released from her latest incarceration at one of the local psychiatric facilities; another model friend of Indus's; and a quiet woman who said almost nothing the whole evening because she had just broken up with her boyfriend.

Jay's roommate, Paul, did all the cooking and serving.

Indus was supposed to bring Phil Everly, the boyfriend with whom she was supposed to be having an affair, but she said he couldn't make it. So, Jay put Indus next to Scott McKenzie since he seemed most interested in her. Krassner and I were supposed to be paired with the other model and the silent girl. Neither of the two extra women seemed interested in either of us, even though we both tried to talk with them. I found it humorous to realize that my hero Krassner, a badly dressed, dumpy little guy with unruly hair, was just another man on the make, looking to get laid. He was having no more success than I was during the Summer of Love on that particular evening.

Scott McKenzie basked in the attention of the two models. They were like vines growing on him. The two model-friends suddenly began competing with each other for the night's prize. Dark-eyed with wavy dark hair and a thick, dark moustache, McKenzie was dressed in his full-stage outfit, looking like an urban cowboy on his first day at a dude ranch.

Krassner was in a good mood. After the May issue with the "Disneyland Memorial Orgy" and "The Parts Left Out of the Kennedy Book," the June issue had taken three months to finish. It had just come out at the end of August. It was the third and last issue that year of a magazine that was normally more or less monthly. [77] [78]

I wanted to talk to Krassner about other articles he'd written, specifically, about the draft and Canada, but those subjects were of no interest to anyone at dinner except me. I was the only one at the party eligible for the draft. In fact, despite Jay's best efforts to get a dinner conversation going, the party appeared to be heading toward total awkward silence as McKenzie shut down after he realized he wasn't interested in either of the two models, and the third woman was drowning herself in wine.

Jay saved the evening by putting on the new Doors album. It was an acetate of the *Strange Days* album. Jay borrowed it from someone in the industry before its release. It contained the eleven-minute masterpiece, "When the Music's Over." The album thankfully took over from the lack of conversation.

The evening faded out with a whimper as Scott McKenzie left alone, and Indus and her model friend and the silent woman left shortly afterward, clearly not interested in Krassner or me. I hung around, hoping to finally get a chance to talk with Krassner, but he was soon yawning and telling Jay he should go, too.

Jay suggested I take him back to his hotel since Krassner didn't drive. He had arrived by cab, and I could save him cab fare.

On the way, we got into a conversation about how both of us had struck out with the two models even though it was supposed to be the Summer of Love. He had been mildly interested in Indus.

I explained how Indus had had a couple of nervous breakdowns in the past couple of months and had spent several weeks in a mental hospital.

"Then, I guess I did get lucky. I need less craziness in my life right now, not more," he laughed. "You know what really bugs me about casual sex?"

"No."

"I get a lot of chicks wanting to sleep with me because of my paper. They think I'm a rich somebody. Or I'm going to make them famous. I tell them I'm not going to fall in love with them. And I'm probably not going to see them again. We end up in bed anyway, but after it's over, they ask me for a free subscription to *The Realist*."

"Do you give it to them?"

"No, never. It would be too much like paying for sex."

I had been dying to ask him about the article in the June issue (published in August) that talked about the US government's concentration camps for hippies and Black dissidents. The article "Legal and Actual Concentration Camps in America" by Charles R. Allen, Jr., confirmed the existence of these sites. The article detailed how the US government had first implemented the *Subversive Activities Control Act* of 1950, popularly called the McCarran Act. It was named after its key sponsor, Democratic Senator Pat McCarran of Nevada, during the height of the Korean War and the Anti-Communist hysteria after World War II. Title II of the Act, which was still on the books in 1967, gave the president, on his own authority, the power to declare a "national internal security emergency" if Congress declared war; if an insurrection occurred within the US; or an invasion was imminent in the US or its possessions. [79]

Apparently, the money to keep these and other facilities active continued to flow through the system. These camps, according to the article, were gearing up to take in the first 10,000 to 12,000 dissidents. Other facilities would be opened later to handle more arrested dissidents.

The thirty-four-year-old Krassner told me the camps were real. He expected to be one of the first rounded up. He was one of the loudest voices against the growing craziness in Vietnam. During the past year, he had provoked considerable controversy at anti-war conferences and other venues by publicly burning Photostats of his draft card. In the June issue of *The Realist*, Krassner explained how he burned one of these copies of his draft card in front of a US Marine guarding the US Pavilion at Expo 67 in Montreal. It made the evening news in both Canada and the US.

I told Krassner about my own dilemma. Elsewhere in the same issue, he had mentioned signing a public statement along with many anti-war activists like Norma Becker, David Dellinger, Grace Paley, and Dwight MacDonald. The declaration said they supported those who were eligible for the draft who were burning their draft cards. The statement declared that the signatories would share with the card burners the risk of arrest, fines, and incarceration.

"The truth is you couldn't do much for me if I burned my draft card or refused induction. In the end, it would be me who'd end up in prison for five years," I said.

"But you'd be doing the right thing."

He suggested I think about applying for conscientious objector status. He had posted lots of information about that including guides on becoming a CO.

"I'm not sure I'm a complete pacifist." I told him about how I had reacted during the Watts Riots. "If someone tried to punch me and I couldn't retreat, I'd punch back like a wild man."

He nodded like he understood.

We were almost at his hotel, and I hadn't told him about my novel, except that I had written one and I was hoping to get it published by Random House.

"If I write something that might fit into *The Realist,* can I send it to you?"

"Sure," he said, sounding less than enthusiastic as I stopped in front of his hotel.

"Do I get a free subscription for driving you home and saving you taxi fare?"

For a second, his eyes narrowed. He thought I was serious. Then, he realized I was joking and laughed.

"You're okay," he said. "Next time I'm in town, maybe we'll get together with Jay again. Call me if you're in New York."

I held up a peace sign, and we exchanged goodbyes.

I drove off wondering if anything I had already written might interest him. I was still hoping to sell something to tide me over until the money from my book came in. My savings were quickly running down. I was spending money faster than I normally would. I had told my mother to cash in the birthday and bar mitzvah bonds I had been saving for a rainy day and send me the money. It was part of my letting go. She had cashed in only half and was saving the rest. It was her way of trying to tell me I didn't know yet what a real rainy day was.

CHAPTER 80

All you need is love, I wrote to my mother when she wrote about how my father was getting increasingly paranoid and angry as the date for his operation grew near.

Without a complaint, she addressed her letters to me by my new name, Anon Amos.

I was one of the only amusements in her life, which was tougher than mine for sure. Work at the fabric store and the furniture store was hell. She wrote how the other salespeople went out of their way to steal her customers when she wasn't there. The silver lining, she said, was working partly on salary. She was looking forward to a week's paid vacation—the first paid time off she'd had since the Great Depression. She was also taking an extra week unpaid so she could visit my father in the hospital while he was recuperating from his operation.

Sadly, my mother's carefully laid plans were turned upside down a week later when my sister Daisy drove my father's car off the road and ended up in the hospital with a severely lacerated knee and chin while my father was just about to be operated on. My mother was forced to run back and forth between my father's hospital in New York and my sister's hospital in New Jersey.

Some confusion also surrounded the results of my father's operation. My mother's letters told me his right hand appeared better, but his left hand appeared worse. And apparently, he needed to get another operation in six months, which either he had not understood, or no one had told him.

"Don't worry," my mother said over the phone in one of our rare phone calls. She sounded exhausted.

I tried not to think about what was happening back East. Surviving whatever was about to come my way was enough.

Just as I heard of the calamity with my family, the air went out of my own big balloon.

I got a call from Charles Bloch to come to his office.

He told me flat out that he thought I was a wonderful writer. "What you've written is powerful in parts. I get it. It's the story of a man driven to spend all his time looking for new women to seduce because he is driven by all the horrors in the world. Seduction is an escape. Sex is a drug. He's addicted. He becomes trapped by his own obsessions. He comes to terms with his own conflicts when he faces his own mortality. It's fresh and raw." He paused. "But it isn't ready to be published."

I wanted to scream. I felt anger surging through me. I silently listened as he patiently explained that the first part of the book, the narrative story, was quite good, but it was way too short for a novel, and even a little too short for a novella.

"The second part...well, I'm not quite sure what that is. It looks like you stuck it on to try to increase the length."

Of course, I had done exactly that. Of course, I denied it. "It's all part of the story."

"It doesn't work," he said gently.

"Everyone else likes it."

He smiled. He had an honest, pleasant face.

He was trying to be helpful.

"It might work if you could find a way to lengthen the first part," he added.

I wanted to trust him.

"By how much?" I forced myself to ask.

"I think you'll need another hundred to a hundred and ten pages. I'll need a manuscript of two hundred pages before I can send it to New York. Even that's a bit short."

I felt like I'd just swallowed a brick. He was suggesting that I double what I had already written.

"I don't want to tell you how to do it," he advised me. "You're the writer. Maybe you could build up the part before Jonathan [my antihero and narrator] ends up in the dungeon with the deformed people. What if the aunt in the story isn't a passive character, and instead, Jonathan had swindled some money from her and others, and she's secretly out to teach him a lesson? The freaks in the dungeon could be people Jonathan wronged in the past and perhaps destroyed in his own quest to better himself. You're a good writer. Your writing shows confidence. Keep going."

"I'm not sure I can make it work," I said feebly. I was humbled and intimidated by his suggestions.

"Give it a try. Add more. Take your time. When you have something longer, bring it back."

I walked out of his office with a sense of failure. I told myself he had only suggested the revisions because of his friendship with Jay. I was deeply upset that my first book had not only failed to sell but it wasn't even a book. It wasn't that I didn't believe him. It was that I wondered what it would mean if I couldn't rewrite this story. Was I done as a writer?

I thought about showing the book to another publisher, but I hadn't a clue how to find one.

I was only weeks away from the start of graduate school and was quickly running out of money.

I tried rewriting my story. There was so much to do. Lose those last pages for sure. Change the tone. It sounded too old fashioned.

I wanted to convert it to third person to get another perspective, but I wondered if the story was even worth rewriting. I didn't have the time to do what needed to be done.

I struck out a second time as a writer when I received the rejection from the *Evergreen Review*. They turned down my best short story, "Friday Night," about the day in the life of an urban pothead. The return envelope contained not one but two pages of notes on little notepad paper. On the first, typed at the top: "Powerful and authentic portrait of stoned hippies at home." It was signed SK [for Seymour Krim]. Lower down on the same page was a second message in a different hand that said, "Revolting and, yes, authentic. But what's the point? It reads like an excerpt with the beginning & the end missing." It was signed FJ [for Fred Jordan, Managing Editor].

Seymour Krim added a second handwritten note on a separate page that said, "Sorry that we can't accept this. I enclose part of the dialogue that went on about it." It was signed "Seymour Krim, Consult. Ed."

I was devastated. I had been counting on something of mine selling over the summer. I also was not sophisticated enough to understand how close I had come to being published. This was no ordinary rejection. Krim, who had championed me at the *Evergreen Review*, was a highly respected author, editor, and literary critic, and one of the literary lions of the beat generation. I should have been greatly encouraged by Krim's comments.

I had no idea who FJ or Seymour Krim were at the time.

The last rejection of the summer came from the man my mother knew who did advertisements for Johnson and Johnson. He told her he hated my idea for different colored, flesh-toned bandages, and he apparently scolded my mother for my bad behavior in trying to start at the top. My mother wrote: "He said that you were telling and not listening. To him, it meant disrespect of elders. That you were very arrogant. I guess he wants you to be a puppy."

I laughed. Mom got it. Different colored flesh bandages for different skin types *was* a good idea.

But it wasn't good enough. I had to get my act together and think about surviving the coming year.

To make ends meet, I took a job at Odie's Market as the assistant butcher, stock boy, and bagger at the checkout counter, working eight hours on Saturday and nine on Sunday for thirty dollars a week. Combined with my fellowship, I hoped I would have enough to cover me during the year while I attended school and tried to rewrite my novel. The pay at Odie's was good money, forty-five cents an hour over minimum wage. I could walk to work in a few minutes and go home for lunch. I was busy the whole time I was at work. The hours flew by. The butcher job took some skill and was dangerous, a little like working in the glove factory. The butcher trusted me enough to leave me on my own for hours at a time.

Jay got me work as an assistant holding reflectors and carrying props on a Pepsi commercial shoot with a young, blond starlet in a bikini and a young, bronzed man in trunks on the beach in Santa Monica. The ice on the bottles was plastic, so it didn't melt. The photographer was Don Ornitz, a quiet, well-mannered man who worked quickly and gave good directions. He was easy to work with. Everyone wanted to do their best. This was Los Angeles where a person never knew when they'd cross paths with someone else who could lead them to more work. [80]

Ornitz was one of the top commercial photographers in Los Angeles. He took roll after roll of film with several different cameras, getting me and the other assistant to move the reflectors and telling the models to move this way or that as he looked for the one in a thousand shot that would yell sex and sell Pepsi.

I got paid a hundred dollars for a pleasant six-hour day. The money was equal to half of my monthly fellowship for the next eight months.

I stopped using my pen name. I needed to return to earth and get through the year.

I finished reading Dostoevsky's *Brothers Karamazov*.

In the last week of September, I received a letter from Bruce who had moved out of my old apartment on University Avenue and settled in Berkeley four hundred miles away. He not only felt sick about being separated from Karen but depressed that he barely had enough money for his rent. He wrote he had to give up meals to be able to afford the materials for his sculpture class.

I was feeling as low as I'd felt in the past year because I could see that the war was likely to consume America for years to come. I wrote back, telling Bruce that our lives had become a form of suicide. I meant it in an intellectual sense. The war and the pressures to stay out of it were destroying our generation. If he hadn't been concerned about the draft, he could have taken a reduced number of classes and found a job to support himself. I could have skipped grad school, fixed my novel, and begun my real life.

CHAPTER 81

We had two classes together. Jennifer was one of about thirty other young men and women in the first year of our master's program at UCLA's school of social work. She was the only part of starting graduate school that I found myself interested in.

She had shoulder-length, wavy brown hair, bangs touching her eyebrows, intelligent eyes that seemed to be taking everything in, and a warm, kind smile that instantly made me want to get to know her better.

I was pleased to see her watching me in our second class together. She hadn't looked away when I looked back. She just smiled.

We introduced ourselves at one of the orientation events. She was from the Midwest and had just graduated from the University of Chicago. She had studied dance for a time. She was new to California and had a new boyfriend, but she wanted me to show her more of the city when we both had time.

The next time we had a class together, she showed up late, sat on the other side of the room, and smiled warmly when she spotted me.

I was hoping to talk with her more after class, but another student stopped me to ask a question. By the time I got outside, Jennifer had disappeared into the sea of students moving between classes.

It was my turn to be late for our next mutual class. Car troubles again. I had to walk from the Glen to school. I slid into a seat at the back while the teacher was already lecturing. It took me a second to spot Jennifer. She was sitting on the other side of the room in front, her eyes buried in her notebook.

When the class was over, Jennifer headed straight for the door without looking at anyone. She appeared upset.

I didn't expect to see her outside, but she was only a short distance away standing on the sidewalk with another young woman from our class. As I approached them, her friend walked off. Jennifer looked like she was about to take off, too, but then, she saw me and waited.

Up close, she looked like she'd been crying.

"You okay?" I asked.

She took a deep breath and shook her head. "I just can't believe it. Che's dead."

She was totally bummed out.

I gave her a hug.

She was trembling.

It took me a moment to realize who she was talking about.

Che was Che Guevara, a young medical doctor from Argentina who had ditched his upper middle-class life to join Fidel Castro at the very beginning of the Cuban Revolution. He rode to victory in Havana as Fidel's righthand man. Outside of political junkies and self-styled revolutionaries like Anna, Che wasn't well known in America before he was captured and killed by the Bolivian Army. Later, it would come out that the Bolivians had help from the CIA.

Unknown to me, the news of Che's death had just come over the radio that morning.

I talked Jennifer into going to lunch with me. We bought sandwiches and drinks at the Gypsy Wagon and sat outside on a bench.

She was struggling to find a way to change the world. She was struggling to understand how she could do good. She told me about a long relationship she had in Chicago with a Black student organizer. He had become convinced of the need for him and his fellow activists to arm themselves against attacks by the police. They saw themselves as part of a global struggle against oppression of Blacks and people of color worldwide. [81]

I told her about my experiences during the Watts Riots. I just couldn't buy into the idea that more violence would change anything in the US.

Jennifer wasn't an adventurer. She was frightened—frightened by the insane and seemingly unstoppable war in Vietnam, frightened by the inequities and poverty she had seen in Chicago, frightened that friends of hers had become so convinced they were going to be killed by police that they had begun to arm themselves, and frightened that people like us, young white people opposed to the war and racial injustice could become targets of a government out of control.

"We may end up having to arm ourselves and fight against the police and government to keep from being rounded up and put in camps," she insisted. She had heard the same rumors that I had. There were lists. We didn't know whether to be proud or scared to be on them.

I had a difficult time imagining middle class young people like Jennifer taking up arms against the US government.

Jennifer had the energy for revolution but not the bloodlust.

Jennifer and I saw each other irregularly as friends. She was hoping social work would provide some answers. I kept wondering what the hell I was doing in school.

She had her first encounter with the California police with me one afternoon when we talked another fellow student from out of town into taking the three of us up the coast through Malibu in his new car. I played tourist guide, pointing out landmarks I had discovered over the years.

Out of the blue, we were pulled over along with dozens of other cars by a crew of sheriffs spot-checking traffic heading north near Zuma Beach. A sheriff looked over our school identity cards and driver's licenses, and we were soon on our way after a brief scare. We had been passing a joint back and forth only a mile before we got flagged to the side of the road.

I brought Jennifer to the Glen because she had seen me sketching in class and wanted to see my paintings. I was pleased to see that she liked my latest work. She asked me if she could have a painting for her apartment. She pointed out several she particularly liked. I felt inspired and promised to paint her something special.

We sat on the floor of the square room with the skylight, smoked grass, and talked like we had known each other a very long time.

Jennifer told me about her older sister, Bernadine Dohrn, who had gotten her law degree from the University of Chicago and joined the National Lawyers Guild, a progressive bar association located in New York. Bernadine was deeply involved in the upcoming March on the Pentagon, scheduled for October 21.

I had heard about the march. It was expected to be a big one. It was the last gasp of the Summer of Love. No one was sure whether it would turn Washington, DC into a Love-In or a battlefield.

I drove her home after dinner, and we made a date for lunch the following week after our first class.

CHAPTER 82

Mom wrote that Daisy had gone off to college on crutches and was expected to make a full recovery, and Dad was home from the hospital after his operation.

Mom was sure he was worse, not better. She had to help him do everything, from dressing and undressing him to getting him in and out of bed. Everything tired him or made him agitated—even sitting in a chair and watching TV. Television had been the one thing that seemed to keep him busy before the operation. After the operation, it only made him nervous and uncomfortable. My mother was running on empty, working both jobs, and trying to look after him as well.

I could do nothing to help them.

I found out about yet another change in the draft regulations during the first weeks of graduate school. Previously, draft eligible students who managed to stay in school with a 2-S—a student deferment—until the magic age of twenty-six, would not be drafted unless an all-out national emergency was declared. The new regulation said that anyone who had a deferment until age twenty-six remained eligible for the draft for years afterward.

Once again, the rules of the game had changed. Staying in grad school would only put off my inevitable confrontation with the draft, not end it.

My thoughts again turned to Canada. The idea of leaving the US was still something so bold, so radical, it remained nearly incomprehensible. I stopped by a table where two anti-war protesters were handing out pamphlets and asked them what they knew about going to Canada.

Not much. Nobody did.

They told me that they had only heard through others about a few people who had gone there but didn't know any personally.

Apparently, the Canadians had established a point system to judge potential immigrants—the first in the world. Apparently, if I were healthy enough to pass a physical exam, had a college degree, and spoke English, I would almost certainly be accepted. If I had relatives there, I would get extra points. If I spoke French, I would get more points.

I had some distant relatives in Canada, somewhere. My brother and sister-in-law had visited distant family or friends of family in Nova Scotia over the summer after taking their trailer to Expo 67 in Montreal.

I had taken a year of French in high school. Although I had forgotten most of what I had learned, I wondered if relearning it might earn me extra points.

"How do I apply?" I asked, recalling the previous year when on a whim, I had visited the Canadian consulate in Los Angeles and taken away a hefty application package on immigrating. It had sat around my old place so long without being opened that I had tossed it during my move to the Glen.

The two students manning the anti-war table weren't sure how to apply, but one of them had heard that the quickest way was to fly to Canada as a tourist. "Once there, go to an immigration office and apply. If you have enough points, you'll be granted a residency card. The card will allow you to work. Or you could apply at the consulate in Los Angeles but that might take forever."

I was in a real funk. Totally bummed out. I didn't want to be in school. The thought of being drafted or signing up just seemed wrong. The thought of becoming part of some mythical disgruntled white student revolutionary army fighting the US government seemed preposterous.

I spent Yom Kippur alone, fasting, searching for something that would put an end to the seemingly endless loop of questions, self-doubt, moral uncertainty, and all the rest that had been festering in my head like a ball of worms for far too long.

I needed a sign. Some Biblical event like God telling me to sacrifice my only son in exchange for his good will, and me agreeing to do it, only to find out God was kidding.

When the sign came, it arrived like a thunderbolt out of the blue, unexpected, and staggering in a way that instantly turned everything upside down.

CHAPTER 83

I had taken Saturday off from Odie's for Yom Kippur. On Sunday, I worked in the butcher shop all day, part of it by myself. The afternoon was busy. We sold a lot of hamburger, steaks, and roasts. I was thankful to be at work. The knives were razor sharp. I had cut myself badly at work at the factory and almost lost the tip of my finger with a chipping knife years before, so I worked carefully, shutting everything else out of my mind except the meat, the knives, and the customers.

Later that night at my place while I was reading my latest assignment and thinking about my class and lunch with Jennifer the next day, I got a surprise call from my mother.

"I wasn't going to phone you, but I finally decided that you ought to know. Daddy's going into the hospital for a second operation tomorrow. I don't want you to worry."

Alarm bells went off in every corner of my brain. Something in her voice was completely off. I sensed that if I had been there in the same room with her, she would have avoided eye contact.

"I thought he wasn't scheduled to have the second operation for another six months. What's going on?"

"Nothing's going on. Just don't worry. That's all."

"I'm going to worry more if you don't tell me the truth."

She said nothing for a few moments, and then started to speak with her voice subdued. "Two weeks ago, I came downstairs in the morning and found your father sitting at the kitchen table. He said he had taken a whole bottle of sleeping pills. He didn't want to live any longer. I called the rescue squad right away. They rushed him to the hospital. The doctors pumped out his stomach. Everything's all right now. I talked to the police.

I told them he's a sick man. He was desperate. They're not going to press charges. I spoke to Dr. Cooper at St. Barnabas. He agreed to do the first half of the operation again. Tomorrow's the first date they had available. Don't worry. Everything's under control."

I felt numb—like the blood had suddenly drained out of me. Finally, I found my voice. "Can I speak with him?"

"He's sleeping. I'll call you tomorrow after the operation and let you know how things went. Okay?"

"Okay."

I got off the phone thinking, *nothing's okay*. This has to be a sign.

If it is a sign, what is it trying to tell me?

Two weeks before I had written to Bruce about the strange thoughts— intellectual musings—about suicide and how letting us be taken to war was a type of death wish. It was the day my father swallowed the bottle of sleeping pills. When I had been driving up the Coast Highway near Zuma Beach with Jennifer, smoking a joint, passing it back and forth with the other grad student, I suddenly had a premonition that police were up ahead. I had grabbed the joint from Jennifer and tossed it out the window and told them what I was thinking. A mile later, with the windows rolled down to air out the car, we went around the corner and were pulled over by one of the sheriffs at the roadside checkpoint. Jennifer and the grad student were both shocked. They wanted to know how I knew about the cops. I told them I didn't know. I just felt something.

Had I entered some unexplainable psychic ether? Were the premonitions simply coincidences?

I couldn't stop thinking about what my mother had told me. I was bummed out and shaken.

I barely slept.

What the fuck is life all about? What do and don't we know about reality? I wondered.

I went to class late in the morning. The lecture had already started. Jennifer was seated toward the front. We were supposed to have lunch and study afterward. The closest seat I could get to her was two over and one back in the next aisle.

She smiled warmly, and I smiled back. I tried to concentrate on the lecture, but my head was a complete mess. I felt like I was having an out-of-body experience.

I waited until Jennifer glanced my way again and then mouthed to her, "I can't see you for lunch. I have to go. I'll explain later."

"Are you okay?" she mouthed back, genuine concern on her face.

The professor was still talking but looking in our direction.

I nodded and smiled, not wanting to attract more attention.

As soon as the professor turned away, I grabbed my books and headed out the door.

I can't do this anymore, I told myself. I can't be here.

I walked down the hill to my bank in Westwood and drew out a couple of hundred dollars. I drove to my place, threw a few things into an overnight bag, and headed straight to the airport.

My father's second operation was already in progress.

CHAPTER 84

I couldn't stay and join Jennifer's revolution.

I couldn't continue in school.

I wouldn't join the Army.

I didn't want to live underground and make surfboards in Aptos.

My father's attempted suicide was a cry for help. I saw no dishonor in what he tried. I saw no bravery either—just weariness and hopelessness.

I looked out the plane window as day turned to night and the lights on the ground came on. I told myself: I'm not going back to school. I'm going to Canada.

I felt a need to do something big, something affirmative, something that would shout that I am alive and in control of my life.

I arrived in New York too late to reach the hospital before the end of visiting hours. I called my Uncle Sam in Great Neck. "How did the operation go?" I asked.

"I just got off the phone with your mother. She got home from the hospital a half hour ago. As far as anyone knows, the operation's a success. Less shaking in both hands."

I explained that I had flown in to visit my father but hadn't arrived in time. I was at La Guardia. I didn't feel like going all the way to New Jersey and asked if I could take a bus to his place.

"Sit tight. I'll drive over and pick you up. It isn't far."

On the way to his house, he asked me, "How long are you staying?"

"I'm not sure. A few days, then I'm going back to California."

"How's school?"

"It's okay but it's not for me. I'm dropping out."

"They'll draft you right away. You're an Eagle Scout. They'll put you right on the front lines."

"I'm going to Canada."

"You sure?"

I nodded and said aloud what I had been telling myself for five hours on the plane. "No good could possibly come from me fighting men I don't know in Vietnam on orders from men I don't trust in Washington, DC."

He laughed. We drove in silence for a few minutes before he spoke quietly. "Joey, you know, going to Canada right now isn't a bad idea. Especially for you. Things are getting pretty rotten around here. This is the wrong war at the wrong time. They're just throwing you kids away. And for what?"

Coming from a combat veteran who had shot at people and been shot at in return was reassuring.

"When are you planning to go?" he asked.

"I'm not sure. I want to spend some time with my father. I have to go back to California, drop out of school, pack up, and then...well, I'm not sure. We have relatives in Canada, don't we?"

"Some on my father's side. Have you told your mother?"

"No. I haven't told anyone except you. I intend to keep it secret for the time being. Mom has enough on her mind."

"Joey, I think you're doing the right thing. This war stinks. I wouldn't trust the president or any of them right now. The way things are going it wouldn't surprise me if we all had to get out of the country before this is over. Do you have a passport?"

"No."

"You're going to need one. We'll get that started tomorrow when we're in the city."

I'm really going, I told myself happily. I'm committing myself to living in the moment.

I wanted to feel what it felt like to make a stand at least once in my life. I wanted to be able to look back someday and say, I wasn't asleep.

"What are you going to do for money?"

"I have some bonds and some savings. I should be all right."

"You let me know what you want me to do."

"I can't think of anything, but that's really nice of you, Uncle Sam."

"You may have to look after Adam. He's fifteen. They'll be looking to grab him in a few years. Who knows? They may even take Jill when she's old enough if they don't stop this damned war."

Adam was Sam's son. Jill was Sam's eleven-year-old daughter. Like me, Sam thought the war would continue for years.

I slept on a cot in Uncle Sam's basement in Great Neck. In the morning I went with him to the city by train. He had appointments in the morning. So, I went to the hospital in the Bronx on my own.

My father's head was shaved bald. Bandages covered the spot where the freezing needles had gone into his skull. Dad was disoriented and couldn't understand what I was doing there.

I told him that I had time off from school and had flown in for a couple of days to see how he was. His face still had the frozen look. It was impossible for me to tell how much he understood when I spoke with him. He had difficulty talking.

He needed to pee. He wanted me to take him to the bathroom.

I wasn't sure if he was allowed out of bed.

I found a nurse. She helped him to the bathroom and back to bed. He was too tired to do more than stare at me through half-closed eyes. I kissed him on the forehead and left.

I took the subway to midtown and headed to the photography studio of Uncle Sam's partner, George Elliott. The studio was located in a townhouse with north facing windows opposite the south side of the New York Public Library.

George and Sam were both there looking over photos George had taken a few days before.

Sam had filled George in on what I was planning.

"You're making the right decision," George told me. "If it was me, I'd go."

At Sam's insistence, I called my mother at work.

I told her I was home because we had a little break in our classes, and I thought I could fly in, see dad, and fly out in a few days.

She told me, "You're up to some funny business. You wouldn't be getting any time off now."

"Don't worry. Everything's fine. I'm here to see Dad. I saw him. I can't tell much from what I saw. A nurse and a doctor told me he was recovering just fine. While I'm here, let's enjoy ourselves."

I arranged to meet her late in the afternoon at the hospital.

I spent part of the afternoon wandering around the city, soaking in the sites, visiting the Met and Central Park. I walked around the Village. I avoided my old friends. I was flying under the radar. The fewer people who knew my plans, the better.

I picked up an application form for my passport and had some snapshots taken at a nearby photo studio.

My father seemed a little improved when I returned to the hospital. He was still wobbly and disoriented, but the shaking in both hands did seem reduced.

My mother arrived late in the afternoon, looking haggard and thin. She tried to be cheerful around my father. He couldn't speak much, but I could see the grateful look he gave her. He was the poor fourteen-year-old she had rescued when she was twelve and gave him direction in his life. She had dressed him up, taught him old world manners, and used her own money from her designing days to finance his first factory. He was crying and laughing. The nurses seemed pleased. "I'm going to get better," he said, his voice still hard to understand.

My mother saved her questions for me until we went to the cafeteria for coffee.

"All right. Now, what's going on?" she asked.

She had leveled with me about Dad, so, I decided to level with her about what I was doing. "I'm dropping out of school and going to Canada. I'm only telling you because I don't want you to worry."

Her eyes narrowed. She thought about it for a few seconds, and asked, "You can't go back to school?"

"I don't want to. I just want to go out and live, find out what life's all about. Find out what I get to do with my life while I'm on this planet. I don't want to end up like Dad."

"You won't end up like Dad."

"I don't want to end up in some jungle in Vietnam either."

She sighed. "The last thing I want is you being a part of this war. It's no good. You know how I feel. In the end, it's your decision. Is it because of a girl?"

Love and war, the two themes that had been most common in my letters home.

"No. I wish there was someone, but it wouldn't matter. This is about me. Me having the nerve to take a chance and listen to something I feel is right." I could see clearly that it wasn't the decision she wanted me to make. I went on as much for myself as her. "I don't want to be a part of what's going on in this country anymore. It's coming apart at the seams, and there's nothing I can do to stop it."

"You think that it's better somewhere else?"

"I don't know. It's worth a look."

"Where will you go?"

"I'm not sure yet. I'm thinking Montreal. We have some relatives there, don't we?"

"We had relatives in Nova Scotia. There may be a cousin in Montreal."

"Who did Ray and Linda stay with over the summer?"

I explained the points system for immigrating.

"They're not blood relatives. They're cousins of in-laws."

I asked about the cousin in Montreal, who Sam had mentioned.

"I don't know her. If she's still alive, she would be old. Sam knows that side of the family better than I do. Most of the cousins moved to New York ages ago. Sam is friends with one of the brothers. Moe. He's a dentist. He lives in Great Neck near Sam. Maybe you can talk with him before you go. Maybe get the lay of the land."

"If I have time."

"When are you going?"

"I'm not sure. I have to return to Los Angeles, pack my things, and sell what I don't want to take with me. I'll probably send a few things home. I'm planning on traveling light."

"Do you have enough money?"

"I have some. I'll be all right."

"Can you just go to Canada and work, or maybe go to school?"

School was out of the question. I didn't want to be in school any longer. I explained that I thought I would fly in like a tourist. Then, if everything checked out, I would apply for my immigration papers. "I should be able to work within days of arriving, provided, of course, I'm accepted."

"If you're not accepted?"

"We'll see."

I didn't tell her that if Canada didn't accept me, I would think about flying to Sweden or France, the two other countries I had heard were accepting US draft resisters and deserters.

I swore her to secrecy. "I don't want you telling anyone, period, especially not Uncle Lew."

Great Uncle Lew would be mad at me. I imagined he might go so far as to turn me in for my own good.

"You're sure you're up for this? You may never be able to come back to the US."

"Mom, do you remember what you used to tell me when I was four or five, and I used to ask you things just to get your attention—like help tying my shoes when I already knew how?"

"I said a lot of things."

"'Make believe I'm dead.' That's what you would say, but only when I was making a pest of myself. Never when I really needed help."

"I was pregnant with Daisy and then busy with her full time."

"You knew I was weak. I knew I was physically and emotionally frail. But I wanted to be tough. You helped make me mentally tough when I was physically weak. You knew I would understand exactly what you were saying. I'm not blaming you. I'm thanking you. You gave me the freedom to look after myself from as far back as I can remember. I'll be able to look after myself."

Make believe I'm dead! She had always said it with a little laugh and a twinkle in her eye, never in anger, never to scare me, but to make me less afraid.

I didn't need to say more. We were a lot alike. We could talk to each other without talking. She understood most of what I told her or was ready to accept it on good faith.

CHAPTER 85

I had entered a danger zone. I was unhappy enough, fed up enough, tired of bullshit enough, to say that I could never be happy with the thought of turning over my mind and body for war. Anyone who could see the future knew violence on a spaceship was suicide. War would be outlawed. Someone far in the future would figure out how to win the peace. If I, with all my advantages, couldn't say no to war, then who could?

I wasn't comfortable looking for trouble. I wasn't rebelling against society. My journey had always been more like a struggle to find a place in the world that made sense to me.

The sensible thing to do was cross a border into another country that wasn't in the middle of a war.

Canada wasn't alone. Britain wasn't at war; the whole of Europe wasn't at war; most of the world was not at war.

I needed to do something on my own, alone, to feel what it was like to take a stand.

If I got that far.

I was half convinced that applying for a passport might trip a wire and send FBI agents out to find me.

Before I made my dash across the border, I had unfinished business to take care of.

I flew back to Los Angeles and started sorting out what I needed to send to New Jersey and what I needed to sell or dump. I stripped a few finished canvases off their stretcher bars and packed them into my old steamer trunk along with the original and a carbon copy of my manuscript. I threw in stacks of my old writings, letters, drawings, and photos.

I packed some clothes and my typewriter. I went to Odie's Market, told them I wouldn't be working there anymore, and picked up my last check. The butcher was sorry to see me go and said he would hire me back anytime.

I stopped by UCLA and officially dropped out. I didn't think I would likely try graduate school again for a while, but I also didn't want to end up with a transcript of incompletes or failures. Dropping out that early in the year would leave me with a clean record.

By officially quitting, I was also starting the clock on getting reclassified by my draft board. I expected they would be after me as soon as the school notified them I was no longer enrolled. That could take a few days or a few weeks.

I stopped by the anti-war table at UCLA. The only thing the two self-styled revolutionaries could add to what they already had told me was an address of someone in Montreal who might be able to provide some advice if and when I got there.

I listened to the news of the March on the Pentagon. Writer Norman Mailer was one of those arrested in the demonstrations. I wondered if Jennifer's sister had been arrested. The march had done nothing to dampen the fighting in Vietnam.

I drove to Jennifer's place. Thankfully, her sister hadn't been arrested. I gave Jennifer the two paintings of mine she liked best. I apologized for not being able to paint one just for her. She was a little shocked and saddened to find out I was dropping out. I told her I was heading to New York for family reasons.

"Be a peacemaker," I said hugging her tight, still worried that she might get sucked into some crazy gun-toting group of American radicals who thought armed insurrection against the US government could possibly succeed.

"I will," she said. "Look after yourself."

I drove away from her place wondering if I'd ever see her again.

As part of my whirlwind tour of goodbyes, I hopped a plane to San Francisco and spent a couple of days with Bruce, sleeping on his floor, walking around Berkeley, eating lunch with his aunt in Chinatown, and talking over the possibility that he and Karen might join me in Canada if the troubles in the US got much worse. I hoped I could find a way to keep in touch with them.

Back in Los Angeles, John Beck and I ate Belgium waffles at a new place on Sunset, The Old World Emporium. He was a little surprised that I had decided to go to Canada without him.

"You can still come," I said.

"I might, but I think I'm still okay here for a little while longer."

I was excited for him. He was a good actor, classically trained. He was learning everything he could from every job he went on.

"Let's not lose touch again," he said when we parted.

I said goodbye to Jay. He told me he wasn't at all surprised I was leaving. "I knew you'd go," he said. Jay had served in the US Army years before, but like my Uncle Sam, he had no use for this war. "It was just a matter of when you'd leave. You're probably doing yourself a favor by getting out before the rush. Don't be surprised if Paul and I end up following you before too long. If I were in the service now, I'd be thinking about deserting."

Garry had moved to England to read and write scripts for the London office of American International Pictures. Carol, his girlfriend and soon-to-be wife, was getting ready to follow him. At the end of the summer, I had been delegated to go to Garry's house once a month and drive his Triumph around the hills for a half hour to make sure the battery wouldn't go dead. I drove my Volvo to Suzanne's, took Garry's car out one last time, and told Suzanne she'd have to find someone else to drive the car the following month.

She fed me one last dinner and gave me a handful of Canadian addresses of Rusoffs in Winnipeg and Vancouver should I ever end up in either place. Having addresses of people in Canada was comforting. I copied them carefully into my address book.

One of the last people I visited was Mike Vosse. He was living on Horseshoe Canyon Road in Laurel Canyon at the time. He was coming out of his house and heading for his car just as I pulled up. A minute later and I would have missed him.

"Come back tomorrow," he said.

"I can't. I quit school. I'm leaving the country and heading to Canada."

"Then, come with me," he said. "I have to deliver something to Derek Taylor. You'll enjoy meeting him."

Why not? I didn't have much planned for the rest of the afternoon. I hopped in Mike's car and went with him to deliver a half a key of Panama Red to Derek.[82]

I had heard about the legendary Beatles' and rock superstar publicist, but I had never met him.

Mike and Derek Taylor were now working together at A&M records. They had landed there after the Monterey International Pop Festival.

I was excited about meeting the man who had been the Beatles' original press agent and Brian Epstein's personal assistant at the start of the Beatles' rise to fame. For the past two years after moving to Los Angeles, Derek had been the public relations man for the Beach Boys, the Byrds, the Mamas and Papas, Paul Revere and the Raiders, Mae West, and other members of Hollywood royalty.

Derek's rented house was high in the Hollywood Hills with a magnificent view of Los Angeles spread out below.

Derek opened the door to greet us wearing a white kaftan.

"This is my friend, Joseph," Mike said and was about to add more when the slight Englishman with a moustache, light brown hair, and gentle eyes put up his hand, palm out to Mike, and said to me in a gentle voice, "I know you. Come inside. I've been waiting to talk with you."

I was certain that I had never met him before. So, I wondered why he thought he knew me. As I followed him into the large living room, I gave Mike a quick glance. He said, "He's on acid. He doesn't know you. He's just tripping. Don't let it bother you. He's perfectly harmless."

"Don't listen to Michael. I *know* you," Derek repeated, staring into my eyes very hard with his face only inches from mine. "Come sit down over here and talk to me. You have interesting vibes."

We talked for a couple of hours. I felt comfortable telling him I was leaving for Canada. Derek, who had been in the British military, said he thought it might not be a bad idea to get out of the US. He was thinking about that himself. "Sometimes it feels like the place is ready to explode," he said.

He had heard others talk about going to Canada but never met anyone who had gone there to get out of the draft.

I could see why the Beatles and so many of the kings and queens of rock 'n' roll trusted him. He listened with real interest. He felt like someone my own age and at the same time fatherly and comforting.

Derek was a full-fledged father in real life. Joan, his wife, had just given birth two months before to their latest child. Kids ran in and out of the living room on a regular basis while Derek spent part of the time tenderly holding the sleeping infant as he continued to talk and listen attentively to me.

I think when he said he knew someone it was because he had a deep and genuine interest in people. I wanted to believe he could sense talent. I wanted to believe he sensed some talent in me. Of course, the acid must have amplified whatever he was feeling.

Mike rolled joints from the grass he'd brought and played disc jockey with Derek's record collection and stereo. Mike would interrupt our conversation once in a while to tell us "You have to listen to this."

Derek's wife Joan appeared now and again, always with a pretty, cherubic smile to make sure we had enough tea and snacks and to cuddle their baby or herd the other children out of the room when they became too boisterous.

I felt safe in Derek's house, surrounded by easy-going people and kids. It made it difficult to leave.

"Good luck," Derek told me as he walked Mike and I outside. "I truly hope I'll see you again."

Impossible, I thought. I'll probably never see any of you again.

CHAPTER 86

I bought a pair of leather pants at a boutique on Sunset. It seemed like a smart thing to do if I was intending to live in snow country. I gave my unfinished canvases and art supplies to Bucky next door. My old baby grandfather clock and statue of Moliere went to Karen. I sold my car to Robin for $150. She gave me $75 and said she would send the rest. Of course, she never did.

As the plane rose above the smog, I gazed out the window at California, thinking of all the good times I had been through and all the good friends I had made. I wondered if I would ever see my adopted home and my friends again.

The sun set behind us when we were halfway across the country. I wondered if I would change as much in the next four years as I had in the past four. I wondered what would become of America.

I flew into La Guardia again. Uncle Sam picked me up and took me to his house. It was right after *The New York Times* broke the story that Admiral John McCain's son, John McCain III, had been shot down over North Vietnam and taken prisoner.

"Now the president and the generals have their excuse for a land invasion of North Vietnam," Sam predicted. "Johnson's just looking for a reason to start World War III." Everything seemed to be a sign of the impending apocalypse.

The next morning, I took the train into Manhattan and the bus to New Jersey and hitched to Warrenville to visit my parents for a few days and say goodbye. My father was out of the hospital. He was still very weak but feeling much better. The shaking in both hands and his pain had been reduced. He was able to read and watch TV again without getting agitated. He could look after himself during the day while my mother was at work.

I told him the truth about my plans. He had less to say than I expected. He asked me if I had thought it through. I said I had.

"I'd take my chances with the Army," he told me.

"I'm going to try Canada first." I was committed, and yet in that moment, I still wondered what going to Canada meant.

The one thing that made me feel good about being with my dad in those final days was that I sensed he felt some hope for himself. I could see in his eyes that he hadn't wanted to die. He loved life. He just hated the physical pain from the illness and the helplessness he had been feeling after everything had been taken away from him. Now, he had enough of his life back that he felt hope. His one desire was never to be a burden on anyone again.

He smiled at me. "You're grown up now. It's up to you."

I felt a strange loss as we both let go. I spent the day watching television with him.

John Beck's commercial for Head and Shoulders shampoo appeared on TV a few times. I pointed it out to my father. John played a football player with such bad dandruff that he had to use his cleats to scratch it—until he tried Head and Shoulders, which, of course, magically cured his condition.

"You know how I feel about guns and war," Dad told me. "If you want to end war, put the politicians on the front lines. The war would be over just like that."

My mother gave me my birth certificate. I made a day trip into New York to hand in the application for my passport, wondering if the application would be cross-checked with the government list of dissidents that I was supposed to be on.

If the FBI is watching me, when exactly would they make their move? I tried to imagine what lies I might tell them if they caught me before I got to Canada.

At the urging of my mother, I had lunch with my Great Uncle Lew at his club.

Since I still hadn't been notified of a change in my draft status, I told him, "I'm going to take some time off, travel, live somewhere else, and experience more. Like Hemingway, Fitzgerald, and Jack London."

"Good luck to you, Joey. You're smart. You have a bright future ahead of you. Don't waste it. And remember, if the draft catches up with you, join the Navy."

This time I refused to take the money he offered me.

"I have to do this on my own," I told him.

He gave me a smile and his usual iron-grip handshake.

By then, I knew most of his secrets. He had spent a year in prison for manslaughter in the 1920s but that was the result of a car accident. A drunk had tried to cross the street at a blind spot on a rainy night while Uncle Lew was driving his Cadillac through the Bowery. Uncle Lew told me he had braked and swerved to avoid the man but wasn't quick enough. Lew clipped the man with his fender, immediately stopped, and tried the help the man, who was in pretty bad shape. The streets were empty. No one was around to call for an ambulance or the police. So, Uncle Lew took the man to the hospital in his car, but the man died. Uncle Lew pled guilty on the advice of his lawyer and expected probation, but the judge sent him to jail in the city for a year. Arnold Rothstein, the gangster who was said to have fixed the 1919 World Series, used to chauffer my Great Aunt Fanny—Great Uncle Lew's wife—to the jail to visit him behind bars.

"I'll write about you someday," I said.

"That will be nice, Joey. Take care of yourself. And tell your mother she'll always be my favorite."

I returned to New Jersey to wait for my passport to arrive by mail. I also had to decide what to take with me to Canada.

My mother had resigned herself to my decision.

"I'll pray for you," she assured me. She said she would continue to talk to her Republican friends and try to get as many of them elected as possible. "The only chance we have of getting out of this war is to have a change of guard at the top. Then, they can come in and say, 'Look, this isn't our war.' And they'll be able to end it."

I hoped it would be that simple, but I had my doubts.

I cashed in the remainder of my US savings bonds. The oldest was from my late Grandma Anna. It was a real war bond, bought when I was born and while the Americans were getting ready to cross the Rhine into Nazi Germany. It was also a month before my Uncle Sam had been captured.

My mother threw herself into trying to protect me as best she could. She wrote a long letter to my Los Angeles address while I was still in New Jersey, wording it carefully as if I were still in school and living there.

"If anyone in the government is looking through your mail, this should throw them off," she said.

My sister Daisy was living on campus at Montclair State. I didn't see her at all. She was still on crutches from her car accident but would soon be off them. She was trying as hard as she could to get away from the family and be on her own.

I saw my brother and sister-in-law briefly. Linda was pregnant. I didn't want to upset them. I said I was just taking the semester off and would either go in the Army or back to grad school in January.

I had been thinking about Montreal for so long that I decided to make it my destiny. I had been there. It was the closest large Canadian city to New York City.

I decided to take my typewriter, a copy of my manuscript, and as much clothing as I could stuff into an old duffle bag. I intended to tell the customs and immigration agents at the Montreal airport that I was a writer, and I was planning to visit for a few weeks—the truth, since I thought I would need time to make up my mind. I stuffed an old pair of ice skates that once belonged to my father into the bag at the last minute. If I had to, I would say I was going skating. That seemed like something Canadian.

Once my passport arrived in the mail, I was ready to go.

My father said goodbye to me at the house. We shook hands.

"Good luck," he told me.

"You, too."

I wondered if I would ever see him again.

My mother drove me to the bus stop in North Plainfield and tried to give me a couple of hundred dollars to tide me over. I refused to take it. I had been in New Jersey long enough to know how tight money was around the house. "I'm fine. I'll have a job of some kind in no time."

I spotted the New York bus turning the corner onto Mountain Avenue and heading toward the stop. I gave Mom a quick kiss on the cheek before hopping out of the car with my duffle bag and typewriter. The weather was already turning cold. I flagged the bus and hopped on. As the bus sped away, I caught a last glimpse out a side window of Mom turning the car around and heading to work.

I should have told her I loved her, I thought.

The Summer of Love had trickled off into the autumn of despair.

The big march on Washington had done nothing to turn back the tides of war. The fighting got worse every day. Almost a thousand young Americans were dying each month, thousands more were being wounded. The Vietnamese were losing many times that number each month with no end in sight.

I stayed at Uncle Sam's place for a few days. He had lined up some work for me with George Elliott. George was shooting a national Chevy print campaign at a vacant estate on Long Island. He needed extra help driving the cars between the estate and the dealership as well as help on the shoot.

At the end of the week, Sam handed me $750, a small fortune for someone like me who had been living on a hundred to a hundred and fifty a month for most of the past four years. It was also three times what I'd been promised. When I protested, Sam told me, "George wants you to have enough when you get to Canada. He kicked in the extra money. Don't say anything. Just take it. He thinks you're a great kid, and he wants to make sure you'll be okay up there. Don't worry. George can afford it."

I had to say something. Later, when Sam wasn't around, I tried thanking George. He told me, "Forget it, but just so you know, only half of the extra was mine. The other half came from Sam. Don't tell him."

"But I didn't earn it."

"Then, think of it as a loan. Someday, if Sam or I need help, pay us back. The way things are going here, we all might be following you up there before too long."

I was continuously surprised by how many of the people, who were much older than me, none of whom were personally threatened by the war or the draft—some who had fought in previous wars—said they might be following young men like me to Canada. Would there be a flood of sane people leaving the US for Canada in the near future?

At that moment, I was the first person they actually knew who was going to Canada. I wasn't exactly a flood of people.

As the day of my departure grew near, Uncle Sam telephoned a graphic artist, Emile Pirro. Sam had done business with Pirro over the summer during Expo 67. Pirro lived in Montreal. Sam had never met the artist, but he had seen Pirro's work and recommended him to some of the agencies in New York. Through Sam, Pirro had gotten a few jobs with American companies producing artwork for print campaigns for Montreal's world's fair.

Sam asked Emile if he might have room for me for a few days until I found my own place. Emile said yes.

I was nearly set. I was packed. I had a passport, money, and a place to crash for a few days.

The last thing Uncle Sam did on the night before I planned to fly out was take me to see one of our Canadian cousins who had moved to the US.

CHAPTER 87

Cousin Moe, the dentist, lived with his wife and three daughters across town from Sam in Great Neck. Moe was my grandfather's first cousin but closer in age to my mother and Uncle Sam's generation.

Moe answered the door and let us in.

Sam had already explained to Moe that I was going to Canada and why.

Moe wasn't very friendly. "I think you're making a mistake," he told me flat out as soon as we sat down in his living room. "The US is a much better place than Canada."

I didn't want to get in a political argument with him. So, I simply asked him what he could tell me about Montreal.

"I haven't been there in years." He took a magazine from the coffee table and handed it to me. "You can probably find out more by getting a subscription to this. It's like a Canadian *Time* magazine."

It was a copy of *Maclean's*. I flipped through the magazine. I thought of asking him if I could take it with me and read it, but I just didn't feel comfortable with him. I turned to Uncle Sam for help, but he remained quiet. I tried another question. "Uncle Sam said you have a sister living in Montreal."

"Lillian. She's a widow. She has a son and daughter-in-law in the suburbs."

Sam asked Moe for her address.

"I'll have to look it up." When he left the room to get the address, I whispered to Sam, "He doesn't seem very friendly."

Sam told me, "Shhh. I'll tell you later."

While Moe was gone, I started looking at several round, river stones sitting on the end table beside me. Each was about four to six inches across and cleverly painted.

Moe saw me looking at the rocks when he came back.

"My daughter paints them," he said, smiling slightly for the first time.

"They're very nice."

"She's a very talented artist," he said, handing me his sister's Montreal address and telephone number.

Sam managed to keep the conversation going for a few more minutes by talking about some of the other family members. No one said another word about Canada.

On the way back to Sam's house, I asked, "What was that all about? Moe doesn't seem to like Canada very much."

"Oh, Joey, I'm sorry. I thought your mother told you the story."

"What story?"

"The story of our family in Canada."

I knew my great grandfather had left Russia with his eleven-year-old son (my grandfather) for Canada in 1903 to live there for a few years to learn English ahead of bringing the rest of his family to the New World.

Sam explained, "Your great grandfather and grandfather lived with Moe's parents in Glace Bay, Nova Scotia for two years before settling in New York. Moe's parents—your great, great uncle and aunt—started out with a little store in Glace Bay at the turn of the century and had become very successful Glace Bay merchants and landlords by the 1940s. Two of their children, including the oldest and next to youngest—Moe—became dentists and moved to New York. The youngest became a psychiatrist and also moved to New York. One sister went to Montreal and another brother came to New York later. The only one who remained with her parents was an older daughter who was so mentally slow she couldn't live on her own. Canada was already at war by the spring of 1941; the US was still neutral. An older police sergeant, who rented a house from your great, great aunt and uncle got behind in his rent and refused to pay. On the advice of his lawyer, your great, great uncle served the police officer with an eviction notice. Later that day, the policeman in uniform showed up and shot and killed your great, great uncle and aunt with his service revolver."

"Moe's parents were murdered by a policeman in Canada?"

"Yes. The policeman was caught. There was a big trial. It was covered in all the newspapers across Canada. The policeman was committed to an insane asylum. He got off lightly because he was a World War I veteran who had been gassed. Moe's family thought it was a coverup. There was a lot of anti-Semitism in Canada in those days."

I was shocked. "I never heard about this."

"No one in the family talks about it. Moe's own kids don't even know the story. It's better forgotten. He seemed happy to talk with you when I spoke with him on the phone. Maybe, he was hoping he could talk you out of going."

"You think he might call the FBI and report me?"

"I don't think so."

It was a little eerie hearing this story on the eve of my departure, but I didn't let it stop me.

Canada isn't at war. That's all that matters, I reminded myself as I began to doze off on the cot in Uncle Sam's basement for what might be my last sleep in America for the rest of my life.

The next day Uncle Sam had to go into the city early for another shoot with George, so Uncle Sam's wife, Aunt Ceil, drove me to LaGuardia. I always liked Aunt Ceil. She talked to me like an adult, even when I was a child. She was smart and beautiful with narrow eyes and short blond hair. She had been a ballerina before she married Sam and had danced on Broadway in companies run by George Balanchine and Agnes de Mille. Like Uncle Sam, she was against the war and thought their son Adam might have to follow me to Canada if the war continued. She was also cautious. She warned me just before dropping me off at the terminal, "Whatever you do, don't ever give up your American citizenship." I wondered if Jewish relatives seeing their loved ones off in the early days of Nazi Germany told them to hang onto their German citizenship.

I wondered if FBI agents hung around the airports looking to catch people like me.

The draft board is probably still busy reclassifying me, I told myself as I boarded the Air Canada plane.

I was technically not yet formally wanted for resisting the draft since I hadn't even been called for my physical.

Did that matter?

Were there FBI agents in Montreal waiting to nab me?

Once I stepped off the plane in Canada, it would be hard to deny my intent to leave the country.

I felt a tremendous sense of trepidation as the plane taxied down the runway and finally lifted off the tarmac. Then, I felt relief.

I'm on my way.

As the plane made a circle over the city, I couldn't help wondering if I was seeing New York for the last time.

I knew enough to tell myself it was okay to be afraid of being afraid. It gave me an edge. Being a little on edge was always good when heading into the unknown.

It didn't take long to fly past the city and suburbs. We were soon passing over autumn fields, farms, and woods all decked out in camouflage colors—brown, tan, black, yellow, rust, olive—almost as if the fall season was dressing in combat colors to get ready to fight winter.

I had a plan. I would get working papers and a job as fast as I could. I would get my own place. I would fix my last book or finish a new one.

I thought about what my next book could be.

The streams flowing into the lakes below created curious forms, like giant tadpoles swimming through the landscape.

As my plane hurtled through the sky, taking me toward what I hoped would be a useful life, I thought about what I'd like to write—an anti-war story with a happy ending that showed peace winning.

Joe hitchhiking from California to New York, June 1965.

Joe at the start of his freshman year at USC at a fraternity rush party, Beverly Hills, September 1963.

Joe's passport photo, October 1967.

Joe and Pinkie at the world's first Love-In, Elysian Park, Los Angeles, Easter Sunday, March 26, 1967.

Joe at the start of his last year at USC thinking about his future and the war, December 1966.

EPILOGUE

I made it safely to Canada and wrote about my first three years in Montreal as a stateless exile, new immigrant, tabloid writer, journalist, and John Lennon's accidental muse in *Life After America, a Memoir about the Wild and Crazy 1960s.*

Garry Rusoff wrote a number of books (*Chariots of Fire, Throne of Fire, Spear of Fire, The Gourmet Guide to Grass,* and *Ripped*) and films (*Marian Rose White*) before finding his true calling as a teacher.

Carol Rusoff became a theater teacher, administrator, and director and producer.

Jeff and Cindy Weiss created a 300-acre private nature preserve in Northern California in sight of Mount Shasta where they grow most of their own food, generate most of their own electricity, and remain committed to trying their best to heal the planet.

Bruce Beery became one of the Central Coast's foremost architects and designers and worked on many projects throughout the West Coast and elsewhere in the US.

Karen Beery ran the guide program at the Hearst Castle for many years before moving to San Diego where until her retirement, she oversaw the state's operations in San Diego's Old Town.

Leslie Moulton Asplund worked in the TV and movie industry as an assistant director (*Charlie's Angels, Cagney and Lacey, Happy Days, Goonies*), earned a Ph.D. in social work and practiced as a psychotherapist for many years in the Seattle area while continuing to write, produce, direct, sing, and act in regional theater.

Michael Vosse continued to work in the music industry and TV production.

David Anderle became an acclaimed record producer and continued to paint portraits.

Buddy became an accountant and later a successful entrepreneur and pioneer in cloud computing.

Anna became a writer and a humanist and turned her back on the Communists after experiencing the deep-seated anti-Semitism of the party in Russia.

Kaye switched universities and majors again, earned a degree in early education, and taught elementary school in a small town in Northern California.

Fred continued to play flamenco and classical guitar professionally. He taught himself computer programing and provided computer services for the many pharmaceutical companies located in the New York–New Jersey metropolitan area.

John Beck had a motorcycle accident speeding along one of the roads coming down from the Hollywood Hills one rainy night in 1969. He went to his Army physical with his leg in a cast and was rejected for service. Having reached the cutoff age of twenty-six before being drafted, he was never called again and continued on with his career. His more than one hundred film and TV credits include *Sleeper*, *Pat Garrett and Billy the Kid*, *Rollerball*, *Dallas*, and *The Big Bus*.

Rick Kaplan, a childhood friend of Garry's, was selling blood once a month to survive when I ran into him in 1973, but shortly afterward, Garry introduced him to Donna Arkoff's first husband, Moody Blues musician Mike Pinder, and Rick began touring with the band, doing light shows for them. Mike Pinder and Rick also created the famous recording studio, Indigo Ranch, in Malibu, which focused on recording with old analog equipment when everyone was going digital. Their clients included many of rock 'n' roll's greatest artists.

George Elliott, the photographer, was killed in a freak airplane accident while filming a commercial for the US Army. My Uncle Sam, who was riding in the plane behind him, survived but suffered both emotionally and financially. I was able to send him enough money to help him out during his worst months when he was living in a teepee in upstate New York at the farm of his friend the artist Peter Max. Uncle Sam continued to represent many of the top photographers and commercial artists. A documentary, called *Sam's War: A GI's Journey*, was made about his military service and death-defying journey as a POW.

Great Uncle Lew was angry at me for several years, not because I had gone to Canada, but because I lied to him. He was right. We made amends, and I continued to speak with him until he passed away at ninety-four from old age after a life of smoking cigars.

Jay Thompson finished his book, and it was published under the title of *I Am Also a You* with a drawing by John Lennon as an introduction. Almost none of the celebrity photos nor the photo Jay had taken of me, ended up in the book.

Palmer Jan Ward, the young musician who had triggered the bust at the 32nd Street house, did get a record contract and continued to play music.

Rick Smith became a psychologist and still plays blues harp with local California groups.

Garth Bixler finished his military service, became a psychologist, husband, and father, and became a patron of the arts and LGBTQ initiatives.

Clementine "Pinkie" Van Deusen Black continued to be a fashion setter, designer, confidante, and muse of artists, filmmakers, and writers in California, New York, and elsewhere until her passing in 2016.

Richard Brownell, the star punter of the USC football team in 1963, worked as a stockbroker for a few years before moving with his wife and children to Lake of the Ozarks in Missouri where he became a land broker.

Kim Charney became a successful surgeon in Orange County, California. Like me, Kim lost his copy of the Beatles Butcher cover years ago.

My fraternity big brother Dan became a successful clinical and forensic psychologist in Southern California.

Donna Arkoff became a feature film producer (*Benny and Joon, Grosse Point Blank*, and six other films).

Lou Arkoff became a film and TV producer (*Inspector Gadget, The 13th Warrior*, and *George of the Jungle*).

William Phelps became a producer, director, and writer best known for the feature film, *North Shore*.

Jennifer Dohrn became a national leader of the Weather Underground's above ground support group, the Prairie Fire Organizing

Committee, spokeswoman for her sister Bernardine Dohrn, and a much lauded professor of nursing at Columbia University.

My later, week-long meeting with Derek Taylor and telephone conversations with Allen Ginsberg during John and Yoko's Montreal Bed-In in 1969 are documented in my book *Life After America, A Memoir about the Wild and Crazy 1960s*.

My father lived only six more years and succumbed at sixty-two in January 1973 from heart failure possibly from medications he was taking for his Parkinson's disease.

My mother remarried a year after my father's death to a close family friend, retired from her two jobs, and continued her many civic and political activities. She was honored on many occasions for her civic work by the township.

My brother continued to teach middle school in the township we grew up in until the late 1980s before moving first to California and then Wisconsin where he remained active in rendezvous and mountain men reenactments and gun shows. Linda earned a Ph.D. in public health nursing and later a nurse practitioner's degree and continued to work in nursing.

My sister Daisy became an occupational therapist, teacher, artist, and writer.

ACKNOWLEDGMENTS

I would like to thank the following people who read early versions of *California 1963-1967 Spaceship Earth* or corresponded or spoke with me and offered insight and advice on the telling of this story: Al Abramson, Salem Alaton, Leslie Moulton Asplund, Rosemary Aubert, John Beck, Bruce Beery, Karen Beery, Shulamit Beigel, Kenneth and Debby Bitticks, Garth Bixler, Sam Brody, Richard Brownell, Kim Charney, Fred Dilzell, Barbara Headley Dinger, James Dubro, Carl Emerich, Alan Glazner, Raymond and Linda Glazner, Terry Guerin, Linda and Bill Hatch, Carolyn Heitmann, Fred Jordan, Daniel and Kay Kramon, Iris and Bill Leigh, Robert Levin, George Perabo, William Phelps, Carol Rusoff, Garry Rusoff, Joan Shirriff, Rick Smith, William Stone, John Sullivan, Elizabeth Vihnanek, Michael Vosse, Diane Wanat, Palmer Jan Ward, Jeff and Cindy Weiss, Doug West, Jon Wolfe, and others who I unintentionally may have missed.

ABOUT JOSEPH MARK GLAZNER

Joseph Mark Glazner is an internationally acclaimed American-Canadian memoirist, crime writer, and counterculture chronicler. In addition to *California 1963-1967 Spaceship Earth*, he is the author of *Life After America, A Memoir about the Wild and Crazy 1960s*, and eight crime novels, written under his own name (including *MurderLand*) and his pen name, Joseph Louis (including the Shamus and Crime Writers of Canada nominated *Madelaine*).

Raised in rural Warrenville, New Jersey, he lived in his late teens and early twenties in Los Angeles. He earned a bachelor's degree in psychology (*magna cum laude*) from the University of Southern California and was elected to the Phi Beta Kappa Society in 1967. In addition to writing crime novels and memoirs about the counterculture, he has worked as a journalist, screenwriter, futurist in a think tank, and communications adviser to corporations, governments, and NGOs in Canada. the US, and the Bahamas.

He lives in Toronto, Canada.

END NOTES

[1] The University of Southern California, founded in 1880, was built on land donated by a Protestant, a Catholic, and a Jew. It was five miles away from downtown in what was farmland on the northern border of the county's first agricultural fair grounds, later called Exposition Park. The neighborhood around the school was known as West Los Angeles in the teens and Roaring Twenties and was considered very upscale. The neighborhood went into decline in the 1930s, a decline that continued well into the 1960s.

[2] USC's Doheny Library was built in remembrance of Edward "Ned" Doheny, Jr., the only son of the renowned oil baron, Edward Sr., the Rockefeller of California. I had heard of Doheny, the father, in high school when I read about the Tea Pot Dome Scandal, a crooked deal involving government lands and oil drilling rights in the 1920s. Ned, the son, the one who the library was dedicated to, was allegedly shot by his deranged male secretary before the secretary took his own life. The murder-suicide provided Raymond Chandler with inspiration for his third novel, *The High Window*, and remains fodder for conspiracy theorists to this day.

[3] On November 1, 1960, seven days before the presidential election, presidential candidate John F. Kennedy visited the heart of the USC campus, stood on the steps of Doheny Library, and spoke to a gathering of 20,000 at the university's First-Time Voters Convocation. He referred to his own alma mater, Harvard University, as "the University of Southern California in the East." I was still in high school at the time, but I always felt JFK was speaking directly to me. I was one of those students Kennedy spoke of. I was one of those who had the "longest stake in the great Republic," who were "the most concerned with the search for truth," and had "the least ties to the present and the most ties to the future...."

---

[4] Veteran child actor and teen singing star Kim Charney had had a small part in *How the West Was Won*, which was released earlier in 1963 and was still playing around town that fall. It was Kim's last film before retiring and entering USC to fulfill his childhood ambition to become a doctor.

[5] Kim Charney had a curious connection to the assassination of President Kennedy. A child actor with fifty movies and TV episodes to his credit, Kim's first major role in film was in a black-and-white feature film thriller, called *Suddenly*, when he was nine. Kim played a little kid in a happy-go-lucky family in small town America. Kim and his family become prisoners in their own home when a gang of hired assassins take over their house because it is the perfect location for shooting the President of the United States, who is expected to arrive by train in the next hour. The head of the band of assassins is Frank Sinatra, a ruthless, psychopathic, hired killer and war veteran, who ends up smacking Kim in the movie to shut him up. Lee Harvey Oswald, an ex-US Marine, apparently drew some of his inspiration for killing President Kennedy after watching reruns of the movie on television in Dallas in the months leading up to the assassination.

[6] The film *Suddenly* became controversial for another reason. It was one of the first black-and-white films to be colorized. It quickly became one of the main poster children for the anti-colorization forces because Frank "Old Blue Eyes" Sinatra's blue eyes were turned brown by the process. It was also rumored that Frank Sinatra was so outraged by a possible link between *Suddenly* and President Kennedy's assassination that he used his legal team to make sure the film wasn't broadcast again for decades.

[7] Three weeks before the assassination, while walking across Exposition Boulevard late one cloudy night, Richard had gotten me as close as I'd come to being arrested since landing in Los Angeles.

We had gone out to try to find a diner still open where we could get some hamburgers.

While crossing the wide boulevard south of the campus, Richard spotted a car far in the distance coming toward us and decided to show me how to hold up traffic.

We stopped in the middle of the otherwise empty street and stood there while the oncoming car's headlights played on us.

We were in no danger of being run over. I figured the car would just swing around us and be on its way.

Only when it was nearly upon us did we realize it was a cop car.

"Should we run?" I asked.

"Don't move," Richard advised. "Don't worry. I'll handle this."

I stood still, wondering if he was going to bolt at the last second, and if I should follow or stay if he did.

The patrol car slowed down to a roll and pulled up in front of us, the bumper twenty feet away.

Two burly cops got out. Both cops were taller and broader than Richard.

"What's going on here," the driver and older of the two cops asked as he came toward us.

Richard spoke with the ease of a snake oil salesman. "Nothing to worry about, officer. I was just showing my friend here from New Jersey how polite our drivers are to pedestrians in our great state of California."

The driver asked for our student IDs and driver's licenses. We handed them over. When the cop finished checking our IDs, he looked up at Richard and asked, "Pomona's your hometown?"

"Yup," Richard said. Pomona was a small city thirty miles to the east.

"Tell me something, Richard. Would you have pulled a stunt like this at home?"

Without hesitating, Richard grinned from ear to ear, "Heck, yes. My father's the mayor."

The passenger-side cop could barely keep from laughing. The driver wasn't as amused. He gave us both five-dollar jaywalking tickets and a warning that if he saw either of us again in the middle of the street, he'd haul us downtown.

Three weeks later, the incident seemed like a lifetime had passed; a time of innocence that had vanished. Both of us were silent as we crossed Exhibition Boulevard and headed to the Coliseum to see if anything was going on there.

[8] Kennedy was nominated as the Democratic candidate for president at the Sports Arena, which was a few blocks away from the Coliseum. He gave his acceptance speech, introducing the New Frontier concept at the Coliseum on July 15, 1960, three years before his assassination.

The New Frontier was supposed to be my generation's hope and challenge, our equivalent of the New Freedom of President Woodrow Wilson, the New Deal of President Franklin Roosevelt, and the Fair Deal of President Harry Truman.

The New Frontier was supposed to win back America's lead in space and reverse its waning influence in Asia, Latin America, and Africa.

The New Frontier was intended to win peace in a world where mankind, as Kennedy said, had the means to "exterminate the entire species some seven times over."

The New Frontier was supposed to stir us to face the challenges and new prospects of revolutions in technology, the urban population explosion, medicine, automation, and "a peaceful revolution for human rights—demanding an end to racial discrimination in all parts of our community."

The question of the New Frontier, said Kennedy, was "the choice our nation must make—a choice that lies not merely between two men or two parties, but between the public interest and private comfort—between national greatness and national decline—between the fresh air of progress and the stale, dank atmosphere of 'normalcy'—between determined dedication and creeping mediocrity."

[9] A few of the Beatles' songs had been released in the US earlier in the year, but they had disappeared without much notice. Within weeks of the December release, the Beatles were dominating the airwaves. By February 1, 1964, "I Want to Hold Your Hand" was number one on the US Billboard chart.

[10] Side A of the single was "I Want to Hold Your Hand; side B was "I Saw Her Standing There."

[11] *The Ed Sullivan Show* was a very popular Sunday night variety show that attracted the whole family and usually had the largest audience of any show on Sunday nights. Most homes only had one TV, so watching television was something the whole family did together. That night a record 73 million Americans, or an estimated 45.3 percent of the US population with televisions watched the Beatles perform "All My Love," "Till There Was You," "She Loves You," "I Saw You Standing There," and their first US number one hit "I Want to Hold Your Hand."

Instantly, a large portion of the female population from preteens to women in their early twenties fantasized about one or more of the Beatles as boyfriends. The same cohort of males wanted to be Beatles, or at least, look and act as cool as the Beatles looked and acted on stage and in interviews. Boys and young men grew their hair longer.

[12] The judges for USC's Songfest in 1964 were music and Hollywood professionals, including Nelson Riddle. Our number, "Tobacco Road", won first place in the Variety Division and second in the grand sweepstakes after a reputed wrestling match between the judges, which forced a second vote. The show was recorded, and a record album was made of the concert.

[13] Another exhibit I helped put together a year later with librarian Jean Reif in the library's treasure room was about the humanist, Dr. Albert Schweitzer. The job included sifting through some of his letters and books and topping the display off with one of his pith helmets worn in one of the leper colonies where he served. Jean and I had our pictures taken for a nice writeup in the school paper *The Daily Trojan*.

[14] One question left unanswered for me by the assassination of President Kennedy was whether he would have gotten the US deeper into the civil war in Vietnam.

As a US Congressman, Kennedy visited Vietnam in October 1951. Kennedy traveled with his brother, Bobby, and sister, Pat, who accompanied him mainly to keep an eye on his secret health issues, which at one point on the seven-nation tour nearly killed him.

The then-thirty-four-year-old Kennedy was hoping to return to the US from his seven-nation, Asian, fact-finding mission as an influential voice in international affairs and containment of Communism in Asia.

Containment was the position favored by the right-of-center Democrats and Republicans, including Wisconsin radical, Senator Joseph McCarthy, who felt President Truman was not being tough enough on Communism.

Kennedy was planning to run for Massachusetts Governor or US Senator in 1952. He was hoping to raise his profile. He visited Saigon at a time when the Vietminh guerillas were throwing grenades and carrying out bomb attacks on the French colonial rulers while pro-French agents were assassinating and beheading suspected Communists. The Vietminh were Communist-dominated nationalist guerillas fighting in Vietnam when it was still under Colonial French rule. The Viet Cong were Communist guerillas operating in South Vietnam *after* the French had left and the country had been divided into South and North Vietnam in 1955.

Kennedy flew over the countryside where the French Foreign Legion was fighting the Vietminh.

The Kennedy entourage was greeted in Hanoi by a flag-waving crowd.

[15] Officially, Congressman Kennedy was told the population supported the French and the West. Privately he was told by knowledgeable newspaper reporters that the overwhelming majority of the Vietnamese people—as much as 70 percent—would support Ho Chi Minh over the French or the pro-French leaders in the country in a free election. Kennedy was told that the French colonial war against the Vietminh, for which the US was providing 50 percent of the French arms and supplies, would fail. French colonial rule was doomed.

Kennedy concluded that nationalism was the driving force of the times for much of the underdeveloped world, not Communism or capitalism. By siding with the French in Vietnam and other colonialists and autocrats elsewhere, America would increasingly be seen as a colonialist.

Returning to the United States, Kennedy put forward his idea of "a third way" or a third force for Vietnam. The third way called for support for the Vietnamese people against both French colonialism and the Communist insurgents.

American support of a doctrine of counterinsurgency soon became the policy of the US in Vietnam. Americans, he believed, should work behind the scenes with Vietnam nationalists who were not Communists.

[16] A decade later—after the French had been kicked out and Vietnam divided into a North and South Vietnam—Kennedy remained anti-Communist at the beginning of his presidency in January 1961. He continued to subscribe to the Domino Theory, which said if South Vietnam fell to the Communists, other nations around it would fall. Once in the White House, he secretly helped finance the increase of the South Vietnamese Army by twenty thousand men and increased the number of US military advisers by a thousand in contravention of the 1954 Geneva Agreement.

He supported the Strategic Hamlet program of President Diem, which forcibly uprooted villagers around the country and moved them to new locations, increasing the support of the Viet Cong among unknown numbers of local, angry, displaced, rural inhabitants.

Kennedy authorized US military advisers in South Vietnam to return fire if fired upon on Valentine's Day 1962.

Kennedy had increased the number of US military personnel in Vietnam from about 900 when he took office in January 1961 to 11,300 by the end of 1962.

By 1963, the year I finished high school and began university, Kennedy had begun to change his mind. He became convinced that the situation in South Vietnam was becoming uncontrollable. President Diem didn't appear to be the right man to pull the many different non-Communist forces together to effectively stop the Communists. Some believed Kennedy was beginning to favor withdrawing US military advisers from South Vietnam after the US presidential election in 1964. Kennedy, some said, also supported the coup to remove President Diem as part of the strategy of installing new South Vietnam leaders, who, in turn, would ask the Americans to leave. Kennedy appeared to be against an escalation of American forces in Vietnam, including combat ground troops, which inevitably would include draftees.

[17] So, what would a Kennedy-run America have looked like in February 1965? What if Kennedy was still president, unconcerned about ever running for office again, and having no political risks domestically by being called soft on Communism? I had little doubt he would look at the Vietnam War differently than President Johnson did in 1965.

Kennedy was intellectually and philosophically different than Johnson.

Kennedy had been to war and been under fire. He had saved lives and proven himself as brave as anyone. He was smart. He would have done his homework. He would have looked to the polls—not just the polls of public opinion in the US but *the public opinion polls on the ground in South Vietnam among all the Vietnamese, not just the ruling class.*

"How many of you in Vietnam want more US intervention in your country's affairs? How many of you want less?" he would have asked himself. He likely would have demanded answers to those questions.

[18] By 1965, I wanted to believe Kennedy would clearly have seen that the minority in Vietnam would never unite enough to win over the majority. The overwhelming wish of the majority of Vietnamese was to get all foreigners out of Vietnam. The only thing that adding more American advisers, increasing financing, and arming the South Vietnam military had achieved was to encourage America's two Cold War enemies, China and the Soviet Union, to increase their arms shipments to North Vietnam and the Viet Cong.

The Viet Cong's support and ranks continued to swell with villagers and farmers who had been displaced or had come to fear soldiers of all sides moving through their fields and rice paddies.

The numbers would have told Kennedy everything he needed to know. Between 60-80 percent of the people of North and South Vietnam combined wanted the Americans to go. It was about the same number of Vietnamese who were against partitioning their country in the 1950s and now wanted their country reunited again.

For anyone with any sense of the reality on the ground, Vietnam was already lost to Western control by the beginning of 1965. Only Washington and the ruling class in America weren't ready to accept that just yet.

Vietnam wasn't a domino. It was an independent state trying to unite itself. If the US had gotten out of Vietnam by 1965, the Americans probably could have been doing business with it in a few years.

Kennedy knew enough history to be confident that the Vietnamese Communists weren't being run by Moscow or China. Supplied, yes, but manipulated, no. The Vietnamese Communists were fierce local nationalists; many were veterans of their war of independence when they had thrown the French out. What united them against the French and then the Americans was their belief that they wanted to run their own country.

By 1965, Kennedy would have understood enough to find a way out of Vietnam. Any efforts to continue to prop up a minority in the South would inevitably be futile and cost more lives.

Kennedy was wise to prosperity. He understood that peace was better for business than war, except for the military-industrial complex that Eisenhower had warned of. This minority of American businesses made money off of war.

But Kennedy was dead. Johnson didn't understand Vietnam. All he could understand was the American view of Vietnam. The tragedy of my generation was about to unfold.

[19] Unknown to me, Jeff had smoked grass with his cousin Laurie a few months after I had taken my first toke. He hooked up with a couple of USC women studying TV production and continued to smoke through his remaining years at USC. Even though we were very close, the stigma of smoking weed was so great that neither of us told the other we smoked grass until several years later.

[20] Lou Rusoff wrote scripts for *Terry and the Pirates* and *The Rheingold Theater* before beginning nearly a decade-long career in the movies as a writer and producer. Four of his early writing credits were for films directed by Roger Corman—*Apache Woman*, *The Day the World Ended*, *It Conquered the World*, and *The Oklahoma Woman*.

[21] *Mister Ed* was a TV situation comedy in the early to mid-1960s featuring a talking horse.

[22] Sandoz continued to manufacture LSD until the middle of 1965. LSD became illegal in California on October 6, 1966.

[23] After World War II, the pharmaceutical industry exploded with miracle drugs that were legally prescribed across America and also bought illegally by millions. Uppers or amphetamines or black and whites, and downers or barbiturates, also known as yellow jackets, reds, and other names, were showing up with increasing frequency among my friends, especially the girls, often from parents' medicine cabinets or prescribed to someone because some doctor thought they needed speeding up or slowing down. Most of the girls who were having sex were on the birth control pill.

[24] Years later, I discovered the high-rises along Highway 401 were just one of the many new post-war Toronto suburbs. The heart of the city was more than eight miles to the south.

[25] My knowledge of Canada was spotty. While I knew the prime minister had won the Nobel Prize, I also thought Montreal was located on the coast north of Boston. It never occurred to me to look at a map of Canada, not even while riding with Mr. Brewster. Except for the time we got lost, he seemed to know all the roads, so we never used a map.

[26] *The War of the Worlds* was a CBS presentation of Orson Welles and the Mercury Theatre on the Air, a weekly show that presented original radio plays. The radio play of *The War of the Worlds* was an adaption written by Orson Welles, John Houseman, and Howard Koch, of the science fiction book *The War of the Worlds* by H. G. Wells.

[27] Because my father was still in his early fifties and relatively healthy except for his Parkinson's disease, he had been interviewed and accepted as a candidate for cryosurgery under Dr. Irving Cooper in New York's St. Barnabas Hospital in the Bronx in early 1964. Cooper had pioneered a number of surgical techniques for brain-related ailments and had been written up in *Time* magazine in 1962 after his very first experiments had proved successful in reducing Parkinson's symptoms.

[28] Sophie "Jeanette" Brody Glazner Rilley trained to be a commercial artist at one of the city's most important technical schools, an elite public school for gifted children who excelled in art or had a flair for business (Girls Commercial High School, Brooklyn 1926-1930) As a commercial high school, their class trips were to business establishments. Her class trip in the last semester of her senior year (September 1929-January 1930) was supposed to be a routine trip to the New York Stock Exchange. They arrived there on one of the first days of the Great Crash of 1929. She was the only person in the family who could hold a steady job when she graduated in January 1930. She supported her family and members of her extended family as a sketcher and designer on Seventh Avenue and financed her husband's (Louis Glazner's) first factory before leaving the fashion business at twenty-eight to reinvent herself as a full-time mother and small-town civic leader and politician.

[29] I earned all A's, a perfect 4.0, in the first semester of my sophomore year, one of only 68 students in the entire undergraduate, full-time student body of about five thousand, who had achieved this. Only 359 students made the Dean's List, which required a minimum of a 3.5 grade average with at least fourteen credits. I earned a second 4.0 during my second semester after I began to smoke pot on a frequent basis. I had little fear by then of losing my USC scholarship, which only required full-time attendance and a 3.0 grade point average.

[30] From Adlai Stevenson's UN speech: "We travel together, passengers on a little spaceship, dependent on its vulnerable reserves of air and soil; all committed for our safety to its security and peace; preserved from annihilation only by the care, the work, and, I will say, the love we give our fragile craft. We cannot maintain it half fortunate, half miserable, half confident, half despairing, half slave—to the ancient enemies of man—half free in a liberation of resources undreamed of until this day. No craft, no crew can travel safely with such vast contradictions. On their resolution depends the survival of us all." ADLAI STEVENSON, US Ambassador to the United Nations, addressing the Economic and Social Council of the United Nations, Geneva, Switzerland, July 9, 1965, five days before he died.

[31] The Watts Riots had started almost like comic street theater early Wednesday night, two days before I had any inkling anything was wrong.

Around 7 PM, Wednesday, August 11, a Black man in a pickup truck just south of the Los Angeles city limits hailed Lee Minikus, a white motorcycle officer of the California Highway Patrol (CHiP). The Black man reported a car driving erratically. Sunset was about forty-five minutes away, so there was still plenty of daylight. It was also very hot. Temperatures had reached into the mid-90s during the day. The smog continued to hold the heat throughout the basin as the CHiP officer tailed the old gray Buick traveling north along Avalon Boulevard. Minikus clocked the car at fifty in a 35 MPH zone before turning on his flasher and siren. The Buick and motorcycle, now inside the Los Angeles city limits, pulled to the side of the street of the all-Black, low-rise neighborhood between East 116th Place and East 116th Street, and roughly two-and-a-half miles (or a six minute drive) southwest of the commercial heart of Watts.

[32] Watts itself was a strip of some forty-one low-rise stores spread out on either side of the old train station at 1686 East 103rd Street.

[33] The driver, twenty-one-year-old Marquette Frye, got out of the car and had a friendly exchange with Minikus as a few dozen onlookers, some sipping beer, drifted out of nearby apartments and off stoops to watch. At first, the crowd—by all accounts, including Frye's— was more amused than angry as the officer politely and efficiently questioned Marquette Frye, the driver.

Frye was unable to produce a driver's license, claiming he lost it several days before. After smelling alcohol on his breath and after giving Frye a couple of routine drunk driver tests—walking a straight line and touching his nose—Minikus concluded the driver was under the influence and told him he was under arrest. Frye, an inexperienced drinker, who had been knocking back vodka and orange juices during the afternoon, joked with Minikus as he tried to talk his way out of being arrested. The crowd watched with continued amusement.

Minikus called for backup as well as a transport car to take Frye to the station. A dispatch also went out to a tow truck operator to pick up the vehicle.

Frye's home was less than a block from the scene. Some of the crowd knew Frye, and someone went to his apartment and alerted his mother, Rena Frye, who was in the kitchen cooking dinner. She was told Marquette Frye and her twenty-two-year-old-stepson, Ronald Frye, the passenger in the Buick, were both being arrested, even though Ronald hadn't been charged.

Rena, 49, quickly headed to the scene. By then, another CHiP officer on a motorcycle arrived. The officer driving the transport car and a tow truck and driver also arrived.

The crowd had reached a hundred when Rena confronted the tow truck driver, insisting that the car was registered under her and her husband's name—Ronald's father, Marquette's stepfather. Minikus, still amicable and pleasant, agreed to release the car to her.

When Frye wandered over to his mother, she appeared angrier at him than she was at the police, accusing him of not acting normal and being drunk. She pushed him away.

At this point Frye first went ballistic, telling his mother he wasn't drunk and that he wasn't going to let the cops take him to jail. As Minikus tried grabbing Frye's arm to move him to the transport vehicle, Frye yanked his arm away and started swearing at the officer, saying the police would have to kill him to take him in, telling the cops not to touch him, and threatening to kill them. He ran off a short distance as one of the other officers handed Minikus a pair of handcuffs. An 1199 call—Officer Needs Help—was sent to their headquarters. The two motorcycle cops grabbed their riot batons, and the transport officer grabbed an unloaded shotgun from his car.

Frye continued to taunt the police to kill him as two more highway patrol officers arrived.

In the melee to arrest Frye, he was jabbed in the stomach with a baton. When he tried to grab the baton, he was struck on the forehead, the stick making an audible cracking sound. Soon, Ronald was tussling with the police, and little Rena had jumped on the back of Minikus while Frye was being put into the transport vehicle. Rena and Ronald were also arrested and cuffed and put into the back seat. When Frye tried to get out, his feet were cuffed, and it apparently appeared incorrectly to some in the crowd that one of the officers with his back to the crowd slammed Frye's feet in the door, which hadn't happened. Members of the crowd shouted the occasional words of protest and threats toward the police.

By the time the transport car drove off with Marquette Frye, Ronald Frye, and Rena Frye, about fifty police officers had converged on the scene. As the crowd continued to grow verbally abusive, the decision was made to withdraw from the area. Over the next five or ten minutes as the sun sank in the west, the police gathered all their men together and began to leave as a group. As they retreated, the crowd began pelting the officers, motorcycles, and squad cars with rocks and empty and full bottles of beer and soda.

As the last of the police made it through the crowd, a young woman bystander, Joyce Anne Gaines, allegedly spit on one of the cops and the officer tried to arrest her. Soon, the woman was in the middle of a tug of war between several officers and the crowd. Gaines was a twenty-year-old men's barber by trade and had been about to start cutting a client's hair at the barber shop four blocks away when Minikus had first pulled over Marquette Frye and Ronald Frye. Curious when she heard about the confrontation, she left the shop to watch the show, still dressed in her blue barber's smock—which appeared to those who didn't know her like a maternity outfit. The rumor spread that the police were manhandling a pregnant Black woman.

One policeman recalled hearing a cry of "Burn, Baby, Burn" from one of the bystanders as the troops withdrew.

"Burn, Baby, Burn" was the mantra of a popular Black Los Angeles Rhythm and Blues and Soul disc jockey, Nathaniel "Magnificent" Montague, who often used the phrase when he started playing a record.

The chant was soon on the lips of the crowd as it grew well past a thousand and began to spread through the adjoining Black communities, picking up more spectators and angry young men and teenagers throwing rocks and bottles at any passing police and civilian cars regardless of whether the occupants were Black or white.

By 9:30 PM police moved into the area near the original confrontation and set up a command post at Imperial and Avalon. The eighty-two police officers were no match for a mob, now numbering about 1,500, in the four-by-five block area. While police were withdrawing around midnight, a small group of officers counterattacked the mob. The mob began attacking not only white policemen but any whites in sight, including any who had come to the scene as spectators and white newsmen and white motorists innocently passing through the riot area.

A number of Blacks, including many community leaders, mainly older men, tried calming the rioters but were threatened by the mainly young, often teen-aged rioters.

[34] Robert Hall, a Black civil rights worker from the area who worked tirelessly to halt the Black violence, was credited with stopping rioters who were viciously beating Nicholas Beck, a white United Press International reporter. Other Blacks stood up to the rioters to stop beatings of white motorists.

[35] By first light on Thursday, nineteen police officers and sixteen civilians had been injured, thirty-four people had been arrested, and fifty vehicles damaged or burned, but virtually no real estate had been damaged. Most of the stores in the Black communities opened, and most of the residents went to work and carried on with their normal routines.

Amazingly, no shots had yet been fired. Amazingly, I knew nothing about any of this as I went to work, oblivious to what was happening only nine miles to the southeast of me.

On Thursday, the streets remained quiet during the day. When the County Human Relations Commission met at two in the afternoon at Athens Park, Rena Frye, now out on bail, called for calm, but then she gave her version of the arrests which angered the crowd. A teenager told the crowd he intended to take the battle to the white neighborhoods that night. His message was caught by the television cameras and broadcast over local stations, provoking a run on local gun shops by whites. Traditional civic and religious Black leaders were openly dismissed by speakers in their teens and twenties with great contempt. An attempt by the Black leaders of the community to have only Black plain-clothes cops in unmarked cars patrolling the Black neighborhoods that night was rejected by the police as impractical.

The sense of empowerment was palpable in South Central all Thursday afternoon. The small fringe elements of Black nationalists and Black defense advocates talked about open warfare. Some unemployed, restless, energized, bored young people in their teens and early twenties probably saw the coming adventure as a chance to rebel against authority—against their parents and civic and religious institutions just as their white counterparts across town like me were doing by experimenting with drugs, sex, dropping out, and toying with resisting the draft.

The majority of the Black community was shaken and worried as Black youths in the neighborhoods around Watts spent the afternoon preparing for battle, stockpiling rocks and bottles, and making Molotov cocktails.

The police were also preparing for a tough night. By late Thursday afternoon, Avalon Boulevard was filled with police, many armed with long-range tear gas guns. Police Chief William Parker III had made the first call to officials in Sacramento, telling them that he may have to request help from the National Guard. Lieutenant Governor Glenn Anderson was alerted. He was in charge. Governor Pat Brown was vacationing in Greece.

At sunset on Thursday, new rioting broke out. Cops were pelted with rocks; passing cars were stoned. If white motorists stopped on the way through the growing riot area, they were pulled from their cars and beaten, their cars overturned and set on fire.

The first fire to be set in a store occurred near the location where the Fryes had been arrested. More stores were broken into and looted. Guns and ammunition were taken from local army surplus stores and passed around to would-be guerrillas and delinquents, most of whom had never fired a gun in their lives. Firemen were bombarded with rocks and shot at when they responded to the fires. Emergency switchboards were overloaded with reports of violence and arson. False reports sent police to locations where they were ambushed by rioters with rifles. War cries of "Get Whitey" and "Burn, Baby, Burn" were heard everywhere in the spreading war zone.

A small cohort of Black ministers and other civic leaders continued to roam the streets, trying to pacify the crowds. When possible, they tried to rescue whites who were being beaten. Black storekeepers tried to protect their stores by painting "Blood Brother" and "Negro Business" on their shop fronts.

Even light-skinned Blacks were targeted. Any car, even those with Blacks inside, could be a target since no one could see the color of the occupants' skin in a darkened car. Word soon went around that Blacks should drive with the lights on inside their cars so they could be identified by the rioters. "Burn, Baby, Burn," became the password Blacks used to greet friends and neighbors to guarantee safe passage along the streets.

[36] The first forays into Watts proper soon occurred as the stores in the business center along East 103rd Street were broken into and looted, and the buildings set on fire. The more than forty buildings in the center of Watts—virtually all of the non-residential buildings in the neighborhood—were burned except for the train station, leaving the strip with the dubious title of Charcoal Alley.

[37] Later, we found out that around midnight when we had set off for the basin, a speeding car refused to stop at a checkpoint, scattering a group of soldiers, and hitting one of the Guardsmen who didn't get out of the way fast enough, giving him a head injury and a broken leg.

[38] The great hope for quelling the riots that night was the thousand National Guardsmen from the 40th Armored Division on their way in small convoys, heading toward two staging areas in the riot zone. Several thousand more Guardsmen would soon follow.

[39] The old World War I carbine was originally built to take an 8mm cartridge, but it had been retrofitted between the wars (in 1934—hence the M34) to take the more powerful 7.5 mm x 54 mm shells.

[40] The news coverage of the rioting in South Central appeared to be the main cause of comparatively minor copycat rioting elsewhere, including three days of rioting in San Diego, in which eighty-one people were arrested; one day of rioting, looting, and fire bombings in Pasadena twelve miles from South Central; scattered rioting, looting, and burning in Pacoima, twenty miles away; arson in Monrovia twenty-five miles away; rioting that resulted in the death of a Long Beach police officer in Long Beach twelve miles away, and fires in the San Pedro-Wilmington area, also twelve miles away.

[41] Thirteen months before the Watts Riots, on July 10, 1964, a group of mostly Black World War II and Korean War vets formed an armed civil rights group

(adapting the name the Deacons for Defense and Justice in November), in Jonesboro, Louisiana to protect civil rights workers against Louisiana's very active and angry Ku Klux Klan in the wake of the Civil Rights Act of 1964, passed on July 2.

In early June 1965, the first Black sheriff's deputy in Washington Parish, Louisiana was murdered, sparking civil rights demonstrations and violent confrontations instigated by the Klan against mainly peaceful civil rights protests in Bogalusa, the parish's main city. On July 8, 1965, a month before the Watts Riots, a young member of the Deacons, Henry Austan, stopped a Ku Klux Klan mob in its tracks by firing a .38 caliber pistol shot into the chest of Alton Crowe. Remarkably, Crowe survived the wound. Austan was never tried; he was whisked off to the New Orleans Parish prison where Louis Lomax, Los Angeles TV host and patient of my dentist, bailed him out after Austan agreed to an interview with the veteran journalist. The bloodshed also gave the US government the impetus to force the local police to begin defending the civil rights of local Blacks, effectively gutting the power of the Klan. Some say it was also a major turning point in the civil rights and Black power movements, ushering in an era when the armed civil rights movement began to take off and vie for power with the more peaceful non-violent movement advocated by Dr. Martin Luther King, Jr.

The Deacon win over the Klan, now an almost forgotten incident, was big news at the time, covered widely across the US and familiar to many in the Los Angeles crowd that evening, and probably consciously empowering some, unconsciously others.

[42] Dylan's electric sound was mesmerizing, enticing, and evocative in a way that the old folk music could never be. I heard the album before it was released as an acetate record at the Hollywood Hills home of Garry's friend, veteran TV character actor Linden Chiles. Seeing movies and hearing records before they were released to the public and meeting real working actors and people in show business, made me feel like I was close to the center of the world where new ideas were coming from. I hoped I could be a part of this world if I could find a way to make myself useful.

[43] *The Little Prince* was a fantasy novella written and illustrated by a French aviator and author Antoine de Saint Exupéry in 1943 while he was in exile in New York after the Nazis had overrun France.

[44] *The Little Prince* by Antoine de Saint-Exupéry is a love story and a story of the human condition, an allegory, and a fantasy. The part of the story that I knew she wanted me to read was about the little flower—a rose—which the Little Prince plants and falls in love with. He struggles through a relationship with the rose. He leaves her, in part, because she loves him but is unable to express her love because of her own self-involvement. Confused, the Little Prince wanders

the universe, learning about the flaws of adults, the openness of youth, and what he needs to know about love. Finally, he returns with a better understanding of himself and how he and his flower have both tamed each other and how they are both changed by their love.

[45] The Morgan Cox Award of the Writers Guild of America, west, is named in honor of Morgan B. Cox.

[46] Francis Zold was from an old Hungarian noble family with deep ties to the Austrian-Hungarian empire. He had been captain of the Hungarian fencing team at the 1948 Olympics. He had doctorates in law and the Hungarian language. He had been in the Hungarian Army during the second world war until the Nazis took over, and then worked with the International Red Cross for the remainder of the war and was a colleague of Swedish diplomat Raoul Wallenberg, who was credited with saving over 100,000 Jews from the death camps before he was finally captured and died in the hands of the advancing Red Army.

Zold had been a publisher after the war and after the Communist takeover. He escaped to the West with his wife and son in 1956 during the bloody and unsuccessful Hungarian Revolt. A serene and thoughtful man, he was the only person I ever met who taught an athletic program without shouting and who stressed the mind-body connection in the sport.

[47] Garry got caught in the middle of the Second Watts Riot, He was taking a class at Budd Schulberg's USC Watts Writers' Workshop on Beach Street in Watts. He and budding playwright and director Steve Kent volunteered to drive one of the Black women to her home in Garry's TR3, with the Black woman sitting on Kent's lap. A few blocks away from the workshop, a mob forced Garry to drive on the sidewalk to get away. Someone threw a bottle, hitting Garry in the head, but he managed to keep going. The woman's mother stemmed the blood from Garry's cut when they reached her house.

[48] The strict anti-hazing laws, which most fraternities ignored, had come into effect in 1959 after a pledge at USC's chapter of the Kappa Sigma fraternity died from choking while being forced to swallow oiled raw liver. The story had made national headlines, and USC did not want a repeat of that story.

[49] What Dr. Hadwen saw after the riots was what I had seen the few times I had driven past the areas that had been hardest hit. Lots of buildings were still boarded up. Some burned buildings were still waiting demolition. Nothing had changed. If anything, it had gotten worse. Watts was unlikely to see a new breakout of violence. Only a small minority living in South Central participated in the riots. Those Blacks who couldn't flee stayed inside as much as they could as if there was a plague running rampant in the streets. The under-served

community lost many small businesses and ties to the middle class Black and white communities following the riots.

[50] The *Smile* album was supposed to reflect a higher consciousness and spiritual experience, which Wilson believed could be achieved through laughter. The act of laughing was a time when control was lost. Brian became obsessed with the importance of vegetables and began adding vegetables to his lyrics. He became obsessed with all kinds of sounds. At one point, Mike told me he spent a week taping water sounds—sounds of the ocean, sounds of water splashing in a sink, flushing water in a toilet, rain, water from a hose, a kettle steaming on the stove. Brian wanted to stick to the natural sounds but Mike told me he was going to convince Brian that water was a force of nature and it didn't lose its force when it ran through our lives.

[51] In addition to finding and developing talent and running the Beach Boys' new management company, David Anderle was also an aspiring painter, who was working on a large painting of Brian Wilson, painting it from photos and memories of Brian, with whom he was interacting every day. At one point in the evolution of the painting, Anderle asked Garry to pose so David could paint Wilson's hands, which David said resembled Garry's. The hands in the painting didn't turn out very well, due more to David's lack of skill at that time than the shortcomings of Garry's hands.

[52] Written by Stephen Stills shortly after police and freaks battled it out over the closing of a Sunset Strip club, Pandora's Box, the song became one of the greatest protest songs of the times.

[53] Phi Beta Kappa is a national honorary society that elects the top students in the best schools across the country each year. It is the oldest academic honor society in America, founded in 1776 at William and Mary College five months after the Declaration of Independence was signed on July 4. I was one of 27 liberal arts students elected to Phi Beta Kappa in January 1967.

[54] Timothy Leary had begun using the phrase "Turn on, tune in, and drop out" in the fall of 1966. It became one of his most famous quotes. Years later, he said the phrase came from Marshall McLuhan when they were discussing LSD over lunch in New York City, and McLuhan had sung the words in tune to a popular Pepsi commercial of the times.

[55] A teleidoscope was a cross between a telescope and a kaleidoscope. Instead of being a closed system like a kaleidoscope with prisms and colored pieces of plastic or paper that formed different shapes, the teleidoscope had prisms at the end but a clear lens so real images were distorted. Kaye and I had joked that Picasso must have been using one of these when he painted his misshapen faces.

[56] The Picasso collection consisted of 165 works, including ninety-three from five sketch books of which ten were in color; forty-five separate drawings, of which four were in color; twenty-six oil paintings on canvas, and one colored chalk painting on canvas.

[57] I had been allergic to bee stings as a child, running fevers of 104 degrees Fahrenheit and limbs that swelled to twice their size with a big, ulcerated sore around the sting site. I carried pills of some kind around with me at YMCA and Boy Scout camps. I hadn't been bitten in years when I took my AF physical so I had no way of knowing how I would react. I learned years later that bee stings were automatic 4-Fs at one time.

[58] I have a photo that someone took of Pinkie and me at the world's first Love-In March, Easter Sunday, 1967. A little over two years later, I appear in the same yellow coat in various stills and film footage of John Lennon and Yoko Ono's Montreal International Bed-In for Peace. (See *Life After America, a Memoir about the Wild and Crazy 1960s*.)

[59] Taylor Hackford was a pre-law political science major at USC at the time. He would later become a filmmaker and distinguish himself directing such movies as *An Officer and a Gentleman* and *Ray*, the biopic of Ray Charles, for which he was nominated for Oscars Best Director and Best Picture.

[60] Carl F. Emerich later became Associate Vice President, Student Affairs at San Diego State University and a noteworthy artist and poet in his retirement.

[61] John Sullivan went on to direct plays at the Circle Repertory Theater and the Mark Taper Forum, and later held numerous administrative positions in theater and the arts, including deputy director of the California Arts Council, managing director of the American Conservatory Theater, and executive director of the Theatre Communications Group, the American regional theater's service organization.

[62] After the assassination of President Kennedy, an investigative journalist, Robert Sheer, told Paul Krassner, the publisher of *The Realist* that he had uncovered the back door through which the US government had been stoking a civil war in Vietnam. Krassner financed a round-trip ticket for Scheer to Vietnam.

The article Scheer wrote in March 1964 outlined how, over the past decade, the US had been pouring billions of dollars in aid, armaments, and advisers into the hands of the Diem regime. After the Diems and Kennedy were gone, the funds and weapons continued to flow to the new group of generals who had eliminated the Diems. The funnel went through a group of professors at Michigan State University. Their actions went largely unnoticed because of their so-called academic credentials. These professors helped create a police state in

South Vietnam, which created its own Vietnamese Bureau of Investigation modeled after the US FBI, through which the US was funneling funds to the South Vietnamese in contravention of the Geneva Convention.

The discussion of the Vietnam War in *The Realist* by Robert Scheer was a landmark work at the time and forced the main-stream media to begin to take the first critical look at the Vietnam War. Sheer would go on to be, among other things, an award-winning journalist, editor of *Ramparts* magazine, and a *Los Angeles Times* reporter and columnist for three decades.

[63] Paul Thek had studied at the Student Art League, Pratt, and Cooper Union. He was still waiting for his big break. He would be well enough known within a couple of years for one of his most famous wax sculptures, *The Tomb*, also known as *Dead Hippie* and *The Death of a Hippie* featuring the wax sculpture of himself. I saw the write-up a few years later in *Time* magazine and pasted it in my journal. Paul Thek was in Andy Warhol's test shot series. I had seen the wax sculpture of Paul in his kitchen but had not realized it was a self-portrait.

[64] The medical standards for accepting draftees by the summer of 1967 were so low that George was found eligible for the draft in September of 1967. He trained as a paratrooper and made several jumps and became a second lieutenant through the Officer Training Corps program. He was sent to Vietnam in 1969 and three weeks after arriving in country was wounded in the leg in a fierce firefight. He was awarded a Purple Heart. He spent many months in rehab and eventually regained most of the use of his leg. He became a poetry professor at a junior college in New Jersey, married his best friend, Mary, and had three wonderful children.

[65] Raised in London by American parents, Bill Phelps had been refused entry to Yale despite a long history of family members who had attended and donated small fortunes to the school. (He was a direct descendent of the donors of the Phelps Gate and the Sheffield Scientific School at Yale.)

[66] Bill "Buffy" Phelps was one of Warhol's test shot subjects in 1965 as was Paul Thek.

[67] I didn't know it at the time, but Bill's friend was part of the Rindge/Adamson family that owned Rancho Malibu. The ranch at one time covered the entire Malibu coast. Large portions of the estate were still in the family's hands and operating as one of the world's largest dairy farms in 1967. The hillside was all grazing land, scrub, or woodland. The land gift to Pepperdine College had not yet been made.

[68] Anitra Ford, a very tall, dark-haired, exotic looking woman a few years older than me, had made herself look even more dramatic for Dick Dunn's party

by using blue and green eyeliner pencils to draw a flower on the right side of her face—the petals of the flower surrounded her eye, and the stem and leaves ran down her cheek. At the time, she was trying to break into TV and film. Her exotic, Jewish look helped open doors for more ethnic diversity in the modeling field. By the start of the 1970s, she would achieve her goal of becoming a successful actress, with roles in TV and films.

[69] Nico had sublet the Castle from actor John Phillip Law, who held the lease from the owner and had been renting it to rock 'n' roll groups off and on for some time. Bob Dylan stayed there. This Castle is sometimes confused with another Castle on Melrose where Warhol and his entourage stayed the year before in 1966 while in Los Angeles.

[70] The Castle was across the street from the Ennis House, designed by Frank Lloyd Wright in the mid-1920s in Mayan style. The house looked Egyptian to me at the time, and I referred to it as the Egyptian house. The outside of the Ennis home was used in many films and TV productions including the 1959 production of *The House on Haunted Hill* starring Vincent Price.

[71] Nico was the adopted name of Christa Paeffgen, another of Andy Warhol's superstars. By the time I came to be sitting unwanted in her living room, she had been a sought-after European fashion model and acted and played herself in a dozen or so films including Fellini's *La Dolce Vita*, Warhol's *Chelsea Girls*, and *Strip Tease*. She had also traveled across Europe with Bob Dylan, recorded her first single, Gordon Lightfoot's, "I'm not sayin'," and had been the occasional lead singer for the Velvet Underground.

[72] Nico's first album, *The Velvet Underground and Nico*, which included Lou Reed, John Cale, Sterling Morrison, and Maureen "Moe" Tucker, had been released earlier in the year. Nico was at the time awaiting the October release of her first solo album, *Chelsea Girl*, which included the Dylan-written single, "I'll Keep It with Mine," which was supposed to be about her.

[73] Leslie, three years younger than David Crosby, later of the Byrds, was still in high school when she met the future folk-rock star. Their paths crossed while working on a play together at The Repertory Theatre, a local community theater in Santa Barbara. David was in several plays in town. Leslie sometimes worked as part of the stage crew. That's how David came to be the first boy who ever kissed her. They were at a party together, and someone told David that Leslie had never been kissed. So, he walked up and surprised her.

[74] Leslie was dividing her time between Crosby's house and her parents' place, lured by Crosby's creative energy, and spending many hours listening to songs as he was writing them. Crosby was doing a lot of coke at the time. Leslie wasn't,

which in a strange way probably added to her attraction. She was normal, down to earth, loving. She was part of David's past but hip enough to be part of his present, too.

[75] Part of the reason for the misinterpretation of the most controversial parts of Paul Krassner's "excerpts" was that he mixed known truths and complete fabrications together in the piece. Krassner began with the fact that Johnson had tried to undercut John Kennedy at the Los Angeles Democratic Convention in 1960. Johnson had attacked the young, handsome, and charismatic Kennedy by reminding Kennedy supporters that JFK's father, Joseph Kennedy, while ambassador to Great Britain, had been a Nazi sympathizer and had urged President Franklin Roosevelt to withhold aid to the English because he thought Germany would beat them.

In another so-called excerpt reputed to have been removed from the Manchester book, Krassner also recounted stories well-known by reporters but never written in the mainstream press at the time. These included the story that Kennedy was using the Secret Service to aid and abet him in his frequent sexual liaisons with models, actresses, and other beautiful women. The Krassner piece mentioned Marilyn Monroe and suggested that Jackie was aware of JFK's affairs, but she joked about it. Krassner was the first to air Kennedy's extra marital shenanigans in public.

Although Krassner took some serious swipes at Kennedy, his real target in his story was President Johnson, who Krassner exposed as someone known to have meetings with cabinet members and staff while sitting on the toilet and otherwise engaging in activities that were meant to demean and humiliate others.

Most of this would have resulted in the article being laughed off or ignored if it weren't for the last excerpt consisting of five paragraphs. Krassner started these paragraphs by taking a swipe at the schizophrenia of the American press which wanted to expose and not expose the human frailties of its leaders. (See next endnote.)

[76] Krassner created a scene in his May article, which he attributed to something that Gore Vidal allegedly said. Vidal, said Krassner, had recounted a story of Jacqueline Kennedy discovering Johnson defiling JFK's corpse at the back of the plane as the president's body was being flown from Dallas to Washington, D.C.

Krassner ended with Jacqueline Kennedy concluding that she didn't believe Johnson had anything to do with killing her husband (though Krassner mentioned elsewhere in the issue that the idea of LBJ's complicity in the assassination was nothing new), but Jacqueline Kennedy said JFK had taught her about the nuances of power. If Jack miraculously came back to life, the first thing Johnson would do would be to kill him, she said (or rather, Krassner had her saying). To drive home the "joke", she added that the only thing that would stop him would be if Bobby Kennedy, the president's brother, beat him to it.

This story that Krassner had concocted was awful, disgusting and yet, if pornographic, then it was less pornographic than the shock I had felt when I had seen the photos of Vietnamese monks burning themselves to death in protest of repression and the constant stream of photos and footage of the dead and wounded on both sides in the war constantly showing up on TV and in magazines. Krassner wanted everyone within reading distance to hate Johnson and Johnson's policies in Vietnam as much as he did.

[77] Krassner had written lengthy explanations of the made-up Kennedy-book story in the June issue (published in August). He had not been sued because, he said, he hadn't broken any laws. He recounted how someone publicly asked why he had not labeled his piece on Johnson as satire. He pointed to Jonathan Swift, who didn't need to tell anyone he was kidding when he wrote about eating Irish babies as a solution to famine and overpopulation in his *Modest Proposals*. Allegedly, Disney didn't sue because they didn't want to draw more attention to the cartoon.

[78] On page 21 of the June 1967 issue, Krassner mentions visiting the Renaissance Pleasure Faire near Los Angeles with Jay Thompson and taking photos with a pretty young women they met there.

[79] The McCarran act was originally sponsored by the liberal bloc of Congress, which included, among others, not only McCarran, but Senators Hubert Humphrey and Paul H. Douglas, and Congressman John F. Kennedy. In 1952, the Justice Department set aside a million dollars for six federal prison campsites for the detention camp program, including sites in Pennsylvania, Florida, Oklahoma, Arizona, and California.

[80] I learned later that Don Ornitz's father, Samuel Ornitz, Hollywood screenwriter and one of the co-founders of the Screen Writers Guild, was one of the famous Hollywood Ten, a group of blacklisted film people who had been accused of being Communists in the 1950s during another dark period in America's history. In addition to commercial photography, Don Ornitz was also one of Hollywood's most famous celebrity photographers and had photos displayed at the Museum of Modern Art, New York and elsewhere.

[81] Self-defense movements among Blacks had been mushrooming around the country for several years. Unlike the Deacons for Defense and Justice, who were World War II and Korean War veterans, the new movements were largely driven

by young Black students fed up with the slow progress of the non-violent movement. The Black Panther Party for Self-Defense had been founded the previous year in Oakland, California by college students Huey P. Newton and Bobby Seale. The group practiced citizen patrols to monitor the police. The patrols had carried loaded firearms until the Mulford Act came into effect at the end of July 1967. The legislation gained widespread support from Democrats, Republicans, and the National Rifle Association earlier in the spring when armed Black Panthers marched on the California legislature in Sacramento in protest of the bill. Signed by Governor Ronald Reagan, the Mulford Act was created in direct response to the Black Panthers' policy of open carry cop watching. It repealed the law that had previously permitted Californians to carry loaded firearms in public.

[82] Most of the time, the grass we got came in nickel or dime bags—plastic sandwich bags containing a half ounce (nickel) or an ounce (dime) of greenish leaves, stems, and seeds, rarely a bud, smuggled from Mexico. A half ounce cost five dollars and an ounce ten dollars.

The trade routes and methods were so primitive that once Garry and a few of his friends ended up with a half kilo that had been smuggled in someone's gas tank. It smelled of gasoline when smoked.

Every once in a while, I'd hear of someone who smoked hashish, but it was rare. Occasionally, maybe two or three times a year in the past two years, one of two distinct high quality grasses turned up in the city—Panama Red, allegedly from Panama, and with a reddish brown tinge to the leaves, and Acapulco gold, from somewhere in Mexico, and with a distinct yellow-brown color to the leaves. The two premium strains usually came with fewer twigs and seeds and cost about thirty dollars for an ounce.

A hit of Acapulco Gold or Panama Red got a person higher faster, so those smoking it needed to treat it with a little more respect, or they'd end up spending six hours eating everything in the house and listening to the same record a hundred times.

Made in United States
North Haven, CT
26 April 2023

35904201R00213